Officially Hispanic

Officially Hispanic

Classification Policy and Identity

José Enrique Idler

WITHDRAWN

LEXINGTON BOOKS

A division of
ROWMAN & LITTLEFIELD PUBLISHERS, INC.
Lanham • Boulder • New York • Toronto • Plymouth, UK

LEXINGTON BOOKS

A division of Rowman & Littlefield Publishers, Inc.
A wholly owned subsidiary of The Rowman & Littlefield Publishing Group, Inc.
4501 Forbes Boulevard, Suite 200
Lanham, MD 20706

Estover Road
Plymouth PL6 7PY
United Kingdom

Copyright © 2007 by Lexington Books

All rights reserved. No part of this publication may be reproduced, stored in a retrieval system, or transmitted in any form or by any means, electronic, mechanical, photocopying, recording, or otherwise, without the prior permission of the publisher.

British Library Cataloguing in Publication Information Available

Library of Congress Cataloging-in-Publication Data

Idler, José Enrique.
  Officially Hispanic : classification policy and identity / José Enrique Idler.
    p. cm.
  Includes bibliographical references and index.
  ISBN-13: 978-0-7391-1969-3 (hardcover : alk. paper)
  ISBN-10: 0-7391-1969-9 (hardcover : alk. paper)
  1. Hispanic Americans—Race identity. 2. Hispanic Americans—Ethnic identity. 3. Race—Classification. 4. Ethnicity—United States—Classification. 5. United States—Race relations—Government policy. 6. United States—Ethnic relations—Government policy. 7. United States—Social policy. I. Title.
  E184.S75I35 20007
  305.868'073—dc22
                                                        2007005740

Printed in the United States of America

∞™ The paper used in this publication meets the minimum requirements of American National Standard for Information Sciences—Permanence of Paper for Printed Library Materials, ANSI/NISO Z39.48–1992.

Contents

Preface		vii
Introduction		ix
Part I: Federal Standards and Ethnoracial Classification		
1	Classification Policy: A Very Basic Framework	3
2	Classifying Race and Ethnicity	15
3	The Presumption of Relevant Membership	33
Part II: Membership and Groups		
4	Theorizing Membership: Culture, Value and Recognition	59
5	Identity and Basic Membership	81
6	The Conditions of Relevant Groups	101
Part III: Hispanic Identity		
7	Nationality and Hispanics	125
8	Hispanic Identification and Common Identity	147
9	Hispanic Identity Making	167
10	Are All Minorities Equally "Minorities"?	187
11	Government, Classification and the Recognition of Hispanics	205
Index		225
About the Author		243

Preface

This is a book about philosophical questions underlying public policies. Although it is a theoretical book, that addresses questions of political philosophy, these questions are addressed as they arise in the practice of public policy. And thus the findings will hopefully shed light on and impact the policy topic under discussion. At the same time, the reader should be forewarned that given the nature of the book—addressing philosophical topics intertwined with public policy—it is probable that both philosophers and public policy scholars will be dissatisfied with the result. Many of the themes addressed in the book—classification policy, Hispanics and identity, for example—are the object of vast literatures within various disciplinary boundaries. As an illustration, the topic of identity, immensely complex and rich, has large and sophisticated literatures in the fields of philosophy, sociology, law, ethnic studies and political science. In crafting the book, I have at times ignored significant debates within disciplines and also sacrificed *disciplinary* rigor. My hope is that the final result is deemed, partially at least, to compensate for my latitudinarian approach. If the book stimulates strong reactions and strikes further insights on Hispanics and the public square, it will have fulfilled its purpose.

A book of this sort could only have been written as a result of extensive interaction and conversations with both philosophers and those who do research in public policy—or better yet, those who combine interests and try to answer questions at the intersection of the two fields. A generous fellowship from the National Research Initiative, a program designed to bridge the gap between academia and the world of public policy at the

American Enterprise Institute for Public Policy Research in Washington D.C., provided a perfect opportunity to do research and undertake this project. Special thanks go to Chris De Muth, David Gerson, Kim Dennis, Henry Olsen, Courtney Myers, Edward Blum and Abigail Thernstrom. Also, an important conversation with Stephan Thernstrom led me to materials that became essential.

I have many intellectual debts to record, as the ideas in this book have been tried out in many conversations and in front of audiences. Jorge J. E. Gracia, who has pioneered work on the philosophy of Hispanic identity, has been instrumental for my own research and writing. In a way, this book results from an attempt to answer questions first raised by him. Jorge L. A. Garcia has likewise been a significant source of insights and stimulating conversations. Among those who commented on earlier drafts, I specially thank Judith Lichtenberg, Robert Fullinwider, Norbert Hornstein and David Crocker. The final book was substantially improved by their comments. Charles Abernathy led me to see the relevance and complications of the legal angle, which is often lost or not fully taken into account, in discussions of political philosophy. I also thank the four referees who read earlier versions of the manuscript. Many people have indeed shaped the direction of this book, but one of my biggest debts is toward Christopher Morris. Numerous chats with him and ongoing discussions have been essential in helping to clarify the topics I tackle and to avoid embarrassingly obvious pitfalls. As usual, the caveat of sole responsibility for the final result applies. As a matter of acknowledgement, some of the material used in the book appeared in *Public Affairs Quarterly* 21,1 (January 2007) in an article entitled *Federal Classification and Ethnoracial Identity*.

Lastly, my thanks go to Sara and our children Ana Luisa and Mateo Enrique. Sara, more than anyone else, has influenced my writing and has been an indispensable companion, providing both encouragement and critique as necessary. Ana Luisa and Mateo Enrique have been a constant source of joy and gratitude. This book attempts to answer some of the questions that they, as the children of a Latin-American immigrant to the U.S., might have to grapple with. It is to Sara and our children that this book is dedicated.

Introduction

It is true that the task of policy-making is oftentimes a messy and complex one. Policies come into existence for different reasons and under varying circumstances; and they frequently seem to have unforeseen consequences. Additionally, many factors come into play when designing and enacting policies—we may count, for instance, partisan reasons, organized and influential enclaves, sheer political pragmatism and pressure from interest groups. But the question we need to keep raising is this: why should certain policies be enacted and implemented? Public policies need to be justified based on their reasonableness. This means that policies need to be constantly tested and examined. It is with this frame of mind that I approach the classification of one particular group in the American political system.

One of the categories officially recognized by the American government through the Standards for the Classification of Federal Data on Race and Ethnicity is that of Hispanic or Latino. The category stems, to a large extent, from the attempt of the government to identify and gather data on populations that have historically "experienced discrimination and differential treatment because of their race or ethnicity."[1] Considering that classification policies—related to issues of identity and civil rights—are a salient feature of American politics, and that Hispanics are now a significant group within American society, we may raise a number of questions related to the task of classification. In general terms, the sorts of questions one might bring up include the following: should ethnoracial classification be a governmental task? When is it legitimate, if ever, for states—and more specifically, the American government—to classify citizens according to race and ethnicity? How should the American government react toward immigrant groups? What is the meaning of Hispanic identity? Should Hispanic identity—or any other specific ethnoracial identity—be publicly recognized by the government? These are the general questions that frame my inquiry.

Let me now narrow down the scope. In this book, I examine the reasons for classifying and collecting data on ethnoracial groups and probe the justification for the Hispanic category. This will lead me to raise the following specific questions: what are the ethnoracial classification policies of the U.S. federal government? What do they assume? With regard to one particular category, who are Hispanics? What is the meaning of Hispanic identity? Is the government justified in classifying and collecting data on Hispanics? Do Hispanics merit official and public recognition?

Hispanics are not the only group classified by the American government, but as noted my inquiry will focus on this group. Except for remarks in the first few chapters and chapter 10 in part 3, I will not have much to say about other groups. And even chapter 10 focuses primarily on African Americans and looks at blacks and Hispanics from a comparative perspective. A full-scale comparison between all the groups currently classified by the American government requires a different study. If I had attempted to produce such a study, I would have not been able to focus on Hispanics at the level of detail in which I have done. My hope is that ensuing studies also raise questions on the justification for categorization and classification, and the meaning of membership, and look at other groups as case studies. There are good reasons for focusing on Hispanics. The Hispanic phenomenon is an established fact of American society due to continued immigration since the 1960s. In a nation historically characterized by immigration, just over 18 million of its current immigrants—roughly 50% of the foreign born population—were born in Latin America. But first-generation Latin-American immigrants are not the only Hispanics. We must also add American citizens of Latin-American descent, which makes the actual count of the overall Hispanic population much higher. Over 40 million Hispanics currently live in the U.S., constituting almost 50% of the population in California and Texas. Other states also have a considerable Hispanic presence: a total of 13 states, including California and Texas, have at least one million Hispanics. The group, according to projections from the U.S. Census Bureau, will represent close to 25% of the general population in 2050 with a figure of 102.6 million people.[2] While projections depend on many factors and variables, the actual number may be even higher due to higher fertility rates among Hispanics compared with the general American population.

STRUCTURE OF THE BOOK

In general terms, my inquiry starts out with an examination of the governmental guidelines for ethnoracial categorization, and leads me to explore the nature of membership, identity and ethnic groups. Subsequently, I examine the nature of Hispanic membership and raise the question of whether the Hispanic category ought to be included in the federal standards for ethnoracial classification. In a nutshell the argument and structure of the book run as follows. I argue first that the federal standards for ethnoracial classification rely on what I call the *presumption of relevant membership*. Briefly, the presumption says that someone is a member in group X and such a membership is central to her identity. I then raise the question whether Hispanic membership is of the relevant kind and argue that it is not. Hispanic identity does not seem to be what the American government thinks it is. Thus, given the identity variable in the federal standards for ethnoracial classification, the case for classifying Hispanics, which entails an official category and datacollection, is not as clear and obvious as it might seem. It is necessary to emphasize that the central claim of the book, that the Hispanic category as used by the government is not justified and thus needs modification, derives from the premise of identity assumptions. The claim does not imply that all forms of Hispanic or immigrant classification ought to be eliminated under all circumstances. So, strictly speaking, the case I present is not necessarily a "color-blind" one. Some forms of classification for certain groups, under some circumstances, are necessary for the sake of policy intervention strategies with regard to, for example, health and education. It is just that Hispanics are not classified simply based on grounds of policy intervention strategies. As I mentioned, an important element of Hispanic classification is the notion of identity. My claim is that given the identity assumptions of the government and the way the current Hispanic category is defined, the category as such is not justified.

Going into more detail now, the overall argument of the book is developed over eleven chapters in three sections. After making a few introductory remarks in chapter 1 on why states find it necessary to classify its citizens, I review in chapter 2, Classifying Race and Ethnicity, the Standards for the Classification of Federal Data on Race and Ethnicity. In looking at the document, first issued in 1977 as OMB's Policy Directive 15 and then revised in 1997, I point out two reasons to explain the interest of the federal government in collecting ethnoracial data. First, the government aims to obtain an accurate demographic profile of its population. Based on the stated goals of the federal standards, I argue that the demographic objective is guided by what I call the "principle of diversity"—i.e., the notion that a certain kind of diversity is a good and it is thus necessary to keep records that accurately reflect the demographic profiles of diverse populations. The second, and most important, reason has to do with civil rights enforcement in the context of groups that have experienced differential treatment due to race and ethnicity. I point out that group inclusion in the federal standards presumably depends on whether the second reason applies or not.

But ethnoracial classification is not only driven by demographic profiles and civil rights enforcement. In chapter 3, "The Presumption of Relevant Membership," I argue that in order to explain the government's interest in collecting ethnoracial data, as stated in the federal standards, we need to look at what I call the *presumption of relevant membership*. I start out with a weak claim—simply, that the presumption of relevant membership helps to explain why the federal government is interested in ethnoracial groups and memberships. A question that arises is whether the federal government, independently from identity considerations, may still have an interest in compiling ethnoracial data in order to monitor and enforce civil rights legislation. In addressing this question, I argue that the presumption of relevant membership is actually necessary for understanding the government's interest in the ethnoracial dimension. I then advance a strong claim, arguing for a necessary connection between the presumption of relevant membership and ethnoracial classification. I adduce two reasons for this connection. First, the extension of subgroups that experience discriminatory treatment differs from the extension of all the subgroups covered under a particular category in the federal standards. Second, the preferred method of identification for the federal standards is self-identification.

Ethnoracial classification presumes that membership in this kind of group is highly significant. Is membership in ethnoracial groups always central to members' identities? To answer this question I turn in chapter 4, Theorizing Membership: Culture, Value and Recognition, to one of the theorists of multiculturalism and the value of ethnic membership I mentioned above, Will Kymlicka. Kymlicka has helped to shape cotemporary debates by bringing to the forefront of political theory the cultural and identity component.[3] He has also been a prominent defender of policies of multiculturalism in Canada. And although the U.S. does not have an official multicultural act or policy, unlike Canada or Australia, the federal standards are a form of membership and group recognition. Discussing Kymlicka will help us to understand the theoretical justification for the value and recognition of particular memberships and groups in the public sphere. The question I look at, in the context of Kymlicka's theory of multiculturalism, is whether membership in ethnic or national minority groups is always highly significant and valuable to group members. I argue that highly significant and valuable membership is not always confined to national or ethnic minority groups and thus membership in group-types other than ethnocultural ones may be a primary source of meaning and direction for group members. If my view is right, I incidentally point out three problems that arise for Kymlicka's model of multiculturalism.

I have talked so far about membership and identity. I have made claims about relevant membership as the sort of membership that is central to someone's identity. We now need to examine further membership and identity by looking at the following question: what kind of membership is central to members' identities and under what conditions? This is the topic of chapter 5, "Identity and Basic Membership." Drawing on G. H. Mead's symbolic interactionism, I begin the chapter with a discussion on the general meaning of identity and then discuss the conditions under which membership is central to members' identities. To this purpose, I introduce the notion of *basic membership*. Briefly, membership is basic when certain group traits are essential to a member's self-understanding and make her a member in a particular group. I explain in this chapter the first part of the claim, i.e., that certain traits are essential to someone's self-understanding.

In chapter 6, The Conditions of Relevant Groups, I turn to the second part of the claim, i.e., membership is basic when someone is a member in a particular group. What kind of group? I argue that groups in which membership is basic satisfy three conditions. The first condition, *relevant identification*, posits that, based on identifiable properties that make it possible for people to recognize group members and nonmembers, we are able to distinguish the sorts of properties that make membership in a particular group basic. The second condition, *differentiation*, says that when membership in a particular group is basic, this membership is necessarily connected with the difference-sensitive attributes of the group. According to the third condition, *intrinsic identification*, groups in which membership is basic are identified from the "inside," i.e., members identify their own group.

With the previous chapters in mind, the book now transitions into the phenomenon of Hispanic identity. If the federal standards are based on the presumption of relevant membership, according to which there is a strong identity dimension to the groups included, the question is whether the Hispanic category satisfies the presumption of relevant membership. Another way of raising this question is by asking whether membership in the Hispanic group is basic. Chapter 7, Nationality and Hispanics, examines the basicness of Hispanic membership. After establishing that Hispanics have various nationalities and membership in national groups is generally basic for Hispanics, I turn to whether Hispanic membership is also basic. I make three points. First, whereas nationality meets what I call the criterion of pervasive basic membership, Hispanic membership does not. Second, Hispanic membership only meets a much weaker criterion that I call partial basic membership. Third, according to the criterion of robust membership, national membership is robust with regard to Hispanic membership. My conclusion is that comparing national and Hispanic memberships shows that the former has a higher degree of basicness than the latter.

In order to fully answer the question on the basicness of Hispanic membership, we need to look in chapter 8, Hispanic Identification and Common Identity, at whether the Hispanic group satisfies the conditions of relevant groups outlined in chapter 5. I argue that Hispanic membership is not basic because it is an epiphenomenon of national membership. Given that the Hispanic category is defined by virtue of national criteria, the traits that allow for basic membership among members of the Hispanic group are first and foremost national. Thus, while nationality satisfies the condition of relevant identification, Hispanic membership does not. I suggest further that Hispanics do not have a common identity. Jorge Gracia and Angelo Corlett have attempted to show that Hispanics do have a common identity. I examine these two attempts and argue that they fail.

Nonetheless, I suggest in chapter 9, Hispanic Identity Making, that Hispanic identity may be a tipping phenomenon. So although Hispanic membership is not basic and Hispanics do not have a common identity, a process of external Hispanic identification may create and strengthen a particular group identity. In looking at external identification and the process of identity making, I focus on the American state using the Hispanic Heritage Month presidential proclamations as a case study. I suggest that, if the Hispanic group internalizes identification and identity making, Hispanics may become the sort of group that could come closer to satisfying all the relevant identity conditions. I also suggest, however, that although this might be a possibility, Hispanic identity making will not yield a meaningful identity until national identities subside.

When one speaks of Hispanics, ostensibly the largest minority in American society, comparisons with another large minority, African Americans, is inevitable. Thus in chapter 10, Are All Minorities Equally "Minorities"? I compare both groups and argue that there is no clear analogy between the two groups. My general thesis in the chapter is that whereas African-American membership is indeed basic, Hispanic membership is not; and thus questions about public recognition for the two groups will lead to separate answers.

Finally, in chapter 11, Government, Classification and the Recognition of Hispanics, I draw some conclusions. I began my inquiry by probing the reasons why the federal government attempts to categorize and classify certain ethnoracial groups—to produce accurate demographic profiles and to enforce civil rights legislation. I argued further that these reasons hinge on the presumption of relevant membership. In subsequent chapters, I show that the presumption of relevant membership does not apply to Hispanics. If Hispanic membership is not relevant, the question arises whether there is a strong justification for including the Hispanic category in the federal standards. Although Hispanics do not satisfy the presumption of relevant membership, it may be argued that given the statutory protection of Hispanics as a minority group, the government must, in any case, monitor civil rights enforcement in relation to the group. This task would seem to require categorization and data collection. Nonetheless, using the legal vocabulary of "suspect classes" and "strict scrutiny" for purposes of ethnoracial classification, I argue that the justification for the Hispanic category, as it is now used in the federal standards, does not seem to be strong enough—which would require reasonable modifications with regard to the current standardized category and how Hispanics are classified for public policy purposes. I finally close this chapter with a few remarks on group classification and public philosophies.

A NOTE ON TERMINOLOGY

In an attempt to characterize nationhood and culture in his classic *Nations and Nationalism*, Ernest Gellner remarked that definitions are notoriously difficult to come up with. In fact, it is better to approach the phenomenon to be examined, in his case culture, "without attempting too much in the way of formal definition, and looking at what culture *does*."[4] In the same vein, I will look at definitions but will focus primarily on how the phenomena I am interested in operate. For the sake of clarity, however, terminology and its consistent use are extremely significant. I have tried to be sensitive to and highlight, albeit not always successfully, significant distinctions. Just as nations and states are not always identical, despite the fact that we live in a world of nation-states, governments and states are not always the same—the state apparatus, for instance, includes the armed forces of a country, whereas the government does not. In some discussions, it helps to distinguish these terms.

One particular distinction made by some is that of "Hispanic" and "Latino." There is a debate on whether the group under consideration should go by one term or the other. Those who propose Hispanic argue that the term highlights the linguistic commonality of all members, which would seem to exclude non-Spanish speakers. Those who propose Latino argue that the term Hispanic has colonial overtones and Latino suggests a closer connection with Latin America, and may include non-Spanish-speakers. It has become customary to use both terms interchangeably—a practice officially sanctioned by the federal standards for ethnoracial classification.

The terminological debate is revealing and important, but it is for the most part ignored in this book. I have decided instead to use a single term, Hispanic, for the simple reasons that it was the term first used to describe the group in the federal standards for ethnoracial classification and still seems to be the one more commonly used in policy circles. Although I do not directly address the terminological debate, which is precisely a reflection of how ambiguous and indeterminate the identity of the group is and how imprecise the membership boundaries are, some of the tensions that such a dispute reflects are indirectly discussed in several sections. Interestingly, journalists such as Michael Barone believe that the term Latino is more commonly used than Hispanic.[5] I have the opposite impression.[6] But be that as it may, I am more concerned with the phenomenon of group identity as such than with terminological tendencies. Lastly, I use the term "America" to refer to the United States of America and not the whole continent named after Americo Vespuccio—which is now spoken of in the Anglo-American world as "the Americas." When speaking of countries south of the United States, I usually use the term "Latin America"—not a good term, but a commonly used one.

NOTES

1. See "Revisions to the Standards for the Classification of Federal Data on Race and Ethnicity," in *Federal Register*, vol. 62, no. 210 (Thursday, October 30, 1997, Notices, 58782).

2. See the U.S. Census Bureau's Facts for Features on the Hispanic Heritage Month. <http://www.census.gov/Press-Release/www/releases/archives/facts_for_features_special_editions/007173.html> (November 15, 2006). For recent literature discussing the future of Hispanics, see Marta Tienda and Faith Mitchell, eds., *Hispanics and the Future of America* (Washington D.C.: The National Academies Press, 2006); and its related report, *Multiple Origins, Uncertain Destinies: Hispanics and the American Future* (Washington D.C.: The National Academies Press, 2006).

3. In addition to the level of influence he has exerted in contemporary debates, and the cogency in exposition and argumentation in his writing, a good reason for focusing on his work has to do with his attempt to implement and justify his own theoretical work in the sphere of public policy. His theoretical work is developed primarily in three books. See Will Kymlicka, *Liberalism, Community, and Culture* (New York: Oxford University Press, 1989); *Multicultural Citizenship: A Liberal Theory of Minority Rights* (New York: Oxford University Press, 1995); and *Politics in the Vernacular: Nationalism, Multiculturalism and Citizenship* (New York: Oxford University Press, 2001). For a more applied policy perspective, see *Finding Our Way*.

4. Ernest Gellner, *Nations and Nationalism* (Ithaca: Cornell University Press, 1983), 7.

5. Michael Barone, *The New Americans: How the Melting Pot Can Work Again* (Washington, D.C.: Regnery Publishing, 2001), 4.

6. Although it is a fact that newspapers such as the Los Angeles Times prefer the term Latino to Hispanic on the grounds that it is more commonly used on the West Coast.

I

FEDERAL STANDARDS AND ETHNORACIAL CLASSIFICATION

1

✣

Classification Policy: A Very Basic Framework

THE IMPERATIVE OF INTEGRATION

One of the central questions for the modern state is how to integrate successfully all of its citizens. The question arises in circumstances such as when there are, or have been, disenfranchised groups within a political unit. Take the example of blacks in the U.S., who were formally granted the right to vote in the second half of the nineteenth century, by two Amendments to the U.S. Constitution, but did not begin to achieve any significant progress—particularly in the Deep South—until the 1960s, when the Voting Rights Act was passed. And even to this day, how much progress has been made with regard to participation in the political process is a matter of intense debate. The topic of political participation also arises in places such as South Africa, where disenfranchisement has been drawn along racial lines, or in places where indigenous groups are in effect excluded from political participation, as in some Latin-American countries like Mexico and Bolivia.

The question of integration also has to do with newly arrived immigrants. Think of how the topic of immigration reform has become a pressing issue in the United States, due to mass migration from primarily Mexico and other Latin-American countries in the last few decades; and how countries like Canada and Australia grapple with the integration of immigrants through official policies of multiculturalism that have generated both enthusiasm and strong criticism. In addition, countries in Western Europe such as Germany have realized that what started as a guest-worker program in the sixties and seventies has generated immigrant communities that are more or less settled in the host country; and despite this settlement, immigrants have not been successfully integrated into the host society.

The condition of permanent "immigrants" then brings us to another set of situations in which integration becomes a pressing concern. Within the mainstream of a political unit, there are those who have been marginalized socially, racially, culturally or economically. They are members of a given unit, sometimes even in equal terms with other citizens from a formal point of view. Culturally and economically, however, these members have limited access to resources that should in principle be open to all citizens. This situation creates the insular minorities we see in some European countries leading to, for instance, the phenomenon of the alienated and angry youth and events such as the nationwide riots in France in 2005. Blacks in the U.S. and other countries might be said to be in a comparable situation of marginalization, and indigenous groups in places as dissimilar as Australia and Peru are in many respects on the fringes of the mainstream. Groups that are racially, culturally or economically marginalized are often groups that have also been disenfranchised or denied privileges of citizenship. But often, even long after the right to vote or citizenship status is granted, the groups remain without access to economic and social resources, or culturally excluded from the mainstream.

Integration also moves to the center stage of multinational, multireligious, or in some sense multicultural states.[1] In the case of multinational states, countries like Canada and Spain immediately come to mind. With different national groups subsisting under the same state—sometimes with overt and violent separatist goals as has been the case, for instance, of actions undertaken by some Basque organizations in Spain—the problem that needs to be solved is that of competing interests under the same overarching legislative body. This situation, which puts the topic of federalism in the forefront, raises questions and concerns about the success or limits of the modern nation-state and the meaning of, say, national identity and the right to self-determination. In the case of multireligious and multicultural states, we are confronted with accommodation rights and the steps that governments ought to take in order to integrate people with multiple religious and cultural backgrounds. When a particular religion is dominant, as in the case of countries with established national churches, or when the state is explicitly secular, as in the case of France, the question of religious accommodation becomes pressing—which is the situation, for instance, generated by Muslims in parts of Western Europe. But in states that have not achieved the measure of success that industrialized countries have, the need for the integration of varying religious and cultural groups becomes even more acute. The case that immediately comes to mind here is that of African states. As a byproduct of colonization, and living under the legacy of political lines drawn without much regard for salient group boundaries, the topic of integration is extremely sensitive and creates a sense of heightened emergency. Countries like Nigeria and the Sudan are besieged by internal conflicts, which result from religious, ethnic and cultural variables that have become impossible to reconcile within the unit of the nation-state.

The matter of integration takes different forms depending on the context in which it is raised, ranging from situations that require full incorporation into the political process, and also cultural or economic incorporation, to arrangements that try to develop a form of federalism or mitigate religious conflict. Efforts to achieve integration can also take many different forms. Perhaps one that has been pressed with results that have both strong advocates and foes is that of cultural recognition, or more commonly, multiculturalism.[2] The phenomenon of multiculturalism is much more complex than it seems at first, and varies from one country to another, and even from one sphere to another—for instance, speaking of multiculturalism in education is often different from talk about multiculturalism in the workplace or with regard to celebrations in the public square. Generally speaking, multiculturalism posits that certain marginalized groups ought to be accorded public recognition.[3] But then the hard questions begin. What are cultural groups? Do, say, gender and race count as criteria for distinguishing cultural groups? Should all cultural groups be recognized? What is cultural identity? What does public recognition mean and what kinds of policies does it entail? Another related question follows from the last one: how does this recognition happen—e.g., does it require group rights in addition to individual rights? Questions of this kind have been addressed by leading multicultural theorists like Iris Marion Young in the U.S., and with more straightforward policy implications, by Will Kymlicka in Canada and Bhikhu Parekh in Great Britain.[4]

The phenomenon of multiculturalism is often confused with other distinct phenomena that happen to be particularly salient in American society. The first one could be called the diversity movement, and the second one is known as the civil rights revolution.[5] Although all these phenomena are interrelated, it helps to distinguish them in order to see how the question of integration takes shape.[6] The phenomenon of diversity is a paradoxical one, since the main claim of the diversity movement is that integration is achieved when differences are recognized and celebrated.[7] The diversity movement may overlap with multiculturalism, but whereas some multiculturalists could emphasize accommodation on grounds of fairness, those in the diversity camp tend to focus on celebration. Integration is then measured not so much by how much access there is to social or political resources, but rather by how much differences of some type are publicly celebrated. Some hard questions, such as what is the source of diversity and what kinds of differences do we celebrate, are bound to come up.[8]

In the case of the civil rights phenomenon, perhaps the most single important question with regard to integration is: what does the principle of equality entail? There was a time in U.S. history in which equality was seen as being compatible with racial segregation. From *Plessy v. Ferguson*, the Supreme Court case that formulated the infamous "separate but equal" doctrine in 1892, American society came to a turning point with *Brown v. Board of Education* in 1954.[9] But if *Brown* made equality and racial segregation incompatible, civil rights legislation in the sixties and a host of ensuing court cases have brought up the similar concerns and questions time and again.[10] Although race still plays a prominent role, the matter of equality now extends beyond racial discrimination. At the center of this legislation is the question, what does the Equal Protection Clause that guarantees equal protection of the laws for all citizens, as found in the Fourteenth amendment of the U.S. Constitution, mean?[11] As illustrated, for instance, by the famous 2003 affirmative action cases arising from admissions policies at the University of Michigan—at both the undergraduate college and the Law School—the meaning and application of equality principles in legislation and public policy are notoriously complex.[12] The question of equality raised by these kinds of situations is really the question of whether certain groups, generally construed as minorities, have been fully and successfully integrated into society.

Along with varieties of multiculturalism and phenomena such as the diversity movement and the civil rights revolution, solutions on how to achieve integration also take another form. Here we find claims that marginalized residents, primarily immigrants, ought to assimilate, which happens either by their own initiative in making an effort to blend in, or also policies that encourage immigrants to learn the new language and mainstream habits. These claims, which have been standard in the republican and civic French model, tend to be associated with concerns for national unity and identity.[13] The U.S. has also had its share in calls for national unity; but unlike France, the imperative of unity by assimilation has been widely discredited—although the U.S. has been more tolerant in general of the public "cultural" factor than the French.[14] Now, whatever one might make of the theme of assimilation, the topic is much more complex than it seems at first. To begin with, questions such as who is eligible for assimilation are likely to come up. In so-called ethnic nations, ethnicity is a precondition for becoming a member of a society. In civic nations, ethnicity might not be necessary, but then, what does full membership entail?[15] Incidentally, themes of this sort tell us just as much about the conditions for membership as they do about the nations or groups into which new people, namely immigrants, integrate.[16] But also consider what assimilation might involve. Suppose it is sufficient for immigrants to learn the new language, which many immigrants are anxious to do in order to gain access to economic benefits derived from better jobs often requiring linguistic skills. Does this count as assimilation or is there something else involved, which would perhaps require a degree of homogenization and complete integration into the mainstream. If so, one has to examine what exactly is the mainstream.[17]

CLASSIFICATION AS A MEANS FOR EVALUATING INTEGRATION

Grappling with integration, states often find it necessary to classify their citizens in order to enact or assess policies. Many actions undertaken by states, including legislation, entail some sort of classification.[18] Modern states, for instance, grant a set of rights and protective measures to children that are not extended to adults—where an adult may be defined, for statutory purposes, as a person who is eighteen years old. Sexual intercourse, for instance, between an adult and a seventeen-year-old teenager—legally, considered a member of a protected class—constitutes grounds for liability, although perhaps such intercourse may have been consensual. Similarly, in many modern states people who reach their sixties are eligible for certain retirement entitlements that take the form of state or private pensions and medical benefits. People in this age bracket are also usually protected by a set of legislative measures that aim to correct age discrimination in the workplace, whereby a job candidate is not immediately disqualified for employment by virtue of her age. In order to design and apply all these measures coherently, states find it necessary to classify people according to their age, defining and singling out the age groups—e.g., children and the elderly—that will be the beneficiaries of state-sanctioned procedures. Virtually any action undertaken by states requires some type of classification—male and female, guilty and innocent, wealthy and poor, those who should pay more taxes than others and those who are exempted from paying taxes, foreigners and citizens, etc.

Perhaps the oldest and most conspicuous form of classification is the census.[19] Governmental institutions, preceding the modern state, have for many centuries gathered data and classified their citizens according to particular attributes—e.g., freemen, members of religious communities and foreigners. Historically, before the advent of the modern census, salient purposes for classifying and counting the population had to do with taxation and military conscription. And although these purposes continued to be prominent in the era of nation-states, the development of the modern census, which was initiated by the 1790 American decennial census, more acutely raised the question of who should count. As an illustration, the question of which civic status was necessary in order to count "was debated several times by the International Statistical Congress, a body that met every three years or so in Europe between the 1850s and the 1880s, and its recommendation to count the *resident* population became standard practice." But perhaps even more conspicuous than the question of civic status was the question of origin and racial groups. With regard to origin—a question that was crucial for determining the membership boundaries of the national group—French, British, American, and Australian census-designers became highly "interested in ascertaining the country of origin of their residents."[20] With regard to race, colonial ideology and beliefs on groups distinguished by phenotypic traits made racial categorization a standard feature of many censuses.[21] The American census has included a question on race since its first count in 1790—one that was not only based on beliefs about race but was also designed to assess the taxable population. So collecting racial data has always been one of the U.S. federal government's tasks. For the most part, the drive behind this task has been exclusionary. The goal was, in part, to identify particular racial groups, which were not white. Between 1790 and 1840 the census categories were more or less divided according to White and Colored people, free or slaves (with the sporadic inclusion of nontaxed Indians). Beginning in 1870 the categories were further diversified and started to include categories such as White, Black, Indian and other Oriental groups (e.g., Japanese, Chinese, etc.).[22]

As I have mentioned, questions about race, which often included "ethnic" groups as well, were motivated by an exclusionary or discriminatory purpose. Again, the American case—in which blacks were not considered full citizens and did not acquire the right to vote until the second half of the nineteenth century—is telling. But due to the minority or civil rights revolution, began in the middle of the twentieth century, categories that were once designators of blatantly excluded groups—distinguished by race—have become means for assessing social and political integration.

Consider how the situation has changed. First, the purpose of racial and ethnic data is now to identify groups that have been historically excluded with an eye toward inclusion and integration. So classification and policy-making now have, based on principles of equality and justice, not an exclusionary purpose but on the contrary an inclusivist one. Second, the task of gathering data has only intensified in the civil rights era. Official racial categories no longer belong to the decennial census but are now pervasive. Direct or indirect encounters with the federal government will often raise the question of one's racial or ethnic identification. All federal agencies collect this type of data, either among their constituencies or employees. Similarly, the birth of a son or daughter is immediately followed by a form that includes an item asking the parent or guardian to report the child's race or ethnicity. Schools, under federal law requirements, collect data on the racial and ethnic makeup of their student body. Practices having to do with employment, contracting, housing, voting and education are seen through the prism of race and ethnicity. Part of this, undoubtedly, is the result of federal expansion over the decades. The size of government in our time, the number of agencies and employees, is greater than what it was in, say, 1950. But the main cause for the change in how ethnic and racial categories are viewed and the purposes they serve has to do with new sensibilities and beliefs. So Melissa Nobles, who has studied the racial categories embedded in the American census, and their shifting meanings throughout history, describes the transformation this way:

> The Civil Rights Movement and resulting civil rights legislation of the 1960s dramatically changed the political context and purposes of racial categorization. Federal civil rights legislation, most notably the Civil Rights Acts of 1964 and 1968 and the Voting Rights Act of 1965, dismantled the most egregious discriminatory mechanisms: namely, black disenfranchisement in the south, rigid residential segregation, and wholesale exclusion from certain occupations and American institutions. These new laws and programs required racial and ethnic data for monitoring legislative compliance and the delivery of new social services and programs.[23]

Under the current state of affairs, the U.S. federal government, like other governments such as Canada and Great Britain, routinely collects data on race and ethnicity. The decennial census and all kinds of questionnaires designed to collect data include a section enquiring about the respondent's racial or ethnic identity. In a society defined by civil rights principles, knowing which groups ought to be the target of nondiscriminatory or affirmative action policies constitutes an extremely important matter. These categories and form of classification become a means not for discriminating but for assessing equal access and integration.

CLASSIFICATION, MEMBERSHIP AND RECOGNITION

The act of classification is extremely significant. The very practice of classification has contributed toward generating, consolidating and reinforcing identities, as census scholars have shown, and plays a prominent role in singling out particular groups in contemporary society. Classification is based on certain beliefs and assumptions about the groups and memberships that serve as the basis for or result from the action of classification. We know that groups are classified for different purposes. Some classifications, however, seem to assume that membership in a certain group is of a special kind.[24] Then classification may take the form of political and social recognition—or the basis on which further acts of recognition will take place. Public recognition is sometimes associated with protection or accommodation. Although the two factors are not necessarily related, they often go together: recognition takes the form of protection and measures of social accommodation; and statutory protection of certain groups, which entails governmental action toward the group, is a form of recognition. Recognition could be taken in a weak sense—the government simply takes action by, say, classifying citizens in order to achieve certain ends with regard to the group, e.g., statutory protection or the implementation of educational policies; or recognition could also be taken in a stronger sense—the government believes, implicitly or explicitly, that membership in the group is a good.

This state of affairs leads us to consider questions having to do with, first, the nature of recognition, and, second, the meaning of membership. Consider question about recognition. Which kinds of groups or memberships, if any, should be recognized? Similarly, when should they be recognized? Under what conditions and for what purposes should some groups and not others be classified and recognized? Should we recognize politically memberships distinguished by the criteria of, say, gender, sexual orientation, ancestry, religion, culture or race? And if that is the case, under what circumstances and in what ways should these memberships be the recipients of public recognition? Additionally, supposing that these groups have been, and are, marginalized from society or the political process, is a certain type of robust public recognition, other than statutory protection, necessary for integration?

As I have said, when memberships are recognized, it is normally done on the grounds that these sorts of memberships are more significant than others and thus require recognition in the form of, say, protection, some type of accommodation, or public celebration. Think now of membership and the question that arises here is: what are these types of special memberships that may merit, under some circumstance, protection or celebration? Additionally, what does a special kind of membership entail? In other words, why is it special? And similar to the questions I raised above: even when the conditions for significant membership are met, which of these memberships warrant, and under what circumstances, some type of recognition? And is this recognition a precondition or necessary means for integration?[25]

By laying out these sorts of questions, I think we are able to see how a cluster of themes is intertwined: integration, classification, recognition and the meaning of membership. As I suggested above, the topic of classification policy raises what is perhaps one of the central questions for modern states: how to integrate its citizens. In the following chapters, I wish to address this topic by looking at a particular form of classification toward one specific group that brings up a number of pressing questions for American society.

NOTES

1. When I speak of "multicultural" states in this chapter, I use the adjective descriptively, i.e., to depict the kind of state that, as a matter of fact, includes several cultures. When I speak of multiculturalism, as a means for integrating citizens, I use the term, a noun, normatively, i.e., to refer to a program on how citizens ought to be integrated.

2. The kind of multiculturalism I am referring to has integrationist aims, although different in mode from the "assimilationist" view. "It is important to distinguish assimilation from what we might call 'multicultural integration.' Both involve fashioning a new transcendent identity—the identity of citizenship, or full, equal membership in the state. And both seek to integrate people from various ethnic backgrounds into common social and political institutions. However, multicultural integration does not have the intent or expectation of eliminating other cultural differences between subgroups in the state." Will Kymlicka and Wayne Norman, "Citizenship in Culturally Diverse Societies: Issues, Contexts, Concepts," in *Citizenship in Diverse Societies*, eds. Will Kymlicka and Wayne Norman (New York: Oxford University Press, 2000), 14.

3. This claim is different from, and may contrast with, arguments that make a case for unity on the basis that a shared national identity and a robust common public space are "important to a well-functioning democracy." Margaret Moore, "Liberal Nationalism and Multiculturalism," in *Canadian Political Philosophy: Contemporary Reflections*, eds. Ronald Beiner and Wayne Norman (Ontario: Oxford University Press, 2001), 184. Her essay reviews recent arguments for national unity, presumably necessary for facilitating goods related to justice in liberal-democracies, along with arguments for the cultural recognition of diverse groups, which often go by the name of "multiculturalism," also on grounds of justice.

4. See particularly Will Kymlicka, *Finding Our Way: Renegotiating Ethnocultural Relations in Canada* (Ontario: Oxford University Press, 1998); and Bhikhu Parekh, *Rethinking Multiculturalism: Cultural Diversity and Political Theory* (Cambridge, MA: Harvard University Press, 2000). In ensuing chapters, I will draw extensively on Kymlicka's theoretical work.

5. On the topic of diversity, see Peter H. Schuck's book, *Diversity in America: Keeping Government at a Safe Distance* (Cambridge, MA: Harvard University Press, 2003). On the topic of the civil rights revolution and how it transformed American society, see John D. Skrentny, *The Minority Rights Revolution* (Cambridge, MA: Harvard University Press, 2002).

6. Other interrelated phenomena include what goes by the labels of "identity politics," the "politics of recognition," or "the politics of difference." See "The Rise of Identity Politics," *Dissent*, 40 (1993): 172–77; Michael Walzer, *What it Means to Be an American: Essays on the American Experience* (New York: Marsilio Publishers,

1996); and Iris Marion Young, *Justice and the Politics of Difference* (Princeton: Princeton University Press, 1990).

7. Claims of diversity may also take a different shape: it is necessary to homogenize a particular population in order to create diversity. This is typically the case with racially-based gerrymandering in the U.S., which has resulted from the application of the Voting Rights Act and a body of court decisions that are notoriously difficult to interpret. Schuck puts it this way: ". . . courts sometimes require an election *district* to be drawn so as to pack racially similar people together in order to diversify the racial composition of the *legislature* by assuring that such districts will elect minority representatives" (original emphasis). Schuck, *Diversity in America*, 313. Lani Guinier critically refers to this practice as "tokenism." See Lani Guinier and Stephen L. Carter, *The Tyranny of the Majority: Fundamental Fairness in Representative Democracy* (New York: The Free Press, 1994), 41–70.

8. For a discussion on the different kinds and sources of diversity, see Schuck, *Diversity in America*, 19–36.

9. The case overturned *Plessy* and ruled that children in segregated schools are deprived of the equal protection of the laws because "separate educational facilities are inherently unequal." 347 U.S. 483, 495 (1954).

10. For a list of representative cases that have raised the question of equality with regard to racial classifications, see *Regents of University of California v. Bakke*, 438 U.S. 265 (1978). The Court ruled that the dual track admission's policy—designed to favor minority applicants—in the University of California at Davis Medical School was unconstitutional because it unduly discriminated against nonminority applicants. See also *Shaw v. Reno*, 509 U.S. 630 (1993), a voting rights case that found a racially-based North Carolina districting plan unconstitutional since it violated the right to equal protection of some residents. Finally, see also *Adarand Constructors, Inc v. Pena*, 515 U.S. 200 (1995). This is a contracting case, which ruled that unqualified race–based presumptions in subcontracting violate the equal protection of the laws. I refer to these cases in the final chapter.

11. According to Section I of the U.S. Constitution's Fourteenth Amendment, ratified in 1868, no State shall" . . . deny to any person within its jurisdiction the equal protection of the laws."

12. The cases I refer to are *Gratz v. Bollinger*, 539 U.S. 244 (2003); and *Grutter v. Bollinger*, 539 U.S. 306 (2003). Using the criteria set out in *Bakke*, the Court upheld one set of admission's policies and struck down the other. See Charles Fried, *Saying What the Law Is: The Constitution in the Supreme Court* (Cambridge, MA: Harvard University Press, 2004), 235.

13. Independently from claims about assimilation, concern for national unity has been a theme of commentators on both sides of the political spectrum, i.e., the "left" and the "right." See, for instance, the work of Arthur M. Schlesinger, Jr., a "liberal" author, *The Disuniting of America: Reflections on a Multicultural Society*, rev. ed. (New York: W. W. Norton & Company, 1998). See also Samuel P. Huntington, an author of the "right," *Who are We?: The Challenges to America's National Identity* (New York: Simon & Schuter, 2004). For a more elaborate and developed defense of national unity, as a necessary condition for the delivery of certain goods, see David Miller, *On Nationality* (Oxford: Oxford University Press, 1999 [1975]).

14. In recent times, social theorists such as Richard Alba and Victor Nee have formulated sophisticated theories of assimilation that examine various layers of membership and models of social integration. See Richard Alba and Victor Nee, *Remaking the American Mainstream: Assimilation and Contemporary Immigration* (Cambridge, MA: Harvard University Press, 2003).

15. States as "membership communities" have different kinds of self-understandings reflected in their membership notions and integration models. Here I use the terms ethnic and civic memberships to denote two general conceptions deriving from the French and German models of nationhood. See Rogers Brubaker, *Citizenship and Nationhood in France and Germany* (Cambridge, MA: Harvard University Press, 1992).

16. For a comparative approach to the relationship between national self-understandings and immigration policy, see Christian Joppke, *Immigration and the Nation-State: The United States, Germany and Great Britain* (New York: Oxford University Press, 1999).

17. In other words, what exactly is the body that represents the object of assimilation? Even when the claim is made that "newcomers [to the U.S.] find themselves facing an ambivalent public that questions their willingness to assimilate and doubts their assimilability," the question is: into what should newcomers assimilate? See Min Zhou, "The Changing Face of America: Immigration, Race/Ethnicity, and Social Mobility," in *Mass Migration to the United States: Classical and Contemporary Periods*, ed. Pyong Gap Min (Walnut Creek: Altamira Press, 2002), 83.

18. On this point, see Fried, *Saying What the Law Is*, 209.

19. The census is a very old instrument of authority, with the first recorded census-taking place in ancient Babylonia around 3800 B.C. In contemporary times, the "census is inextricably bound up with the administrative needs of the welfare state." See Peter Skerry, *Counting on the Census? Race, Group Identity and the Evasion of Politics* (Washington, D.C.: Brookings Institution Press, 2000), 11–12.

20. David I. Kertzer and Dominique Arel, "Censuses, Identity Formation, and the Struggle for Political Power," in *Census and Identity: The Politics of Race, Ethnicity, and Language in National Censuses*, eds. David I. Kertzer and Dominique Arel (Cambridge: Cambridge University Press, 2002), 8.

21. "As a product of the ideology of colonial and modern states, the project of dividing populations into separable categories of collective identity inevitably intersected with the division of populations into racial categories. The two efforts share a common logic, a kind of categorical imperative, in which people must be assigned to a category and to one category alone. The history of racial thinking is a history of cultural categorization, of seizing on certain physical characteristics and inventing a biological category for those people who manifest them." Kertzer and Arel, "Censuses, Identity Formation," 10.

22. For a historic review of census categories, see *Measuring America: The Decennial Censuses from 1790 to 2000*, U.S Census Bureau, September 2002. See also Melissa Nobles, "Racial Categorization and Censuses," in *Census and Identity*; and her book, *Shades of Citizenship: Race and the Census in Modern Politics* (Stanford: Stanford University Press, 2000), 25–84.

23. Nobles, "Racial Categorization and Censuses," 57.

24. Membership may be of a special kind for a number of reasons having to do, for instance, with identity, the fact that a class has been discriminated against and thus merits protection, or the fact that certain memberships consist of immutable traits. For example, a Supreme Court decision, discussing dependent policies with regard to a female Air Force officer, considered the merits of the case under the following assumption: ". . . since sex, like race and national origin, is an immutable characteristic determined solely by the accident of birth, the imposition of special disabilities upon the members of a particular sex because of their sex would seem to violate 'the basic concept of our system that legal burdens should bear some relationship to individual responsibility . . .' [. . .] And what differentiates sex from such non-suspect statuses as intelligence or physical disability, and aligns it with the recognized suspect criteria, is that the sex characteristic frequently bears no relation to ability to perform or contribute to society." *Frontiero v. Richardson*, 411 U.S. 677, 686 (1973).

25. This is an extremely significant question. For some, classification and recognition is a means for integration, and for others it has a divisive (and thus undesirable) effect. Still for others, official recognition has a perverse effect in that it creates rigid identities; and what we need is a post–ethnic model that conceptualizes membership in a different way, highlighting choice over ascription, moves beyond the paradigm of particularized identities and emphasizes the nation as a unity-laden community of solidarity. For a development of themes in this last position, see David A. Hollinger, *Postethnic America: Beyond Multiculturalism* (New York: Basic Books, 1995). See also Amy Gutmann, *Identity in Democracy* (Princeton: Princeton University Press, 2003), 86–116.

2

✦

Classifying Race and Ethnicity

Anyone who has used in recent years a public service—and many private services too—has probably noticed that facilities and organizations generally collect data on race and ethnicity. When applying to school, being admitted into a hospital, applying for work or a house loan, one will have to check a box reporting whether one is White, Black or African American, Asian, Hispanic or Latino, Native Hawaiian or Pacific Islander, or American Indian—or sometimes check "other." Generally one would be asked about one's ethnic affiliation and racial identification. The previously mentioned categories are the minimal categories set, standardized and used by the federal government and also other private organizations. The minimal categories are not meant to be exhaustive—so, for instance, the 2000 census added "Chinese," "Filipino," "Korean," and "Japanese."[1] But the minimal categories are, nonetheless, *standards* that need to be used in order to show compliance with government-related reporting.

These categories, used for purposes of data gathering and classification, are outlined in a document entitled Standards for the Classification of Federal Data on Race and Ethnicity. In looking at the practice of ethnoracial data collection, several questions arise. Why do the federal government and other organizations currently classify certain people according to their race and ethnicity? Why use the ethnoracial membership criterion for classification? Why not use other criteria such as political affiliation, religion, sports preferences, etc.? There are many ways and many criteria according to which people could be classified. What then is it about ethnicity and race that makes them conspicuous? The answer to these questions is partly historical and has to do with the civil rights movement and legislation. Although the history is important, I will not look at these questions from a primarily historical dimension.[2] I am more interested in reasons and justification. In the next two chapters, I will address these questions and query the reasons that explain the classification of citizens according to race and ethnicity.

I will begin this chapter with a survey of the Standards for the Classification of Federal Data on Race and Ethnicity and then discuss the government's reasons for the implementation of these standards. Briefly, the two reasons have to do with producing an accurate demographic profile, reflecting the diversity of the national population, and civil rights enforcement. I end the chapter by discussing some political considerations that bear in the objective of producing an accurate demographic profile.

FEDERAL STANDARDS ON RACE AND ETHNICITY

In 1977, the Office of Management and Budget (OMB) issued Policy Directive 15—entitled "Race and Ethnic Standards for Federal Statistics and Administrative Reporting"—setting out standardized categories for collecting data and classifying the population according to race and ethnicity.[3] The immediate goal of the standardized categories was to produce nonduplicated data that could be exchanged across different federal agencies. Although the categories and data were essential for civil rights enforcement, Directive 15 was quick to point out that these classifications should "not be viewed as determinants of eligibility for participation in any Federal program."[4] So, in other words, although the categories were meant to classify people on the basis of the ethnoracial criterion, the categories by themselves did not entail eligibility for programs. The primary purpose was to provide standardized data and record keeping. The point is important because data collection as such, by itself, is not enough grounds for administrative decisions leading to minority classification or affirmative action. In order to get to affirmative action, it is necessary to have several more links in an argument.[5]

Just as the Directive refrained from determining eligibility for federal programs, the document also made it clear that the purpose of the categories was neither scientific nor anthropological.[6] So it should not be read as a document that tells us anything about the meaning or biological basis of race. According to the document, "the racial and ethnic categories set forth in the standards should not be interpreted as being primarily biological or genetic in reference. Race and ethnicity may be thought of in terms of social and cultural characteristics as well as ancestry."[7] Its purpose was, at least apparently, strictly related to policy matters. In view of the fact that different agencies collected data using disparate categories, Directive 15 was meant to standardize categories for practical data collection, thus solving the problem of nonexchangeable information.

The document defined five categories dividing them by race and ethnicity, a distinction that would be maintained in a subsequent revision. In order of alphabetical appearance, the first category was called "American Indian or Alaskan Native." It was defined as "a person having origins in any of the original peoples of North America, and who maintains cultural identification through tribal affiliation or community recognition." The second category was "Asian or Pacific Islander," including people "having origins in any of the original peoples of the Far East, Southeast Asia, the Indian subcontinent, or the Pacific Islands." Examples of the areas under this category were specified: "China, India, Japan, Korea, the Philippine Islands, and Samoa." Third came "Black"—defined as "a person having origins in any of the black racial groups of Africa." In the fourth place, "Hispanic" was defined as "a person of Mexican, Puerto Rican, Cuban, Central or South American or other Spanish culture or origin, regardless of race." Whereas the Hispanic category referred to an "ethnic" group, the rest of the categories pointed to "racial" groups.[8] The last category, "White," was defined as "a person having origins in any of the original peoples of Europe, North Africa, or the Middle East."[9]

Different formats could be used for collecting data. So administrators could, for instance, combine race and ethnicity in a questionnaire. The preferable format, however, separated race and ethnicity—which is still currently the case. In this format, administrators would include the four racial categories, American Indian or Alaskan Native, Asian or Pacific Islander, Black and White, followed by the ethnic options: "Hispanic origin" and "not of Hispanic origin."

A significant feature of the original categories is that they were meant to be exclusive, which generated significant debates and was eventually changed. Dual racial identification was not possible. So, for instance, individuals who belonged to two racial groups, e.g., Black and Asian, had to be identified by a proxy standard. According to the document this should always be the case: "the category which most closely reflects the individual's recognition in his community should be used for purposes of reporting on persons who are of mixed racial and/or ethnic origins."[10] Interestingly, by looking at the context, it seems like the standard for single-category classification is not self-identification, but rather the "individual's recognition in his community." I will examine in the next chapter some implications arising from the method by which data is collected.

Due to criticism of the original five categories, after the 1990 census, "OMB announced in July 1993 that it would undertake a comprehensive review of the current categories for data on race and ethnicity."[11] With members representing over 30 agencies, OMB set up an Interagency Committee for the Review of the Racial and Ethnic Standards. The review process contemplated two elements: public comments expressing concern over the original standards and testing assessing the consequences of possible changes. The result of this review was a long report by the Interagency Committee published on July 9, 1997 that made recommendations for changes in the Statistical Policy Directive 15. Along with the report, OMB requested comments before proceeding to modify the old standards. Finally, in October of that same year OMB issued the revised standards, which were to be used for the 2000 decennial census and at all federal agencies immediately (and no later than January 1, 2003). The name of that final document, which made the official changes to the old standards, was "Revisions to the Standards for the Classification of Federal Data on Race and Ethnicity."[12]

The revised standards were in many ways similar to the original ones. Most proposals for new categories were rejected, including Middle Easterner or Arab, and, with the exception of a new racial category, the changes were primarily terminological. Several categories retained the original definition but slightly changed their names or added new terms. So, for instance, Hispanics could now check either "Hispanic" or "Latino." Similarly, blacks now had two options: "African American" or "Black." Another minor change was that the term "Alaskan Native," which goes with the "American Indian" category, was changed to "Alaska Native." The most important change with regard to the categories themselves was that the Asian or Pacific Islander category became two different categories. This added an additional category to the standards—so now there was one ethnic category, Hispanic or Latino, and a total of five racial categories.

Under the new and current standards, there is the "Asian" category, defined as "a person having origins in any of the original peoples of the Far East, Sotheast Asia, or the Indian subcontinent including, for example, Cambodia, China, Indian, Japan, Korea, Malaysia, Pakistan, the Philippine Islands, Thailand, and Vietnam." And the new additional category is now "Native Hawaiian or Other Pacific Islander" defined as "a person having origins in any of the original peoples of Hawaii, Guam, Samoa, or other Pacific Islands."[13] The final categories and current of the federal standards then have one ethnic option Hispanic or Latino, and the following five racial categories: American Indian or Alaska Native, Asian, Black or African American, Native Hawaiian or Other Pacific Islander, and White.

Perhaps the most significant feature of the revised federal standards is that they allow individuals to check multiple races. As I mentioned, under the original standards, individuals could only check one racial category. During the review process, the proposal for adding a "multiracial" option that reflected the mixed background and identifications of many people was widely discussed. After conducting extensive research, the Interagency Committee recommended, "when self-identification is used, a method for reporting more than one race should be adopted," and this method "should take the form of multiple responses to a single question and not a [new] 'multiracial' category."[14] OMB accepted the recommendation and so in the revised standards "respondents shall be offered the option of selecting one or more racial designations."[15]

REASONS FOR FEDERAL STANDARDS

Now that we have seen the categories themselves, we need to ask this question: what explains the government's interest in collecting data and classifying people according to their race and ethnicity? In order to answer this question, we need to look at the two reasons for having certain categories and data for classification purposes.

First, the goal is to have an accurate demographic profile of the national population. When the Interagency Committee decided to revise the standards, the official objective, as described in the document that effectively changed the standards, was "to enhance the accuracy of the demographic information collected by the Federal Government."[16] The objective presupposes that there is a given population from which data will be collected, and such population comprises the sum total of the nation's residents. A crucial question is: how is this national population, from which a demographic profile will emerge, socially configured?

Later on, the document paraphrases the same objective adding a few new elements. The second mention goes like this:

> OMB also finds that the Committee's recommendations are consistent with the principal objective of the review, which is to enhance the accuracy of the demographic information collected by the Federal Government by having categories for data on race and ethnicity that will enable the capture of information about the increasing diversity of our Nation's population.[17]

In addition to the idea of accuracy in demographic information, two additional elements are mentioned. First, demographic accuracy entails having ethnoracial categories. Second, these categories reflect, or ought to reflect, the "increasing diversity of our Nation's population." It seems then that given the ethnoracial diverse configuration of society as a whole, enhancing accuracy requires examining whether the categories truly reflect such a social configuration or not.

It is important to bring up at this point one of the causes for revising the federal standards. Since the 1990 census, the standards came under growing criticism from those who thought "that the minimum categories set forth in Directive No. 15 do not reflect the increasing diversity of our Nation's population that has resulted primarily from growth in immigration and in interracial marriages." Then, "in response to the criticism," OMB announced that it would undertake a comprehensive review of the standards.[18] The task of the revision was to modify the standards so that they would reflect more accurately the makeup of American society. Thus the conjecture was that the general demographic profile of the population could have enhanced accuracy by closely reflecting the social makeup of the national body.

Underlying the purpose of the federal standards we find the notion that the general population consists of subgroups of a certain kind and that such a state of affairs is a good. This is what I will call the *principle of diversity*. My claim is that the objective of having an accurate demographic profile is guided by the principle of diversity.

Let me begin with the notion that the national population consists of diverse subgroups. According to the report recommending changes to the standards, the U.S. government has long collected statistics in an effort to have records of its diverse population and monitor changes in these groups. So data on race and ethnicity "have been used to monitor changes in the social, demographic, health and economic characteristics of various groups in our population."[19] The picture that emerges is that of diverse groups with different characteristics within the larger national body. So the profile provided by the data not only contains general demographic patterns of the nation as a whole; but also, more specifically, patterns of *particular* subgroups within the larger national group. It is then more precise to say that the purpose of classification and data gathering is to show the demographic profiles of subgroups within the national body. Unsurprisingly, as those subgroups change so should the categories used to collect data on those groups.

The goal, however, is not simply to collect data on different sub-groups. Differences by themselves are not necessarily significant. When classifying people, generating data that reflects differences among groups, or sub-groups, in a political or national body is natural. After all, unless there is perfect homogeneity in the population's characteristics, one should expect some degree of difference between subgroups within a larger group. Thus, for instance, children are not adults and males are not females. Similarly, nationals are not foreigners and the rich are not poor. When, say, a census questionnaire or a hospital form asks what your income is and what your gender is, it is already assumed that some difference between groups (wealthy and poor, male and female) exists and will be reported.

Classification and data gathering then presumes differential qualities. Interestingly, the qualities that the federal standards address seem to have some value. We read that: "federal data collections, through censuses, surveys, and administrative records, have provided a historical record of the Nation's population diversity and its changing social attitudes, health status, and policy concerns."[20]

To see the value of the "population diversity," think of the sorts of differences that are not generally conceived of as a good. No one, including governmental agencies, would seem to think that in most cases having two groups in the same social body is a good by virtue of difference alone. The mere differential condition of single and married people is not necessarily valuable. Something similar occurs with the difference between high income individuals (which could be defined arbitrarily as those who earn a salary over $100,000.00) and low income individuals (defined as those who earn a salary below $9,570.00).[21] Given the presence of different groups, one might be able to speak of some kind of "diversity" within the larger population. But the diversity created by these two groups, based on marital status or income level, would not generally be seen as a good.[22]

I pointed out above that ethnoracial groups are thought of as a set of subgroups within the national body. And we know that there is "a historical record" of these subgroups, which have or create policy concerns and which presumably constitute "the Nation's population diversity." Why should we be interested in a historical record that reports group differences? Why be concerned about subgroups that seem to have social attitudes and policy concerns? Married or wealthy people presumably have specific social attitudes and policy concerns, thus creating group differences; but keeping a historical record of these group differences would not seem to have much social value. In contrast, the "Nation's population diversity" is worth recording because the kind of diversity created by various ethnoracial groups is thought to be a good.

Note that the diversity of ethnoracial groups in U.S. history, according to the diversity principle of the federal standards, is a good by virtue of the fact that these groups are and have been part of the national body. It is true that corporations and institutions of higher education would value and encourage the presence of, say, women in their bodies—this would indeed be a significant component of their bodies' diversity. But diversity in this last case consists of group *representation* within a specific institution and not simply the fact that there are various groups within the national population.

For the federal standards, ethnoracial diversity is presumably a good by virtue of having continually existed, and be still existing, in the national body. Thus the value of diversity springs not only from different groups having been represented in, say, education or political positions—although this too is a very important consideration, as we will see below when discussing civil rights. The value of diversity is more basic than representation in specific groups that entail some type of achievement, as is the case in educational or professional groups. That an African American becomes a Supreme Court Justice is highly valuable. But the value of diversity in the picture that emerges from the federal standards consists in the fact that the American nation has, for instance, an African-American population, which is different from other communities. The mere presence of African Americans, and other groups, in the national body is considered a good.

We are thinking then not only of achievement groups, but also nonachievement groups. Access to a university is an achievement, whereas membership in the African-American group—or any other racial group—is not an achievement. Membership in nonachievement groups is a fact of life, something that occurs naturally. The presence of these nonachievement groups and memberships throughout American history and society is thought to have great value. Incidentally, one of the important tenets of a certain version of multiculturalism is that non-achievement groups have made important contributions to American history. Thus members of nonachievement groups also become members of achievement groups. In this context, achievement groups may be formal. So one must think, for instance, of Catherine Brewer, one of the first women ever to be granted, in 1840, a baccalaureate degree (at Wesleyan College in Georgia); or W. E. B. Dubois, the first African American to receive a Ph.D. from Harvard University. Achievement groups may also be informal. So, for instance, Frederick Douglass, the black escaped slave, was a notable speaker and author and a very significant contributor to the abolitionist cause. Douglass is part of the group of notable contributors to the cause of freedom. The set of contributors is an achievement group, but not a formal one.

So far I have discussed the picture behind one of the purposes for classifying groups and gathering data on race and ethnicity. The purpose is to produce the demographic profile of the national population. This national population is atomized by diverse ethnoracial subgroups. Thus there are distinct groups that have or create specific concerns, and that are differentiated by particular traits. This state of social differentiation generated by groups of a certain kind seems to be a good. Given this picture of ethnoracial groups, it makes sense to have and revise categories that accurately reflect the population's diversity. As I put it earlier, the principle of diversity guides the effort to produce an accurate demographic profile.

I want to focus now on a second, an in many ways a more important reason for collecting data and classifying people according to their race and ethnicity. Data is collected for the purpose of assessing law compliance toward groups that have been discriminated against. Thus, one of the main reasons for having ethnoracial categories in an official and standardized form has to do with civil rights monitoring and enforcement. This reason is directly derived from civil rights legislation forbidding discrimination in voting, education and employment. Legally, it is prohibited for all federally assisted programs to discriminate on the basis of race, color or national origin.[23] The Revisions to the Standards have an instructive description of why its ethnoracial categories were first created. According to the document, the standards were developed in order to provide consistent data across agencies. And "development of the data standards stemmed in large measure from new responsibilities to enforce civil rights laws." The following sentence is then quite descriptive of the situation: "Data were needed to monitor equal access in housing, education, employment" for historically excluded populations. These populations had "experienced discrimination and differential treatment because of their race and ethnicity."[24] If not the only purpose for collecting data on ethnic and racial groups, compliance with civil rights law is still a fundamental reason for having the current categories. So in their present form, "these standards shall be used by all Federal agencies in either the separate and or combined format for civil rights and other compliance reporting from the public and private sectors and all levels of government."[25]

A set of groups have been discriminated against and received differential treatment based on their race and ethnicity and so the public and private sector must report that previously excluded groups are no longer excluded. In order to do this reporting and show compliance, it is necessary to have categories and data showing the state of affairs. So the standards include not only categories of groups characterized simply by racial or ethnic traits, but also ethnoracial groups that have been treated unfairly.

The consideration having to do with discrimination is an important piece for arguing that African Americans ought to be included in the standards, whereas, say, German Americans, another ethnic group, should not be included. The argument would go like this. African Americans are a racial group that has been discriminated against in the past. Hence legislative measures and monitoring ought to be enacted in order to make sure that African Americans are not treated unfairly. These measures and monitoring activities entail official and standardized categories, classification and the gathering of data. In contrast, German Americans are an ethnic group, but since they have not been subjected to differential treatment, there is no reason to include German Americans in the official classification and data.

Assuming, somewhat hypothetically, that German Americans (or any other group not currently recognized) are indeed an ethnic group, an obvious retort could be that such an ethnic group is part of America's diversity. This reply would assume that the principle of diversity is reason enough to grant a group public recognition by means of classification and data collection.[26] In this picture, diversity is a good and thus all ethnically differentiated groups should be recognized. The federal standards, of course, do not recognize the vast range of possible ethnoracial groups. This seems to indicate that the principle of diversity is significant, but not sufficient for purposes of public recognition. In addition to creating diversity, a group must have received differential treatment in order to be publicly recognized. I will return to a similar point in the next chapter and examine whether differential treatment of ethnoracial groups is sufficient grounds for inclusion in the federal standards.

Let me now mention what I consider to be two varying versions of the civil rights enforcement criterion. In the first version, which can be considered of a minimalist type, a particular group of people have been unjustly excluded from mainstream society and political participation due to their race and ethnic affiliation. The purpose here is to rectify exclusionary policies from the past and prevent intentional exclusion, or discrimination, in the future. A good example of this version comes from the reasons behind the enactment of the Voting Rights Act. Given the constant evasion of voting rights for blacks in the South, the Voting Rights Act sought to create a mechanism that eliminates every "qualification or prerequisite to voting."[27] Moreover, section 5 of the Act requires "preclearance" from the federal authorities for states or counties with a history of discrimination before making any changes to voting procedures.[28] The provision ensures that new changes will not be in fact subtle discriminatory practices.[29]

The second version, which belongs to a more aggressive type of corrective measures, posits that some groups are disadvantaged with regard to other groups due to their race and ethnicity. The civil rights enforcement criterion then wants to close the gap between groups and level the playing field. This aim, to level the playing field, is the rationale behind affirmative action. A good example of this version is found in the regulation of government grants for public works. Under these regulations, it is the case that no grant shall be made for "any local public works project unless the applicant gives satisfactory assurance to the Secretary that at least 10 per centum of the amount of each grant shall be expended for minority business enterprises." A "minority business enterprise" means "a business at least 50 per centum of which is owned by minority group members or, in case of a publicly owned business, at least 51 per centum of the stock of which is owned by minority group members." In the statute, the reference to minority groups is specified. Thus, "minority group members are citizens of the United States who are Negroes, Spanish-speaking, Orientals, Indians, Eskimos, and Aleuts."[30] These are, in a rough and approximate form, the categories in the federal standards—although we must remember that categories and classification alone do not necessarily entail or lead to affirmative action.[31]

POLITICS AND CLASSIFICATION

We have seen that the government classifies people according to race and ethnicity due to the aim of having an accurate demographic profile and enforcing civil rights legislation. In the rest of this chapter, I want to look at the first goal, having an accurate demographic profile, and suggest that this goal, which is presumably achieved by a neutral or impartial statistical procedure, is actually based on political considerations. It is not only about counting people in an accurate way; it is also about determining who counts—and this determination is a political one.[32] In the next chapter, I will have much more to say about civil rights enforcement.

Earlier, I argued that the objective of increasing demographic accuracy, which prompted in part the revisions to the old standards, is guided by what I called the principle of diversity. I also pointed out that the principle of diversity, by itself, would not be enough grounds for including a certain group in the standards—since, say, German Americans can be construed as an ethnic group, but the group is not included in the standards. Presumably, you need an additional criterion, civil rights enforcement, in order to justify the inclusion of a group in the standards. This line of thought, as we will see in the next chapter, is not entirely true.

But what I wish to suggest now is that even if we isolate the principle of diversity and consider this enough grounds for counting people, some important political decisions come into play. The question of who counts cannot be answered by simply looking at different groups that are in existence. It can only be answered by taking into account the political considerations for determining who counts. Given different political considerations, the outcomes will vary. The basic claim is that classification depends on politics. Another way of stating the point is this: the principle of diversity, which guides the accuracy objective, is itself a political principle. And since the principle guides the objective, this objective of demographic accuracy is based on political decisions. In referring to census bureaus, Melissa Nobles puts it like this: "Counting by race is as much a political act as it is an enumerative one. Census bureaus are not simply producers of racial statistical data; they are also political actors."[33]

Consider first that the principle of diversity is a novel assumption in American history. It is true that "the United States Government has long collected statistics on race and ethnicity." The first decennial census in 1790, for instance, distinguished whites and people of color (whether free or slave). Nonetheless, the claim that "such data have been used to monitor changes in the social, demographic, health, and economic characteristics of various groups in our population" needs to be qualified.[34] The belief that data collection, censuses and administrative surveys provide a record of the population—showing a demographically diverse profile in American history and society—makes sense if you assume that diversity of a certain kind is a good. This is, nonetheless, a modern-day assumption that has not been present throughout much of U.S history. Consider the original constitutional purpose of census-taking. The goal was apportionment of representatives, which is still one of the purposes for collecting census data. The U.S. Constitution stipulates, "Representatives and direct Taxes shall be apportioned among the several States which may be included within this Union, according to their respective Numbers . . ." Moreover, the distinction was made between free persons, Indians (not taxed), and black slaves, who counted as three fifths of a person.[35]

In the second place, even if one accepts the assumption that the larger national body consists of a set of subgroups, one has to recognize that some of these groups shift over time. So, for example, let us assume that at some historical moment a given subgroup is very significant and thus should be included in the decennial census in order to record the demographic profile of this subgroup. But due to the phenomenon of assimilation by former immigrant groups, this subgroup ceases to be significant. This is the case because the group becomes indistinguishable from other similar groups. A clear example is that of the Irish. Between 1820 and 1924, approximately 4,578,941 Irish immigrants came to the U.S. The highest point of immigration in terms of raw numbers was the 1850s, with 914,119 immigrants coming in. The lowest point was in the 1820s, which had a total of 54,338 immigrants.[36] During that same time the general U.S. population oscillated between 9,633,822 and close to 105,710,620. For the 1860 decennial census the general population was 31,443,321. If we take this number as a rough approximation of the population throughout the 1850s this means that the Irish immigrants represented a little over 3 percent of the population, without including the second generation born in the U.S. If we do the same for the 1820s—the general population in 1830 was 12,866,020—the percentage of Irish immigrants is a little less than 3 percent. Again, this does not take into account the second generation. Consider that in the 2000 decennial census Native Hawaiians and Pacific Islanders—an official category of the federal standards—represented 0.3 percent of the general population.[37]

These rough facts show that the Irish group must have been a noteworthy bloc within American society—representing 3 percent of the population.[38] The Irish were clearly a group with distinguishing traits; some of which must have been passed on to their own children, born in the U.S.

Nonetheless, even for the people born in the U.S. from Irish parents, the second generation and beyond, there was never an official category in the census questionnaire to recognize their "Irish-American" identity. And what is more important, as time went on and new generations of Irish-American children came, their Irish identity became weaker and mainstream American identity stronger. This is illustrated by the fact that one single category, "white," would be enough to encompass all the formerly immigrant European groups that are now mainstream "American." Here we have a good example of shifting national subgroups and their identities. The question then is, at what point should the federal government include certain groups and drop others? If you think of the increasing levels of immigration from Muslim countries, and the emerging Muslim-American identity, would it not make sense to accord this group public recognition? The "Arab-American" category has been explicitly rejected by the federal government. But given the apparent growth of an emerging Arab-American bloc, would it not make sense to include this category in the federal standards? Likewise, at what point do you drop, say, categories that cease to be relevant? Suppose immigration from Latin America stops, five generations later all the children from formerly Latin American parents have blended into mainstream American society and have only a vague recollection of their "Hispanic" or "Latino" background. In this process, at what point does the federal government drop the Hispanic category from official documents? The important point is that as groups change, the possibility and decision of including certain people or not is an administrative and political one.

In the third place, one has to contend with the question of why the ethnoracial criterion. Under the assumption that we live in a diverse society, with different subgroups within the national body, why organize the subgroups according to an ethnoracial criterion? We could, for instance, arrange subgroups so that we have different color preferences. In this new arrangement, group A prefers white, group B prefers blue, group C prefers orange, and so on. This would be neither an acceptable arrangement of group differences for purposes of public recognition nor the type of diversity that we could consider a good. One could answer here that the reason for classifying people according to their race and ethnicity has to do with past discrimination according to ethnoracial traits. This is true, but as I will show in the next chapter the matter is much more complicated than it seems. What I want to highlight now is that the decision has been made, based on the ethnoracial criterion, to include certain categories and not others in the federal standards.

Then another subtler question arises. Even if we confine the subgroup measure to ethnoracial groups, why accept some particular groups and not others? Why instead of having a broad and encompassing category, Hispanic, not have more localized group identities? The census, for instance, does recognize to some extent particular nationalities within the Hispanic category. But now think of someone from Peru who happens to be Quechua. Why make, say, the Hispanic or even Peruvian-American category acceptable and not accept the Quechuan-American category? Drawing the boundaries for groups that will then become part of the classification scheme is a political decision.

The attempt to achieve accuracy is filtered through political considerations.[39] The first thing we need to see is that the goal is based on an assumed principle. On the basis of that principle, group diversity is a good. Only by assuming the principle can we then move on to classifying different groups and, more importantly, attempting to achieve an accurate representation of those groups. But group boundaries also change over time and the question arises: when do official categories cease to represent accurately the group that has either come into existence or began to fade? Lastly, groups are recognized according to a certain criterion, e.g., ethnoracial. So the attempt to achieve demographic accuracy comes after the criterion whereby groups will be recognized has been determined. The upshot is that group classification, for policy purposes, is based on previous beliefs and criteria that determine who is to be counted in the political landscape.

CONCLUSION

I started this chapter by reviewing the Standards for the Classification of Federal Data on Race and Ethnicity. As we saw, there are standardized categories for collecting data and classifying the population according to the ethnoracial criterion. Two reasons explain the interest of the federal government in collecting ethnoracial data. The first one has to do with accurate demographic profiles. Here, I discussed the notion that a certain kind of diversity is a good and it is thus necessary to keep records that reflect accurately the demographic profiles of diverse populations. More importantly, the second reason has to do with civil rights enforcement in the context of groups that have received differential treatment due to race and ethnicity. Presumably, group inclusion in a classificatory scheme depends on whether the second reason applies or not.

But even if one assumes that the first reason, having accurate demographic profiles, is enough grounds for classifying groups, it is necessary to take into account the political dimension of the task. Population profiles are based on a series of political considerations that contribute toward determining how to categorize groups and also which ones ought to be classified. Thus in the final part of the chapter, I suggested that the statistical task of counting people is preceded by a political process of categorization and decision-making that determines who should count and why. I now turn to a significant underlying assumption for determining why certain groups ought to be the object of classification and enumeration.

NOTES

1. See *Measuring America: The Decennial Censuses from 1790 to 2000* (U.S Census Bureau, September 2002), 100.

2. For historical accounts and considerations, see Peter Skerry, *Counting on the Census? Race, Group Identity and the Evasion of Politics* (Washington, D.C.: Brookings Institution Press, 2000); John D. Skrentny, *The Minority Rights Revolution* (Cambridge, MA: Harvard University Press, 2002); and Terry H. Anderson, *The Pursuit of Fairness: A History of Affirmative Action* (New York: Oxford University Press, 2004).

3. For the full text, see appendix 1 in "Recommendations from the Interagency Committee for the Review of the Racial and Ethnic Standards to the Office of Management and Budget Concerning Changes to the Standards for the Classification of Federal Data on Race and Ethnicity," in *Federal Register*, vol. 62, no. 131 (Thursday, Wednesday, July 9, 1997, Notices, 36876–36877).

4. "Recommendations," 36876.

5. For some popular misconceptions about the standards, see Skerry, *Counting on the Census?*, 54–57.

6. "Recommendations," 36876.

7. "Revisions to the Standards for the Classification of Federal Data on Race and Ethnicity," in *Federal Register*, vol. 62, no. 210 (Thursday, October 30, 1997, Notices, 58782).

8. The distinction between race and ethnicity is a complicated one. One of the discussions in the standards emphasizes this point. "Recommendations," 36909–36910. Nonetheless, the standards maintain the distinction due primarily to the fact that Hispanics or Latinos could be of different races. So instead of considering them a "racial" group, they are rather considered an "ethnic" one.

9. "Recommendations," 36876.

10. "Recommendations," 36876.

11. "Recommendations," 36874. For a brief historical overview of the review process for the standards, see Katherine Wallman, "Data on Race and Ethnicity: Revising the Federal Standard," *The American Statistician*, 52, 1 (1998): 31–33.

12. "Revisions," 58782–58790.
13. "Recommendations," 58789.
14. "Recommendations," 36937.
15. "Revisions," 58789.
16. "Revisions," 58783.
17. "Revisions," 58785.
18. "Revisions," 58782.
19. "Recommendations," 36879.
20. "Recommendations," 36879.
21. See the U.S Department of Health and Human Services' 2005 Poverty Guidelines. <http://aspe.hhs.gov/poverty/05poverty.shtml> (September 15, 2006).
22. For different ways of conceptualizing diversity, see Peter H. Schuck, *Diversity in America: Keeping Government at a Safe Distance* (Cambridge, MA: Harvard University Press, 2003), 19–27.
23. The two landmark pieces of this legislation are the 1964 Civil Rights Act (particularly Titles I, IV, VI, VII) and the 1965 Voting Rights Act. See also 42 U.S.C. 1973, 42 U.S.C. 2000d, 42 U.S.C. 2000e-2.
24. "Revisions," 58782.
25. "Revisions," 58789–58790.
26. Following the standards, when I speak of recognition, I generally refer to any type of governmental action that highlights and acknowledges particular groups and members in a public way. The reference to recognition in this context overlaps but is not identical with Charles Taylor's notion of recognition. Whereas Taylor explicitly links recognition and identity, the U.S. government does not. Precisely, my point is that despite the lack of an explicit link for the U.S. government, ethnoracial recognition is motivated by identity considerations. See "The Politics of Recognition," in *Multiculturalism: Examining the Politics of Recognition*, ed. Amy Gutmann (Princeton: Princeton University Press, 1994).
27. 42 U.S.C. 1973.
28. 42 U.S.C. 1973c.
29. Despite this original intention, Abigail Thernstrom, for instance, argues that the provisions have been interpreted and applied in a way that has turned them, in fact, into another affirmative action program. See *Whose Votes Count? Affirmative Action and Minority Voting Rights* (Cambridge, MA: Harvard University Press, 1987).
30. 42 U.S.C. 6705.
31. Affirmative action is a very complicated subject and the legislation in this regard is difficult to understand. See, for instance, *Adarand Constructors, Inc. v Pena* 515 U.S. 200 (1995) for a discussion on the standards under which race-based contracting should proceed without violating the equal protection of the laws. Moreover, the claim that the federal standards do not lead to affirmative action gets very thin at times, for although the federal standards are not affirmative action as such, the data generated by the standards are the basis on which affirmative action is construed and assessed. I return to this point on the final chapter.
32. For useful literature on this point, see Skerry, *Counting on the Census*, 9–42; and Melissa Nobles, *Shades of Citizenship: Race and the Census in Modern Politics* (Stanford: Stanford University Press, 2000), 1–24.

33. *Shades of Citizenship*, 1.
34. "Recommendations," 36879.
35. See the U.S. Constitution, Article 1, Section 2. See also 13 U.S.C. 141.
36. See Roger Daniels, *Coming to America: A History of Immigration and Ethnicity in American Life* (New York: Harper Collins, 2002), 129.
37. See Elizabeth Grieco, *The Native Hawaiian and Other Pacific Islander Population: 2000* (U.S. Census Bureau, December 2001), 1.
38. For general population estimates, see *Measuring America*, appendix A, A-1.
39. The political considerations are extremely significant because the classification scheme "has *expressive* or *symbolic* significance beyond its explicit purposes" (original emphasis). Judith Lichtenberg, Suzanne Bianchi, Robert Wachbroit and David Wasserman, "Counting Race and Ethnicity: Option for the 2000 Census," in *Report from the Institute for Philosophy and Public Policy* 17, 3 (1997): 19.

3

✣

The Presumption of Relevant Membership

We have seen that ethnoracial classification is driven by demographic profiles and civil rights enforcement. In this chapter, we will see that classifying people on ethnoracial grounds also has to do with what I call the *presumption of relevant membership*. Briefly, the presumption says that membership is relevant when someone is a member in group X and such membership is central to her identity. I will argue that the presumption is necessary for understanding the government's intention of classifying people according to ethnoracial criteria. In this chapter, we will then see the connection between identity politics and data collection.

I start out with a weak claim—simply, that the presumption of relevant membership helps to explain why the federal government is interested in ethnoracial groups and memberships. A question that arises is whether the federal government, independently from identity considerations, may still have an interest in classifying and compiling ethnoracial data in order to monitor and enforce civil rights legislation. In addressing this question, I then argue that the presumption of relevant membership is actually necessary for explaining the government's interest in the ethnoracial dimension. So I advance now a strong claim, arguing for the necessary connection between beliefs on identity and ethnoracial categorization.

A SPECIAL KIND OF MEMBERSHIP

Let me then begin with the weak claim that the presumption of relevant membership may help us understand why the federal government is interested in ethnoracial groups. Suppose a certain kind of membership has a special status, making such a membership highly significant—so much that we want to recognize it and cherish the diverse groups that play such a crucial role in citizen's identities. If that were the case, what is the kind of membership that would seem to have a special status? Let us compare different groups to see what this kind of special-status membership should look like.

First, compare two groups, American Indians and members of the Libertarian party. An American Indian is someone who generally has a set of traits—having to do with ancestry and adherence to certain myths and customs—that make her a member in a minority group. A Libertarian in American society is also someone with a set of traits—e.g., views on government and certain social practices—that make him a member of another minority group: the Libertarian Party. In comparing both groups, I use the term "minority" simply to indicate that with regard to the sum total of the American population both groups are a numerical minority.

One could feasibly claim that American Indians are a species of an ethnic group; that ethnic identity is extremely significant for a sense and affirmation of who I am; and thus my ethnic identity ought to be recognized and upheld by means of, say, legal group rights and preferential treatment.[1] This sort of claim, however, would be extremely odd in connection with membership in the Libertarian Party. We do not normally think of the Libertarian Party as an ethnic group, or, more importantly, as a kind of identity that is extremely significant for a sense and affirmation of who I am. We neither think of being a libertarian as a kind of identity that ought to be publicly recognized or receive preferential treatment. The libertarian way of life might be protected under, say, the first amendment (just like many other views and ways of life), but it would be odd to say that legal provisions must exist in order for my "libertarian identity" to be publicly recognized —the American state does not have, for example, a Libertarian Heritage Month.

There is then apparently a degree of significance in someone's ethnic membership that does not seem to be present in someone's political affiliation. I might have two overlapping memberships: ethnic and political (I am an American Indian and a libertarian). In my layers of identity, one type of identity, i.e., ethnic, will be more important than the other, i.e., political. If you do not publicly recognize my American Indian ethnic identity you would be doing me a great and grievous harm. If, in contrast, you do not publicly recognize my libertarian identity the result will not be consequential; or you might still be doing me great harm, but not to the same degree.

The point is that there is apparently something extremely significant about my ethnic membership—a degree of significance that seems to be absent in other types of memberships. So, in short, whereas my ethnic membership is central to my own identity, the sense of who I am, my political membership, in this case my libertarian affiliation, presumably is not.

In the second example let us compare two groups according to their levels of income. One group is disadvantaged with regard to the other in that people in the first group have a higher income than people in the second group. Let us posit that a particular disadvantaged group ought to be recognized and receive preferential treatment because a society is based on principles of justice. The rationale is that since one of the groups is disadvantaged with regard to others, some type of affirmative action is necessary in order to close the gap. But the assumption here is that the sort of justice that would seem to require affirmative action only acknowledges classifications and groups of a certain kind. Consider that not *all* disadvantaged groups should receive recognition and preferential treatment. To see this, compare now the group of lawyers and the group of musicians, where lawyers generally have greater access to a distributional good such as salaries than musicians do. And so we could say that in a certain sense musicians are disadvantaged with regard to lawyers. Nonetheless, we would not generally say that musicians should have special rights or receive preferential treatment by virtue of the fact that they are musicians. The reason is because musicians are not related to the kind of membership or group that generally qualifies for special treatment.

Let me further illustrate the special kind of membership I have in mind with a third example. Imagine someone applying for a job in which she has no previous professional experience. She then is said to belong to a group that we will call "novices." What all the members of this group have in common is that they have no previous professional experience for the jobs to which they are applying. Suppose now that in the pool of applicants there are members from another group that we will call "experts." Members of this group are highly experienced in their fields. The hiring committee offers the job to one of the experts because they would like to hire someone with previous experience. Now let us suppose that the person applying for the job is both a novice and a member of the Hispanic group. She has reason to believe that she was not offered the job not because she was a novice, and the hiring committee had preferences for an expert. The real reason why she was not offered the job is because she is Hispanic.

Whereas rejection on the grounds that she is a novice, instead of an expert, does not constitute discrimination, rejection on the grounds that she is Hispanic constitutes discrimination. Why is that the case? The first reason is that while the level of expertise might be directly relevant to the task, the person's ethnic or religious affiliation is not. So hiring considerations based on nonrelevant grounds might entail discrimination—although consider that employers sometimes make determinations on grounds that are not directly relevant to the job, e.g., concerns about a long commute. But there is also a second and more important reason. Our applicant is a member in two groups that are different in kind from each other: novices and Hispanics. Her membership in the group of novices may not be very significant, but her membership in the Hispanic group is presumably highly significant for a sense of who she is. So exclusion from hiring due to her Hispanic membership is far more serious than exclusion due to her level of expertise. Real life situations will undoubtedly be more complex since hiring processes are generally murky procedures that take into account many different factors and considerations. This example, however, illustrates an important point. Membership in the Hispanic group, or another similar group, has a presumed status that other memberships or groups do not have.

Although the examples I have used are simple and even trivial, they serve to illustrate how memberships may not only be different, but may also have different degrees of significance.[2] In two of the three examples, I compared memberships and groups of different kinds. American Indians and political parties are two groups that happen to be different in kind from each other. The former receives recognition and the latter does not. Something similar occurs with Hispanics and novices. Musicians and lawyers have an income gap, but the groups are not different in kind from each other since they are both "professional groups"—and more importantly, they are not groups of a special kind. Hence, income gap does not seem to be sufficient grounds for preferential treatment of the disadvantaged group.

What is then the special kind of group I have been talking about? These are presumably nonachievement groups in which members have immutable traits "determined solely by the accident of birth."[3] But more importantly they are, roughly speaking, what we might call "identity groups." These are groups in which membership is very significant because membership in this kind of group is a major source of identity. And indeed, membership in these groups is presumed to be central to members' identities. Identity groups, as I use the term, are characterized by what I will call the "presumption of relevant membership," i.e., membership in group X is central to a member's identity.

Once we bring this presumption into the picture, we can then begin to see what is special about American Indians or other ethnoracial groups in contrast with, say, political groups or clubs. We can then probably see one of the reasons why the government collects data on some groups and not others. If the assumption is that membership in the African-American group, for instance, is central to a member's identity, hence the government has good reasons to recognize and collect data on this population in order to know its demographic profile. The presumption also shows the type of diversity that is a good. This diversity consists in having people from different ethnoracial identity groups sharing perspectives that are essential to their identities and are thus worth knowing about. We can finally then see part of what is so wrong with discriminating against people from identity groups. People are excluded based on traits that are highly significant for their identities, which causes great harm. The general picture is that membership in identity groups, such as ethnic and racial ones, has a special status and such a status constitutes grounds for granting these groups some type of public protection and recognition.

CIVIL RIGHTS COMPLIANCE AND RELEVANT MEMBERSHIP

Note that my suggestion in the first section has been a limited one. I simply conjectured that when it comes to the rationale behind ethnoracial classification and data collection, the presumption of relevant membership may help to explain why the government would want to collect this sort of data. If this hypothesis is true, it would seem that ethnoracial membership merits recognition because it has a special status that other memberships do not have. I have not conjectured or suggested that the presumption of relevant membership is the *only* reason why government officials would think that it is necessary to collect data on certain groups. But if it is not the only reason, what else would we need in order to explain ethnoracial recognition? Consider that certain groups have experienced differential treatment and been excluded from resources that should have been equally open to all citizens. And hence, the civil rights enforcement criterion, in either one of the two versions mentioned in the previous chapter, aims at guaranteeing that these groups are not barred from participating in and having access to certain public goods.[4]

Additionally, one could also claim that although identity might help to explain the motivation for ethnoracial data collection, the ultimate test for the groups included in the federal standards has to do with civil rights monitoring and enforcement. After all, the government does not collect data on Jewish Americans, a type of identity that is presumably important to many members of the group and that could certainly be thought of as part of the diversity we value. Think also of the hypothetical German-American group mentioned in the previous chapter. I suggested that although this group's identity might be indeed highly valuable, given the government's rationales for ethnoracial data collection, the German-American category may not warrant inclusion in the federal standards. The way I put it was that the principle of diversity, in and of itself, is not enough grounds for public recognition by way of classification and data collection. The point is then that a special status might help to explain why the government would want to collect ethnoracial data on certain groups, but the explanation for determining why some groups are included and others ignored needs to turn to the civil rights criterion. In short, it is not about identity, it is about civil rights.

I now want to look more closely at the claim that the civil rights criterion is necessary for explaining the government's interest in collecting ethnoracial data. Suppose that this criterion were not enough or even necessary for explaining the inclusion of certain groups in the federal standards. So, in other words, imagine we could explain the presence of groups included in the federal standards without recourse to civil rights monitoring and enforcement. Based on this consideration, I want to argue that without the presumption of relevant membership, it would be extremely hard to explain the rationale for ethnoracial categories and data collection. My claim is that the presumption of relevant membership is necessary for understanding ethnoracial classification and recognition. Certain groups are recognized not only because they may have experienced differential treatment, but also because they are groups of a certain kind that generate special identities. Thus the explanation for ethnoracial recognition goes beyond civil rights monitoring and enforcement. For a full explanation, we need to turn to certain beliefs about identity groups.

Consider first that certain groups, which are protected under civil rights legislation and may be subjected to discrimination, do not receive public recognition. For groups that have experienced differential treatment and been excluded from resources that should be open to all citizens, the civil rights enforcement criterion aims at guaranteeing that these groups are not barred from participating in and having access to certain public goods. But not all the groups that have experienced, or continue to experience, differential treatment are the object of classification and data collection.

Think of members of religious groups who can be discriminated against and are thus protected under civil rights legislation—e.g., title VII of the Civil Rights Act with regard to employment. Consider also the fact that certain religious groups have been subjected to exclusion—think of the Mormon exclusion from Illinois in 1844. The government, however, does not collect data on religious groups. Differential treatment then would not seem to be sufficient grounds for recognizing the sorts of groups we find in the federal standards.

But supposing for a moment that this is true so far, we can still add another condition in order to see why some of the groups subjected to differential treatment are recognized, whereas others are not. If we now add to the condition of differential treatment the view that ethnoracial membership satisfies the presumption of relevant membership, we could perhaps see more clearly the rationale for collecting ethnoracial information. Since ethnoracial membership is central to members' identities *and* group members have been subjected to differential treatment due to their membership, the government is justified in collecting the sort of data that reflects group members' identities and serves to monitor civil rights enforcement. The obvious question here is: what if religious membership also satisfies the presumption of relevant membership and members of a religious group receive differential treatment? Would it not then be necessary to also collect religious data? In order to answer this question fully, we need to take into account considerations about the separation of church and state.[5] Nonetheless, bypassing these considerations, it is clear that for purposes of public recognition, religious memberships are not generally considered to be relevant. In fact, for purposes of public recognition, religion is not a good.

The line of reasoning I have pursued to this point may not take us very far, since religion imposes certain constraints that trump other factors, including the two we are considering now: members of religious groups may be subjected to discrimination and religious membership may be central to someone's identity. But absent these constraints, I do not see any good reason for not drawing a parallel between ethnoracial and religious groups, especially considering that the boundary lines between both types of groups are sometimes hard to draw. For instance, the American-Indian group, a racial group according to the federal standards, is partly defined by religious practices that are addressed in special statutes. Thus the ceremonial use of peyote is allowed and protected by federal regulation.[6] Leaving, however, those exceptional cases aside, which are precisely exceptional ones, let us assume generally that principles of separation between religion and state trump other factors.

Looking now at other types of groups that have also suffered discrimination and are not recipients of public recognition, we may find that it is much harder to explain why certain nonreligious groups are not publicly recognized. Take, for instance, gays and lesbians. Although the group has been the target of discrimination and could be construed as an identity group, where sexual orientation is central to members' identities, the government does not regularly collect data on sexual orientation. But if gays and lesbians are not an ethnic group, now take Arab Americans—arguably, an ethnic group, which has also been subjected to differential treatment.[7] The category "Arab American" came under review for inclusion in the federal standards on the grounds that "in order to track problems related to discrimination against Arabs or Middle Easterners, some way of identifying them separately is necessary."[8] The proposal to include the category in federal forms, however, was turned down claiming, "the definition of Arab or Middle Eastern is problematic,"[9] given that "currently there is no recognized common identity for this population group—neither a generally accepted name nor a common description." Part of the problem arises from the fact that most Middle Easterners are Muslims but not all are, for there are Christian Palestinians.[10] So according to the current federal standards, people from the Middle East—a complex and problematic category to begin with—are classified under the category of "White."[11] Yet despite the difficulty in identifying an "Arab American" group, which also applies to other groups such as Hispanics, if we assume that Arab Americans are indeed an ethnic group subject to discrimination, it is hard to see why the group is not included in the federal standards.[12]

I have looked so far at instances of groups and classes, determined by sexual orientation and Arab-American membership, which are protected under civil rights legislation and do not receive public and official recognition. This shows that, whether there are good reasons to do so or not, not all legislatively protected classes receive public recognition by way of categorization and data collection. Thus protection under civil rights legislation does not seem to be a sufficient condition for recognition. The lack of connection between civil rights protection and public recognition by way of classification and data collection makes us wonder how strong the relationship is. But all I have suggested to this point is that the link between civil rights enforcement and the reasons for group classification are weaker than we would initially think—protection under civil rights legislation does not necessarily lead to governmental classification. Let me move a step further now and show that the link is even weaker than I have suggested so far. We will see that certain ethnoracial groups that have not suffered, or no longer suffer, discrimination are actually included in the federal standards.

One could immediately think of African Americans and point out that although they were once subjected to violence that is no longer the case. Racism might still be around, but not to the degree that fueled the Jim Crow mindset; and when one thinks of, say, lynching, one has to agree that after the civil rights movement "that world is gone."[13] And yet the African-American case is a very difficult one, since African Americans were subjected to extreme differential treatment for much of the U.S. history and, as some stereo-types still remain, are still subjected to certain forms of racial discrimination. So, if not immediately obvious, the merits for African-American categorization and data collection would seem to have a higher degree of plausibility than other groups.

Despite the degree of plausibility for African-American categorization and data collection, let me point out that the group covered under the African-American category is not coextensive with the group that has historically received differential treatment. Note, for instance, that the category is defined as "a person having origins in any of the black racial groups of Africa."[14] The category, however, is not limited to members of the racial group who have been, under U.S. jurisdiction, subjected historically to differential treatment due to race, and for whom constitutional provisions—e.g., the Thirteenth and Fourteenth amendments to the U.S. Constitution—were enacted. The category explicitly includes any members of a racial group called "black," including, say, black Haitians, Jamaicans and Nigerians.[15] But why should it be relevant whether Jamaican blacks are included? One could say, of course, that given the prevalence of racism, these groups could be *potentially* subjected to differential treatment. I will return to this discussion below, but now, with a similar point in mind, let me turn to the extension of three other groups included in the federal standards, Hispanics, Asians and American Indians.

Let us grant what is a matter of fact: members of the Hispanic group have indeed suffered discrimination. The 1947 report of Harry Truman's Committee on Civil Rights names "Hispanos" as a group that has been discriminated against.[16] And as recognized by the Supreme Court, members of the Hispanic group in the Southwest have been subjected to systematic discrimination. So in 1954, *Hernandez v. Texas* found that the equal protection of the laws, as prescribed in the U.S. Constitution, did not apply only to blacks and whites; it also applied to people of Mexican descent. In view of the systematic exclusion of people of Mexican descent from jury duty, the Court reversed the conviction of Pete Hernandez on the grounds that he was entitled to be tried by a jury in which members of his class, those of Mexican descent, were not excluded. For our purposes, let me highlight that, according to the arguments presented in the decision, people of Mexican descent did indeed constitute a different class from whites. Additionally, although 14% of the general population consisted of people "with Mexican or Latin-American surnames," no one with a Mexican or Latin-American surname had served in a jury commission for the last twenty five years—which established discrimination against the class.[17]

Using this case now as an illustration of the kind of discrimination suffered by Hispanics, note two points. First, the category "Mexican American" is not necessarily coextensive with the category "Hispanic." More precisely, the population of Mexican descent in the Southwest—and more specifically with regard to the case mentioned above, Texas—is not coextensive with the whole Hispanic group.[18] Foreshadowing discussions that will follow in the book, the Hispanic category includes many different nationalities with sometimes little in common. Interestingly, the Truman report mentioned above defines the "Hispano" category in terms of the first Spanish settlers in the Rio Grande Valley. The report also acknowledges a second group, not to be confused with "Hispanos": "persons of Mexican descent" settled primarily in Texas and California,[19] which is the group that often goes by the category "Mexican American." Now note a second point. Even after we grant that people of Mexican descent in certain parts of the country have been subjected to discrimination by virtue of class membership, it does not follow that all members of the Hispanic group have suffered or currently suffer discrimination. If we think of Cubans in Florida, just to mention another "Hispanic" group that has generally flourished culturally and prospered financially, we will immediately see that different Hispanic groups tend to find themselves in very different circumstances.[20] So, for instance, a U.S. Census Bureau report on the 2000 census found that in 1999 "median family income among Hispanic groups varied from a high of $53,000 for Spaniards to a low of $28,700 for Dominicans." The national overall median income for all families in the U.S. was $50,046, and the overall Hispanic median family income was $34,397. The median family income for Cubans was $42,642, which was lower than the national median income, but much higher than the Hispanic median income. South Americans, a category unto itself according to the report, had a median income of $42,824—which is above the Hispanic median, but below the national one—and Spaniards had a median of $53,002—above the national median.

Thus whereas it is easier to see discrimination against people of Mexican descent in, say, the Southwest, it is much harder to see discrimination against Spaniards or Cubans in Miami. To make matters even more complicated, consider, for instance, that the Cuban migration had different patterns with varying profiles. So, for instance, Cubans who migrated before the Castro revolution possessed, for the most part, assets and skills that distinguished them from those who migrated as part of the *Marielito* boatlift in 1980. If my observation is right, it is then the case that although some members of the Hispanic group have suffered discrimination by virtue of class membership, not all members or subgroups within the Hispanic category have been indeed victims of discrimination—or at least to the same degree. Moreover, subsets within the Hispanic group find themselves in differing conditions. Using data from the 2004 American Community Survey as an example, I want to illustrate briefly how dissimilar subsets within the Hispanic category might be. Table 3.1 [at the end of this chapter] looks at the population eighteen and older that speaks a language other than English at home. Furthermore, the table compares the non-Hispanic population with detailed subvariables under the main Hispanic variable. All the variables are officially used by the U.S. Census when breaking down the data collected in censuses and questionnaires. Note, for instance, that among Mexicans who speak Spanish at home, only four percent have completed a Bachelors degree. Turning, however, to Costa Ricans the figure climbs to nineteen percent and among Venezuelans it is twenty seven percent. These are staggering differences. In table 3.2, we find a comparison between Hispanic subsets eighteen and older according to their educational level. This table drops the linguistic variable and thus includes Hispanics who speak English. Notice that, as shown in table 3.2, whereas forty six percent of people eighteen and older with a Mexican background do not have a high school degree, only eleven percent of people with a Chilean background do not have a high school degree. In fact, Chileans compare favorably with the overall American, non-Hispanic population, with the rate of those who do not have a high school degree at thirteen percent.

Accepting my point so far, the justification for including the Hispanic category in the federal standards could not rest solely or even primarily on the grounds that Hispanics have been and are subjected to differential treatment, which would then require civil rights compliance and reporting with regard to members of the group. Something similar occurs with "Asians," another incredibly complex group that subsumes disparate nationalities, e.g., Chinese, Japanese and Indians. It is true that members of the Asian group have suffered discrimination throughout American history. Consider, for instance, the Chinese Exclusion Act, which was signed into law in 1882. The act "was the first significant inhibition on free immigration in American history" and "made the Chinese, for a time the only ethnic group in the world that could not freely immigrate to the United States." And as if limiting immigration was not enough, the 1870 Naturalization Act restricted naturalization for whites and people of African descent, making the Chinese ineligible for citizenship until 1943.[21] Similarly, people of Japanese ancestry received differential treatment during World War II through placement in relocation centers and other discriminatory policies. Some of these measures, curfews and exclusion from several areas, were even thought to be constitutional and necessary on the basis of national defense.[22]

Consider, however, that not all members of the Asian group have been subjected to differential treatment under U.S. jurisdiction or throughout American history. Simply put, the case is that not all the subgroups subsumed under the Asian category as construed by the federal standards—e.g., Malaysians—have had in the past, or even currently, a significant presence in U.S. territory. It follows then, a fortiori, that members of these subgroups cannot have been discriminated against, systematically and regularly, by virtue of class membership.[23] Now, there is also the fact that Asians, in general, and within particular subgroups in the category, tend to have a higher proportion of high school diplomas and bachelors degrees than the general American population, and also tend to have higher median earnings. The U.S. Census Bureau reports that in 2000 "a higher proportion of Asians (44 percent) than of the total population (24 percent) had earned at least a bachelor's degree." The report also points out disparities within the group, which would seem to mask the underperformance of certain subgroups. So, for instance, "Asian Indians had the highest percentage with a bachelor's degree, about 64 percent, whereas about 60 percent of Hmong, and about half of Cambodians and Laotians, had less than high school education."[24] With regard to salaries, the report finds that "on average, Asian Indian, Japanese and Chinese men had higher median earnings than Asian men and all men." Asian Indian, Japanese and Chinese women also had the highest median earnings of the Asian group and "were 14 percent higher than those of all women."[25] If education deficits and below-average median earnings are taken as indications of differential treatment, it would seem that at least certain subgroups within the Asian category, e.g., Indians, are not currently subjected to such differential treatment.

The discussion so far leads me to believe that not all the subgroups subsumed under the Asian category are the same with reference to differential treatment and for purposes of civil rights monitoring and enforcement. Granting that certain subgroups within the Asian category experience differential treatment, given the lack of presence on U.S. soil of certain subgroups and the over-performance of other subgroups with regard to measures of discrimination, it follows that not all subgroups within the category experience discrimination. In short, it seems that the extension of subgroups under the Asian category experiencing differential treatment has to be distinguished from the category's overall extension.

Let us now finally consider a third category in the federal standards, American Indians. In the original 1977 category of OMB's Directive 15, American Indian is defined as "a person having origins in any of the original peoples of North America, and who maintains cultural identification through tribal affiliation or community recognition."[26] But if the original category was limited to the "peoples of North America," one of the questions considered in the 1997 discussion for new recommendations, was whether the category should be changed to include "Indians indigenous to Central America and South America."[27] This would presumably include groups such as the Yanomami, the Mayans, the Quechua and the Guarani, or people descended from any of these groups. The 1997 revisions to the standards actually amended the American-Indian category to include this change.[28] What is puzzling about this category is that it explicitly includes people who have not had any significant presence in American territory and do not seem to be part, as a group, of a current migratory wave. So, as with some Asian subgroups in a previous example, the American-Indian category includes people outside the U.S. jurisdiction. If American Indians, understood as the original peoples of what is currently the U.S., have been and continue to be subjected to differential treatment, those members of groups which have not had and do not have a presence in the U.S.—e.g., the Guarani—cannot be subjected to differential treatment by the American government. Surely then, civil rights monitoring and enforcement with regard to groups that experience differential treatment, or even considerations having to do with the diversity of the *American* population, cannot be the only explanations for the categories in the federal standards.

What explains the discrepancy between the extensions of subgroups subsumed under the same category—one that experiences differential treatment and one that does not? A possible answer is that the category points to a group that could be *potentially* subjected to differential treatment. Hence, these groups have a proclivity to be discriminated against. If that is the case, the question arises whether all groups that could be potentially discriminated against, given the historical precedent, should be classified a priori. One can think, most notably, of one of the cases I mentioned above, i.e., sexual orientation. But it is not necessary to turn here to a comparative analysis of group kinds. I think that a more plausible explanation for the discrepancy between extensions is that members of the group are thought to identify themselves with the racial or ethnic category. And, presumably, people identify themselves with these categories because membership in the group is highly significant for a sense of who they are. This act of identification would seem to make ethnoracial groups a special kind of group, and membership in these groups conspicuous.

Nonetheless, even if what I have suggested so far is correct, I still have not shown that membership in ethnoracial groups is thought to be central to members' identities. I have made the case that ethnoracial groups are thought to be special and membership conspicuous. To move a step further and see the extent to which membership in these groups is significant, let us look at the federal standard's preferred method of identification, self-identification. The revisions to the standards "underscore that self-identification is the preferred means of obtaining information about an individual's race and ethnicity, except in instances where observer identification is more practical (e.g., completing a death certificate)."[29]

The emphasis on self-identification then makes us wonder: why is self-identification so significant? Here we need to remember several points. As I pointed out before, the federal standards collect data of different population groups that make up the national body. These groups create a type of social diversity worth valuing and noting. Why are these differential qualities worth highlighting and recording? Or in terms of how I described the state of affairs before, why is this kind of diversity a good?

Presuming that this diversity is a good because it distinguishes and highlights group qualities that are very significant for group members, we can see why the federal standards are so keen on making sure that the categories actually reflect how people see themselves. People identify with and think of themselves as members of certain groups that have particular social and cultural characteristics,[30] and group identification says something very significant about who people are and how they view themselves. In short, group identification expresses noteworthy traits about groups and personal identities.[31]

This belief makes sense in light of the original reason for revising the standards. The revision was undertaken after the standards came "under increasing criticism from those who believe that the minimum categories set forth in Directive No. 15 do not reflect the increasing diversity of our Nation's population." This enhanced diversity "has resulted primarily from growth in immigration and in interracial marriages."[32] As a matter of fact, while some new groups asked for recognition in the revised standards due to suffering discrimination, others requested recognition because "nationality group seems to be primarily a matter of pride."[33] As acknowledged by the standards, identifying with a cultural group is a deeply personal issue for many people.[34] Thus the discussions for revising the standards in 1997 were very careful to consider how terminology could make any of the subgroups within a particular category feel excluded. As noted with regard to the African-American category, problems could arise "if certain national groups feel excluded by the terms."[35] This consideration was actually one of the rationales for the recommendation that the African-American category should be interchangeable with "black." Whereas blacks of African-American heritage identify with the term "African American," blacks "with roots in the Caribbean or Africa do not identify with the term"—and seem to identify with "black" instead.[36]

Group identification and personal identity was also a major consideration for the discussion whether to include a multiracial category in addition to the previous monoracial categories. According to Directive 15, people had to indicate the category that most closely resembled their identity. Given, however, the increase in inter-marriage rates—e.g., 150,000 in 1960 and 1.5 million in 1990—the objection was raised against the federal standards that monoracial categories did not reflect the identity of some people. The point was made that the new standards should include a multiracial category, since for some people a single category "does not reflect how they think of themselves," and may even "deny their full heritage."[37] The revised standards struck down a multiracial category—although as noted earlier the standards did pass the proposal for checking more than one race. The multiracial category was rejected due to possible undercounts in other categories and logistic difficulties such as data comparability.[38] The discussion, however, on whether to include the category or not was prominent. The most significant point for our discussion is that raising the possibility for including a multiracial category did not focus on civil rights monitoring or enforcement, but rather on identity and how people view themselves.

It would then seem that identity considerations and affiliation in cultural groups are essential for understanding the federal standards. If the point is correct, we can now detect a fuller picture emerging. If not all legislatively protected classes receive public recognition by way of categorization and data collection, the propensity to be discriminated against cannot be the only reason why the government categorizes groups and collects data. Similarly, given that not all the subgroups within the categories currently recognized by the federal standards are subjected to differential treatment, an additional element seems to be necessary for making sense of the categories. That element, I have argued, is the belief that groups and memberships of some kind are special. Under this belief, members identify with these groups because identification expresses something about who they are, which merits public recognition. It seems then that civil rights enforcement and monitoring is not a sufficient condition for inclusion in the federal standards. Beliefs about identity are also necessary. The gap between the civil rights criterion and the actual categories in the federal standards is filled by the presumption of relevant membership. Thus for a full justification of the groups in the federal standards, whom the government recognizes by means of classification and data gathering, we need to turn not only to civil rights monitoring and enforcement, but also to the belief that membership in some group is central to members' identities and thus merits public recognition.

ONE NATION, MANY PEOPLES

The view that ethnoracial groups are a special kind of group and thus ethnoracial membership is central to someone's identity is not confined to the document I have been discussing.[39] This view permeates our contemporary social sensibility. As an interesting case study, take, for instance, the 1991 report released by the New York board of education: *One Nation, Many Peoples: A Declaration of Cultural Interdependence*.[40] Here we find an example of privileged memberships and recognition in education. The assumptions underlying the report are in many ways similar to the ones behind the identity rationale for ethnoracial classification.[41]

The main task of the report is to recommend modifications in order "to inaugurate a curriculum that reflects the rich cultural diversity of the [American] nation." The claim is that there is a "nation" characterized by "cultural diversity." When we reflect on the idea of "cultural diversity" and aim to examine the notion of "culture" in the report, it is possible to notice a correlation with race, ethnicity and national origin. As an illustration, the report claims that "no other country in the world is peopled by a greater variety of races, nationalities, and ethnic groups"[42] We note in this sentence that the nation's diversity consists of a variety of racial, ethnic and national groups. There are two claims that could be put this way: (i) The American nation is *culturally* diverse and (ii) The American nation is characterized by racial, ethnic and national diversity. Placing these two claims next to each other allows us to see that the *cultural* diversity of the nation is its racial, *ethnic* and *national* diversity.

Let us now ask ourselves: what is it about "cultures" that makes them so significant? Why would the New York report take the trouble to suggest recommendations for a curriculum that reflect the cultural diversity of the nation? The assumption underlying the emphasis on cultural membership is that cultural affiliation gives members a sense of who they are. The New York report, for instance, does not define culture, ethnicity or national identity, but it is clear that the emphasis on cultural identity helps students understand who they are. One of the Seven Guiding Principles for the Social Studies Curriculum discussed in the report, the Principle of Diversity, encourages students to ask themselves: (a) "Who am I?;" (b) "What is/are my cultural heritage(s)?;" (c) "Why should I be proud of it/them?;" etc.[43] Nathan Glazer, one of the members of the Committee responsible for the report, puts it this way:

> There are multiple selves, not all of which can be represented in the teachers and the curriculum. The assumption in multiculturalism is that of these many selves, one is dominant. Consequently, it is not necessary to represent the musical, athletic, regional, class or religious self, because the racial or ethnic self is central and decisive. If the racial or ethnic self is not represented in the curriculum, education cannot occur, or cannot occur effectively.[44]

The passage mentions several "selves." But one of them, ethnically or racially understood, is predominant; it is, in fact, a precondition for effective education. The idea is that individuals might have multiple memberships or various layers of identity. There is, however, something special about ethnic or racial identity. This type of identity is so central to people (e.g., school children), that it ought to be recognized in school curricula.

CONCLUSION

I have argued that in order to explain the government's interest in ethnoracial classification and data gathering, we need to turn to what I called

Table 3.1. Educational Attainment and English Fluency (1,000s) for Hispanic Population Eighteen and Older that Speaks a Language other than English at Home

	TOTAL	%	No HS Degree	%	HS Degree	%	Some College	%	BA	%	Grad	%
TOTAL	39,659	100	12,585	32	9,688	24	8,440	21	5,476	14	3,469	9
English*	28,383	100	5,838	21	7,128	25	7,387	26	4,816	17	3,212	11
No English**	11,277	100	6,747	60	2,560	23	1,053	9	660	6	257	2
Not Spanish/Hispanic/Latino	18,225	100	3,110	17	3,924	21	4,348	24	4,039	22	2,804	15
English	14,940	100	1,848	12	2,994	20	3,859	26	3,616	24	2,623	18
No English	3,285	100	1,263	38	929	28	489	15	422	13	181	6
Mexican	13,183	100	6,811	52	3,425	26	2,143	16	578	4	226	2
English	7,693	100	2,742	36	2,443	32	1,831	24	476	6	202	3
No English	5,489	100	4,068	74	982	18	313	6	102	2	24	0
Puerto Rican	1,949	100	618	32	601	31	476	24	169	9	85	4
English	1,638	100	423	26	523	32	450	28	159	10	83	5
No English	310	100	194	63	78	25	26	8	10	3	2	1
Cuban	1,018	100	259	26	274	27	255	25	140	14	90	9
English	632	100	78	12	164	26	208	33	107	17	75	12
No English	385	100	181	47	110	29	47	12	33	9	15	4
Dominican	680	100	262	39	187	28	150	22	58	9	23	3
English	394	100	93	24	117	30	118	30	50	13	17	4
No English	285	100	169	59	70	25	32	11	7	2	7	2
Costa Rican	78	100	14	19	24	31	21	26	15	19	4	5
English	58	100	9	15	14	25	18	30	13	23	4	7
No English	20	100	6	29	10	50	3	14	1	7	0	0
Other Central American***	1,874	100	909	49	489	26	329	18	110	6	38	2
English	988	100	286	29	315	32	273	28	82	8	32	3
No English	886	100	623	70	174	20	56	6	27	3	6	1
Argentinean	125	100	19	15	39	31	32	25	18	14	17	14

(continued)

Table 3.1. (continued)

	TOTAL	%	No HS Degree	%	HS Degree	%	Some College	%	BA	%	Grad	%
English	93	100	9	10	23	25	27	29	17	19	16	18
No English	31	100	10	31	16	50	4	13	0.8	2	1	4
Colombian	456	100	67	15	147	32	128	28	73	16	42	9
English	328	100	32	10	92	28	107	33	61	19	36	11
No English	129	100	35	27	55	43	21	16	12	9	6	5
Venezuelan	117	100	11	10	24	21	31	27	32	27	19	16
English	91	100	6	7	13	14	28	31	26	29	18	19
No English	25	100	5	18	11	45	3	11	5	22	1	5
Spaniard	110	100	18	16	29	27	32	29	19	17	12	11
English	103	100	17	16	25	24	32	31	17	17	12	12
No English	7	100	1	15	4	59	0.8	11	1	16	0	0
Other South American****	779	100	149	19	225	29	223	29	127	16	54	7
English	531	100	60	11	139	26	186	35	100	19	46	9
No English	248	100	89	36	86	35	38	15	27	11	8	3
All other Hispanic	1,066	100	339	32	300	28	272	26	100	9	55	5
English	891	100	236	27	266	30	250	28	89	10	49	6
No English	175	100	103	59	34	20	22	13	11	6	5	3

Source: 2004 American Community Survey, Public Use Microdata Sample.

* Includes those who speak English "very well" and "well."
** Includes those who speak English "not well" and "not at all."
*** Includes Guatemalan, Honduran, Nicaraguan, Panamanian, Salvadoran and Other Central American.
**** Includes Bolivian, Chilean, Peruvian, Uruguayan and Other South American.

Table 3.2. Educational Attainment (1,000s) for Hispanic Population Eighteen and Older

	TOTAL	%	No HS Degree	%	HS Degree	%	Some College	%	BA	%	Grad	%
TOTAL	212,796	100	35,240	17	63,893	30	60,767	29	34,275	16	18,531	9
Not Spanish/Hispanic/Latino	186,236	100	24,775	13	56,592	30	54,982	30	32,244	17	17,643	10
Mexican	16,394	100	7,488	46	4,495	27	3,187	19	897	6	326	2
Puerto Rican	2,579	100	733	28	793	31	687	27	247	10	120	5
Cuban	1,140	100	277	24	305	27	291	26	164	14	103	9
Dominican	720	100	269	37	196	27	163	23	65	9	27	4
Costa Rican	91	100	16	18	26	29	24	26	19	21	6	6
Guatemalan	503	100	252	50	136	27	81	16	24	5	10	2
Honduran	276	100	130	47	72	26	50	18	17	6	5	2
Nicaraguan	180	100	42	23	56	31	49	27	23	13	10	5
Panamanian	89	100	9	11	25	28	31	34	18	20	6	7
Salvadoran	856	100	471	55	205	24	132	15	39	5	9	1
Other Central American	80	100	25	31	22	28	22	28	5	7	5	7
Argentinean	140	100	20	14	42	30	38	27	21	15	19	14
Bolivian	70	100	10	15	10	15	29	42	15	21	6	8
Chilean	81	100	9	11	22	28	26	32	14	17	10	12
Colombian	511	100	71	14	163	32	143	28	87	17	47	9
Ecuadorian	332	100	90	27	90	27	97	29	39	12	16	5
Peruvian	305	100	36	12	97	32	86	28	62	20	25	8
Uruguayan	33	100	9	28	11	34	6	19	5	15	1	4
Venezuelan	123	100	11	9	26	21	33	27	34	27	19	16
Other South American	53	100	5	10	14	26	16	31	12	22	6	11
Spaniard	275	100	35	13	80	29	92	34	45	16	22	8
All other Hispanic	1,730	100	455	26	504	29	502	29	180	10	89	5

Source: 2004 American Community Survey, Public Use Microdata Sample.

the *presumption of relevant membership*. According to this presumption, membership in a certain group is central to a member's identity. This notion of relevant membership views ethnoracial groups as groups of a special kind and membership in these groups as the sort of membership that has a special status. My contention is that along with demographic profiles and civil rights enforcement, the presumption of relevant membership is necessary for explaining the government's interest in classifying citizens according to their race and ethnicity. If I am right, it is then the case that the Standards for the Classification of Federal Data on Race and Ethnicity are not only about demographics and civil rights; they are also about identity politics.

It would seem then that understanding membership and identity is essential for examining which groups, if any, ought to be included in the federal standards and the reasons why these groups should be included. I will then pay close attention to the presumption of relevant membership and raise questions such as, what is relevant? These questions will help us to understand the status of Hispanic membership, its relevance and possible justification, or lack thereof, for purposes of public recognition.

NOTES

1. I use the term ethnicity loosely here. Technically, American Indian is a racial category in the Standards for the Classification of Federal Data on Race and Ethnicity.

2. I will return to this point in subsequent chapters, and particularly in the last chapter. The crucial question is: when, and on what grounds, are classifications permissible? From a legal point of view, there is a body of constitutional provisions and standards of analysis that serve to determine when classifications are permissible and when they are not. In the final chapter, I use part of this doctrine to see what it reveals about the Hispanic category.

3. See *Frontiero v. Richardson*, 411 U.S. 677, 686 (1973).

4. The only way, for instance, to guarantee that schools were, in fact, desegregating after *Brown v. Board of Education* was to provide statistical data. Likewise, to measure voting patterns in the South and make sure that subtle discriminatory measures were not preventing blacks from voting, the Voting Rights Act contemplated several "emergency provisions" with a statistical formula. See Abigail Thernstrom, *Whose Votes Count? Affirmative Action and Minority Voting Rights* (Cambridge, MA: Harvard University Press, 1987).

5. The point is acknowledged by one of the discussions for the revision to the standards. Although religious identification has been requested, this option is not open "because the Federal collection of religious affiliation has been interpreted as possibly violating the separation of church and state." "Standards for the Classification of Federal Data on Race and Ethnicity," in *Federal Register*, vol. 60, no. 166, Monday, August 28, 1995, Notices, 44680.

6. See 42 U.S.C. 1996a.

7. People of Arabic origin have been indeed discriminated against and are certainly protected under the law. For a discussion on why "identifiable classes of persons who are subjected to intentional discrimination solely because of their ancestry or ethnic characteristics" are statutorily protected, see the Supreme Court case *Saint Francis College v. Al-Khazraji*, 481 U.S. 604, 613 (1987). The case addresses discrimination against a professor of Arabic descent who was denied tenure due to his class membership.

8. "Recommendations from the Interagency Committee for the Review of the Racial and Ethnic Standards to the Office of Management and Budget Concerning Changes to the Standards for the Classification of Federal Data on Race and Ethnicity," in *Federal Register*, vol. 62, no. 131 (Thursday, Wednesday, July 9, 1997, 36932). See also "Revisions to the Standards for the Classification of Federal Data on Race and Ethnicity," in *Federal Register*, vol. 62, no. 210 (Thursday, October 30, 1997, Notices, 58789).

9. "Recommendations," 36940.

10. Similarly, "many Moslems do not have race or geographic origin in common—they come from Asia, Sub-Saharan Africa, etc." An additional problem that arises in connection with the category at stake is that it "would it include persons [located in the Middle East] from a non-Arab state such as Israel." See "Recommendations," 36932.

11. "Revisions," 58789.

12. Some scholars speak of Arab Americans as a distinct group with an ethnic identity. As an example, a scholar reviewing the history of Arabs in the United States observes, "World War I affected the Arab settlers in the United States in many ways. Thus, for all practical purposes, it cut off the group from its people in the homeland, and, consequently, intensified its members' sense of separation and isolation—and enhanced its sense of solidarity as a community." Michael Suleiman, "Arab-Americans and the Political Process," in *The Development of Arab-American Identity*, ed. Ernest McCarus (Ann Arbor: University of Michigan Press, 1994), 43. In another illustration, a study on the ethnic identity of Arab Americans opens like this: 'The social processes that constitute the designation of 'peoplehood' among the ethnic group commonly referred to as Arab are examined through an in-depth study of Muslim Lebanese families living in Dearborn, Michigan, which is home to the largest Arab Muslim community in the United States. In particular this chapter examines the interpretations those of Arab descent produce regarding their ethnic identity. What does it mean to be an Arab, and what does it mean to be American? Which identity do they take for themselves and why?" Kristine Ajrouch, "Family and Ethnic Identity in an Arab-American Community," in *Arabs in America: Building a New Future*, ed. Michael W. Suleiman (Philadelphia: Temple University Press, 1999), 129.

13. Stephan Thernstrom and Abigail Thernstrom, *America in Black and White: One Nation, Indivisible* (New York: Simon and Schuster, 1997), 1. See also, 44–46.

14. "Revisions," 58789.

15. See "Recommendations," 36929.

16. Steven F. Lawson, *To Secure these Rights: The Report of President Harry S. Truman's Committee on Civil Rights* (Boston: Bedford/St. Martin's, 2004), 57.

17. *Hernandez v. Texas*, 347 U.S. 475, 480 (1954).

18. Confusing different groups subsumed under a single category seems to be common among scholars who study Hispanics. An example will make the point. In determining whether Hispanics should assimilate into the American mainstream, the claim could be made, with regard to bilingual education, that the Hispanic experience is different from other groups because Hispanics speak Spanish. Hispanics "were in the Southwest as established Spanish-speaking communities long before those territories became part of the United States; and as circular immigrants, large numbers of Hispanics are traveling between two monolingual societies." Pastora San Juan Cafferty, "The Language Question," in *Hispanics in the United States: An Agenda for the Twenty-First Century*, eds. Pastora San Juan Cafferty and David W. Engstrom (New Brunswick: Transaction Publishers, 2000), 79. If I am right, claims like these are built on a fallacy that ignores the makeup of the Hispanic category. Some Hispanics speak Spanish and some do not.

19. See Lawson, *To Secure these Rights*, 57.

20. See Roberto Ramirez, *We the People: Hispanics in the United States: Census 2000 Special Reports*, U.S. Census Bureau, December 2004, 14. For the kinds of factors that help to explain group differences in economic performance, see Alejandro Portes, "From South of the Border: Hispanic Minorities in the U.S.," in *Immigration Reconsidered: History, Sociology and Politics*, ed. V. Yans-McLaughlin (New York: Oxford University Press: 1990), 167–74.

21. See Roger Daniels, *Coming to America: A History of Immigration and Ethnicity in American Life* (New York: Harper Collins, 2002), 245–46.

22. See the two landmark cases, *Hirabayashi v. United States*, 320 U.S. 81 (1943); and *Korematsu v. United States*, 323 U.S. 214 (1944).

23. If we loosely construe X's right to Y as an obligation of the American state to do Z, X cannot be said to be a right-holder in the relevant sense, since X does not have a right to Y under U.S. jurisdiction.

24. Terrance Reeves and Claudette Bennett, *We the People: Asians in the United States: Census 2000 Special Reports*, U.S. Census Bureau, December 2004, 12.

25. Reeves and Bennett, *We the People*, 15.

26. "Recommendations," 36876.

27. "Recommendations," 36922.

28. See "Revisions," 58789.

29. "Revisions," 58785.

30. The standards make it explicit that ethnoracial groups are not biological, but rather "may be thought of in terms of social and cultural characteristics as well as ancestry." "Standards," 44692.

31. A difficulty here is that the groups that people identify themselves with could be characterized differently and create a wide range of identification forms available to people. David Miller, in the context of British identity-politics puts the point this way: "How should people of Bangladeshi origin in contemporary Britain identify themselves? Should they think of themselves specifically as people whose native language and culture is Bengali? Or, taking into account their commonalities with other groups from the Indian subcontinent should they think of themselves more broadly as Asians? Alternatively, since their religious background is Islamic, should they identify themselves as Muslims, in both British and

International contexts? Yet again, when considering the prejudice and discrimination they experience at the hands of the white majority, should they emphasize what they think they have in common with other dark-skinned immigrant groups and think of themselves as blacks? Over and above all this, should they think of themselves as British (or British Asian or British Bengali) or should they stick to an ethnic identification as, for example, a Bengali-who-happens-to-be-living-in-Britain?" "Group Identities, National Identities and Democratic Politics," in *Citizenship and National Identity* (Cambridge: Polity Press, 2000), 69.

32. "Recommendations," 36874. See also "Standards," 44675.

33. "Standards," 44676.

34. Public input with an eye toward revising the categories "served as a constant reminder that there are real people represented by the data on race and ethnicity and that this is for many a deeply personal issue." "Revisions," 58785.

35. "Recommendations," 36929.

36. "Recommendations," 36929.

37. "Standards," 44685.

38. See the discussion on the multiracial category in "Recommendations," 36885–36906.

39. Social norms with regard to race and ethnicity have evolved over time, touching and transforming many areas. One of the interesting areas transformed by new norms on identity is that of constitutional law. For a lengthy and detailed treatment of this transformation, see William N. Eskridge, Jr., "Some Effects of Identity-Based Social Movements on Constitutional Law in the Twentieth Century, *Michigan Law Review*, 100 (2002): 2,069–113. I will return to some constitutional considerations with regard to ethnoracial classifications in the final chapter and will now discuss another area that has been changed by new norms of identity, namely, education.

40. The Report of the New York State Social Studies Review and Development Committee, June 1991.

41. For the history behind the report and its significance for shifting social sensibilities, see Nathan Glazer, *We Are All Multiculturalists Now* (Cambridge, MA: Harvard University Press, 1997), 22–33.

42. *One Nation*, vii.

43. *One Nation*, 9.

44. Glazer, *We Are All Multiculturalists Now*, 49.

II

MEMBERSHIP AND GROUPS

4

✣

Theorizing Membership: Culture, Value and Recognition

In chapter three, I spoke about the presumption of relevant membership and suggested that this presumption has been construed in a particular way in the public sphere. The presumption, in fact, provides an important rationale for ethnoracial classification. We now need to examine the reasons why ethnoracial membership is thought to be valuable. In order to do this, I will turn to one of the most influential theorists of multiculturalism and the value of ethnic membership, Will Kymlicka. A Canadian philosopher, Kymlicka has helped to shape contemporary debates by bringing to the forefront of political theory the cultural and identity component. He has also been a prominent defender of multicultural policies in Canada. And although, unlike Canada or Australia, the U.S. does not have an official multicultural act or policy, we have seen that the U.S. does recognize certain ethnic and racial groups outlined in the Standards for the Classification of Federal Data on Race and Ethnicity, and if not directly justified by the identity factor, I have argued that this type of classification and recognition rests on certain assumptions about membership in particular groups.

Discussing Kymlicka will help us to understand the theoretical justification for the value and recognition of particular memberships in the public sphere. According to the kind of multiculturalism proposed by Kymlicka, membership in a national or ethnic minority is highly significant and valuable to group members.[1] Membership in a minority nation such as, say, Quebec or the Quechua is so significant that the group's culture should be protected for the sake of its members. Similarly, ethnic groups and identities are very significant and so they should receive public recognition in societies based on the principles of equality and justice. Public recognition could generally take the form of according group-specific rights to certain groups—e.g., bilingual education for Spanish-speaking immigrants in the U.S.—and promoting social events and venues that make the heritage and values of a certain group visible to the rest of society—e.g., celebrating the Hispanic Heritage Month or building a museum devoted to American Indians.

The question I wish to raise in the context of Kymlicka's views is whether membership in ethnic or national minority groups is always highly significant and valuable to group members. I will argue that highly significant and valuable membership is not always confined to national or ethnic minority groups. Membership in some type of group is highly valuable to group members and is thus a primary source of meaning and direction to these members, but these are not always national or ethnic memberships. My thesis is that membership in different group types, and not just in national or ethnic minority groups, could be a primary source of meaning and direction. If my thesis is true, there are several implications, discussed at the end of this chapter that raise doubts about Kymlicka's multicultural model.

CULTURAL GROUPS: ETHNICITY AND NATIONALITY

Let me begin with a general discussion of Kymlicka's views. He develops a "sort of 'multiculturalism,' which arises from ethnic and national differences." In Kymlicka's multiculturalism, "culture" is used "as synonymous with 'a nation' or 'a people'—that is, as an intergenerational community, more or less institutionally complete, occupying a given territory or homeland, sharing a distinct language and history."[2] It is important to clarify that the way in which Kymlicka uses the term "culture" precludes other usages of the term. One may speak of cultural groups "where 'culture' refers to the distinct customs, perspectives, or ethos of a group or association, as when we talk about 'gay culture' or even a 'bureaucratic culture.'" Similarly, one may speak of cultures in a broad sense and thus say "that all the Western democracies share a common 'culture'—that is, they all share a modern, urban, secular industrialized civilization, in contrast to the feudal, agricultural, and theocratic world of our ancestors."[3] Kymlicka constrains the usages of the term "culture" and makes it explicit that he does not use the term in a nonethnic sense. The implication is that, as already mentioned, the terms "culture" and "multiculturalism" are used in the context of national and ethnic groups.

We need to emphasize that despite terminological ambiguities, even when "culture" is applied solely to national and ethnic groups, certain specific differences and distinctions have to be made. Kymlicka notes, for example, that "cultural groups" are different from "racial groups" and makes a distinction between the situation and sets of questions that arise with regard to the African-American group in the United States and the aboriginal people in Canada.[4] I will, in fact, follow in this chapter Kymlicka's distinction between racial and cultural groups and focus solely on the latter. I think, however, that much of what is said on the value of ethnic memberships can be applied to the African-American experience and the significance of racial memberships in the U.S. Be that as it may, I will return to racial membership in chapter 10 when I compare African Americans, a racial group, and Hispanics, an immigrant or ethnic group.

Kymlicka also makes an important distinction between "national minorities" and immigrant or "ethnic" groups.[5] National minorities are cultural groups that have a "societal culture."[6] Societal cultures generally have a concentrated territory, a shared language, and a set of public institutions. So Quebec, for instance, is a national minority within Canada because it has a societal culture—a common territory, language, and public culture reflected in governmental institutions, the school system and media. National minorities are generally societal cultures that have been colonized by another group, i.e., a larger nation. Immigrant or ethnic groups, in contrast, are cultural groups that do not have a societal culture. Since immigrants leave their country of origin and move to a different country, they do not live in a concentrated territory of their own or have a set of public institutions reflecting their own culture. In other words, immigrants do not have a societal culture because they are part of a different and new society in which they become an ethnic minority.

Since a national minority such as Quebec is institutionally complete, i.e., has a societal culture, it is entitled to self-government rights. Immigrants, in contrast, by leaving their societal cultures behind and becoming part of a new societal culture, waive their right to self-government. Nevertheless, since the cultural identity of immigrants is important, they are entitled to recognition in the host society. And thus immigrants integrate into a new societal culture, but the host societal culture must make an effort to accommodate the cultural expression of immigrants. National and ethnic minorities are then entitled to different group-specific rights. National minorities are entitled to self-government rights, whereas ethnic groups are entitled to what Kymlicka has called "polyethnic" rights.[7]

Despite the differences in circumstances between national and ethnic minorities and the sorts of rights to which they are entitled, both groups have an important attribute in common. National and ethnic minorities are both *cultural* groups. We must then think of cultural groups as a group type that encompasses groups in different conditions. It is hard to individuate cultural groups—as suggested, the term "culture" can be very ambiguous—but they are generally intergenerational groups that have a cluster of properties in common. I have already noted the way in which Kymlicka uses the term "culture." A cultural group is an intergenerational community, institutionally complete, which shares a common territory, language and history. As indicated above, not all cultural groups are institutionally complete or have a common territory—these are, in fact, the traits that distinguish national and ethnic minorities. Cultural groups, however, are intergenerational communities that share some relevant features, e.g., language and history. We should then think of cultures as groups with a cluster of properties. Some cultures are institutionally complete and some are not. Cultural groups might have a common territory, but this is not always the case. It might even be pointed out that cultural groups such as Hispanics or Asian Americans—if they are indeed cultural groups in the relevant sense—do not have a common language. Nevertheless, Hispanics and Asian Americans could presumably be intergenerational communities that have a common origin and history.

Kymlicka claims that cultural groups are very important. We may see the significance of cultural groups deriving from the fact that they give group members meaning and direction in life. Cultural attachments give people a set of values and a sense of the world. Accordingly, "the causes of this [cultural] attachment lie deep in the human condition, tied up with the way humans as cultural creatures need to make sense of their world. . . ."[8] Note that human beings make sense of the world by virtue of their cultural attachments. These attachments also provide a framework for making meaningful decisions. The importance of cultural membership lies in the following: "we decide how to live our lives by situating ourselves in [certain] cultural narratives." Similarly, "cultural structures" are important "because it's only through having a rich and secure cultural structure that people can become aware, in a vivid way, of the options available to them, and intelligently examine their value."[9] The upshot is that membership in a certain type of group is a precondition for making significant and worthwhile choices. Cultural attachments, which must be understood ethnically or nationally, are then significant because they endow group members with maps of meaning and direction.

Attachments of this kind are so significant that they ought to be publicly recognized and respected. According to Kymlicka, there seems to be a dilemma between two different principles: "people are owed respect as citizens and as members of cultural communities."[10] The problem is that upholding citizens' rights sometimes seems to obviate the recognition of membership in a cultural community—and thus the apparent conflict between individual rights and group rights.[11] Part of Kymlicka's project is minimally to show that these two principles do not preclude each other—as liberals sometimes have assumed. But there is also a more robust claim in Kymlicka's project: respect toward people qua citizens often *requires* respect toward their cultural membership.

One of Kymlicka's discussions helps us to understand further the significance of the groups he and similar multiculturalists have in mind. In discussing recent literature on multiculturalism and minority rights, Kymlicka identifies a position that goes under the name of "liberal culturalism." Liberal culturalism encompasses "liberal nationalism" and "liberal multiculturalism." There are relevant differences between liberal nationalism and multiculturalism, but for our purposes, the point of concern is the way in which liberal culturalism is characterized.

> Liberal culturalism is the view that liberal democratic states should not only uphold the familiar set of common civil and political rights of citizenship which are protected in all liberal democracies; they must also adopt various group-specific rights or policies which are intended to recognize and accommodate the distinctive identities and needs of *ethnocultural* groups [my emphasis].[12]

We note in this passage that group-specific rights are intended to recognize and accommodate the identities and needs of a particular type of group: ethnocultural. The obvious question is, why this particular type of group? Kymlicka himself raises the following questions: "but why is it important to recognize and accommodate ethnocultural identities and practices? Why does it matter whether society is multiculturalist?"[13] Three types of positions are then described. First, there is the "identity" view. "On this view, there is a deep human need to have one's identity recognized and respected by others. To have one's identity ignored or misrecognized by society is a profound harm to one's sense of self-respect." Second, there is the "freedom," "autonomy," or "context of choice" view.[14] "On this view, one's culture determines the boundaries of the imaginable, so that if the options available in one's culture diminish, so too does one's autonomy."[15] The last position is that of "intrinsically valuable diverse cultures." "Different cultures are seen as the repository of unique forms of human creativity and accomplishment, and to let cultures die out is to lose something of intrinsic value."[16] It is important to highlight that the point of departure for all three positions—"identity," "context of choice" and "intrinsic cultural value"—is that ethnocultural membership has a degree of significance that other types of memberships do not generally have.

THE CLAIMS OF MULTICULTURALISM

The sort of multiculturalism I have been discussing makes two claims. First, cultural membership has a degree of significance that other types of memberships generally do not have—which is one of the reasons why cultural membership ought to be publicly recognized. The second claim is that cultural membership—in some particular instances, at least—ought to be publicly recognized by means of, say, group-specific rights, whether self-government rights or polyethnic rights. In what follows, I will first focus my attention on the claim about the value of cultural membership. Then I will examine some of the implications that follow from this claim for the way we think of groups that merit group-specific rights.

The multiculturalist claim on the value of cultural membership entails two points. To begin, cultural membership is a primary source of meaning and direction in the lives of group members. Note that in the multiculturalist outlook under consideration cultural membership is not only a *significant* but also a *primary* source of meaning and direction. Many memberships might be highly significant. For example, someone's membership in the American Civil Liberties Union, the National Rifle Association, a Mason Lodge or the Eastern Orthodox Church might be highly significant. The type of cultural membership, however, the multiculturalist has in mind is different from these other memberships. This type of membership is a primary source of meaning and direction for group members; and thus has a special status.

The second point is that cultural groups are national or ethnic minority groups—a cluster of groups Kymlicka refers to as "ethnocultural" groups. It is necessary always to bear in mind that in the multiculturalist outlook under consideration "culture" is understood in terms of "national" or "ethnic" minorities. The sorts of groups that come to mind are those that generally have a common history, set of beliefs and customs, and language. As noted earlier, these groups might be territorially concentrated, but they may not have a homeland. They might also have a set of public institutions, e.g., school system, but not necessarily. So the cluster of groups under description includes groups like the Basque in Spain, which has a homeland and a set of public institutions—albeit not having a state of its own. Also included are groups such as immigrants in the United States, Canada or Australia who do not have a homeland or public institutions, not even perhaps a common language; but they have a common history, beliefs and customs.

Given these two points, the multiculturalist then says that membership in an ethnic or national minority is a primary source of meaning and direction for group members. The multiculturalist reasons thus: (a) membership in certain groups is a primary source of meaning and direction; (b) these groups are generally ethnic or national minorities—henceforth "ethnocultural" groups for short; lastly it follows then that (c) membership in ethnocultural groups is a primary source of meaning and direction. I now wish to raise the following question: should we single out ethnocultural membership as the preferred type of group membership representing a primary source of meaning and direction? In examining this question, I will suggest that the claims of multiculturalism must not be conflated. I agree with the claim that membership in certain groups is a primary source of meaning and direction. Nonetheless, the claim that *ethnocultural* membership must be singled out as a primary source of meaning and direction is sometimes hard to justify. For my suggestion to be sound, I would have to show that (i) there are types of groups in which membership is a primary source of meaning and direction for group members, but (ii) the groups at stake are not necessarily ethnocultural ones.

GROUP TYPES AND THE VALUE OF MEMBERSHIP

The case against privileging ethnocultural membership as a primary source of meaning and direction has been made against Kymlicka and the multicultural outlook in general. Brian Walker, for example, identifies two nonethnocultural groups in which membership has presumably been a primary source of meaning and direction for some people: the "family farm" and the "urban neighborhood." He points out that "for millennia, most people lived an agricultural life, which had its own folklore and culture, with knowledge and narratives passed down from generation to generation." With the development of agricultural technology, rendering family farming untenable, farmers were forced to assimilate themselves into the urban lifestyle. The result is that urbanization "marked the loss of a rich culture, and generations of people were cast adrift in a foreign world. The disappearance of the family farm marked the death of a lifeway and of a structure of sensibility."[17] Similarly, Walker uses the disappearance of "urban neighborhoods" as "another example of a swift change in institutional structure that has devastating effects on cultural membership and on the life-chances of the people who rely on it." The reason for such a consequence is that "neighborhoods play a crucial role as carriers of culture. They solidify a sense of identity and they serve as a site for groups to create a sense of community and security in a frequently hostile environment."[18]

The first point in these examples is that the decline of certain groups has grievous consequences for group members because the flourishing of group members is bound with the flourishing of the group itself. Note that group flourishing is essential for members' flourishing, but why so? Presumably, the answer is because group membership endows members with maps of meaning and direction. If membership in group G is essential for members' flourishing, then membership in G is most likely more significant than other memberships. Membership in G is then a primary source of meaning and direction. Note, however, a second point in the examples above: family farms and urban farms are clearly not ethnocultural groups. If membership in family farms and urban farms could indeed be a primary source of meaning and direction, it follows that nonethnocultural memberships could represent such a primary source.

The observation I have just made may lead to the view that we should be impartial toward the *types* of identity groups that are worthy of recognition and protection. The implication is that different types of groups may be equally valuable—or more precisely, membership in different types of groups may be a primary source of meaning and direction. So Thomas Pogge observes that

> whatever we demand from a just and fair political process for ethnic minorities, we should also demand for any other minorities: if enough citizens share a certain identification and are willing to form a coalition for the sake of securing representation for themselves in the legislature, then they should be able to gain such representation, *irrespective of the type of their identification* [my emphasis].[19]

The claim in the passage just quoted is concerned with the recognition of minority rights for nonethnocultural groups in a fair and equal system—a thesis that is defended in explicit contrast with Kymlicka's view. What I wish to emphasize here, however, is the assumption that whatever the merits of ethnocultural groups, these groups *per se* should not be privileged before the law. The relevant implication for our purposes is that ethnocultural groups should not be necessarily privileged because membership in these groups might be valuable just as membership in other types of groups might be valuable as well.

The point to be highlighted in the discussion so far is that we should not necessarily think of ethnocultural groups as a *special type* of group because membership in groups other than ethnocultural ones might also be a primary source of meaning and direction. In order to defend the claim that membership in ethnocultural groups is not the only primary source, let me propose that we think of significant memberships modally. The question is: how could we think of the relevant kind of membership without necessarily linking such memberships with ethnocultural groups? My suggestion is that a modal framework pointing to the functional quality of groups will help achieve two purposes. First, we could preserve the view that membership in certain groups is a primary source of meaning and direction. And second, we could also move away from categories such as "ethnicity" and "nationality," namely, the vocabulary of ethnocultural groups and multiculturalism. In my view, this sort of language ends up creating more confusion, instead of contributing to an understanding of what highly valuable membership entails.

The guiding idea of the framework in mind is that highly valuable membership is based on the function that a group has in the lives of group members. As a result, we must think of groups in which membership is a primary source of meaning and direction not as group *types*, e.g., religious, national, ethnic, racial, etc., but rather as groups that have a certain *function* in the lives of group members, i.e., the function of endowing members with relevant memberships.[20] Or put differently, whenever someone is a member of a group with the membership function I have in mind, this membership is central to her identity. This is what I called relevant membership in the previous chapter.

Let us then think of group-type A in a possible world W1. Membership in A is a primary source of meaning and direction and thus membership in A will tend to be more valuable than other memberships. Now imagine that, in possible world W2, membership in group-type B—and not membership in A— is, in fact, a primary source of meaning and direction. A in W1 has the function of endowing group members with the relevant membership, whereas B in W2 has the same function. Membership in either A or B will be central to someone's identity depending on whether we find ourselves in W1 or W2.

To illustrate the point just made with social categories, consider an instance in which membership in a national minority group, e.g., Quebec, is a primary source of meaning and direction for some group member. In this case, Quebecois membership has a degree of significance that other memberships generally do not have. Now imagine another instance in which membership in a religious group, e.g., Muslim, is a primary source of meaning and direction for some group member who also happens to be a Quebecois. In this second instance, the significance of Muslim membership is higher than the significance of other types of memberships, e.g., Quebecois membership. Membership in two different types of groups, national and religious, might be a primary source of meaning and direction for two different people. Both group types, national and religious, might then have the function of endowing group members with the relevant membership in different circumstances. What relevant membership means and when groups have this function is the subject of the next two chapters.

So far we seem to have a neat proposal on the contingency of groups and valuable memberships. But this could all be complicated by the fact that social categories are very hard to characterize. Consider that it is indeed true that religious impulses are often connected with nationalism. The people of a nation can also be the people of a deity or a set of deities.[21] That groups of people belong to deities has been an old theme in human history. There is, for example, a Sumerian poem from 2000 BC expressing grief because the city of Ur has been conquered by the Amorites and Elamites. The poem cries out to the god of the city, Nanna: "As for me, the woman, the city has been destroyed, my house too has been destroyed; O Nanna, Ur has been destroyed, its people have been dispersed."[22] Using more modern examples, we can think of the American "city on a hill," or movements such as the Afrikaans or Zionism. Truly, nations are often thought of as sacred or chosen communities, and one can sometimes see how religious metaphors are connected with national identities, e.g., the Virgin of Guadalupe is a crucial element of Mexican "national identity."

Groups are often complex and so categorization of group types can be extremely difficult. By the same token, however, consider how a certain religious affiliation can be transethnic or transnational, or independent from someone's current ethnic affiliation or nationality. Religion could help us to understand modern nationalism, but religion is also an older phenomenon than modern nationalism. The point is that religious affiliation and national membership do not always overlap. We can then think of situations in which religious membership is a primary source of meaning and direction, whereas ethnocultural membership is not.[23] Consider a Dominican monk in California who happens to be a member of the Hispanic group; or a Buddhist monk in Tibet—a minority nation within China. It is quite possible that membership in the Dominican or Buddhist communities is a primary source of meaning and direction. It is also quite possible that the Hispanic or Tibetan memberships of these monks—or other ethnocultural memberships—will be of relatively little importance. Imagine also a Jehovah's Witness for whom her Kingdom membership is preeminent in comparison with her worldly ethnocultural membership. Ethnocultural membership for a Jehovah's Witness could not only be relatively unimportant, but certain views and practices linked with ethnocultural identities, e.g., saluting or pledging allegiance to a particular symbol, rituals that entail dancing or intoxication, may be associated with idolatry—a grievous sin.

Turning now to other group types, consider a situation in which the identity of a certain small group does not coincide with the larger national identity of the state that the smaller group inhabits. Think of a Yanomami in "Venezuelan" or "Brazilian" territory. The Yanomami will presumably see her place in the world through the lens of her Yanomami membership. The meaning of the term "Yanomami" and what membership in the group entails is explained by the anthropologist Jacques Lizot:

> We can better understand the tendency of ethnic groups to call themselves by a name that, in their language, means simply 'man,' 'folk,' or something to that effect. That is very precisely the meaning of the word *yanomami*. The eth-

nic group is the central focus of the human universe; it is humanity par excellence, around which everything must necessarily converge or gravitate. For a Yanomami, anything that doesn't belong to his own sociocultural world is necessarily alien, *nabfi*. The words *yanomami* and *nabfi* form both a pair and an opposition.[24]

The Yanomami would certainly qualify as an "ethnocultural" group. In fact, these are the sorts of groups Kymlicka often has in mind.[25] Imagine, however, someone who is born from Yanomami parents but is brought up in Caracas, the capital of Venezuela, or Sao Paulo, Brazil. The person in mind attends the public school system in Caracas and one of the national universities, Universidad Simón Bolivar.[26] What is her *primary* source of meaning and direction: her *Yanomami* or her *Venezuelan* membership? The multiculturalist will perhaps be inclined to say that her Yanomami membership is a primary source of meaning and direction. My view, however, is that either group membership—or another group-type membership—might be a primary source of meaning and direction.

In the situation I have in mind, at least four outcomes are possible. First, her Yanomami membership is a primary source of meaning and direction. Second, her Venezuelan membership is a primary source. In the third scenario, her Yanomami and Venezuelan memberships are competing and conflicting primary sources of meaning and direction. In the fourth case, neither her Yanomami nor her Venezuelan memberships are primary sources because a different group-type membership—suppose she identifies strongly with a political party or a religious community—is a primary source of meaning and direction. The point is that different groups might have the function of endowing this person with the relevant membership, which is to say that membership in different groups could be central to her identity.

I have so far mentioned "national," "religious" and "ethnic" groups as types of groups in which membership might be a primary source of meaning and direction. Other groups one might consider include "political parties," "continental groups," or "social classes." Imagine someone growing up in a communist family in Latin America around 1958 strongly influenced by the Pan-American ideology characteristic of authors such as José Martí and Ernesto "Che" Guevara. In the latter scenario, we must bear in mind that events such as the Cuban Revolution created an atmosphere of "commonality," "unity" and "solidarity" in the struggle for liberation across the *Latin-American* continent. In this circumstance, it is plausible to believe that the struggle for liberation is associated with a large continental group in which membership is a primary source of meaning and direction. Thus, in words of José Martí: *"our America* is to show itself as it is, *one in spirit and intent*, swift conqueror of a suffocating past, stained only by the enriching blood drawn from hands that struggle to clear away the ruins, and from the scars left upon us by our masters [my emphasis]."[27] Much to the disappointment of Marxists in the Second International, "social class" did not have the strength to pull the proletariat of different nationalities together.[28] During the 1960s however, the "social class" factor did seem to play an important role in Latin America—although, as we will see later on, still not strong enough to override the "national" factor. But recent conflicts between the "rich" and the "poor" in Venezuela, and other Latin-American countries, seem to be showing that membership in a "social class" could become a primary source of meaning and direction for class members. In subsequent chapters, we will return to similar examples and raise the question of which group types have the function of endowing members of the Hispanic group with the relevant sort of membership.

The purpose of my discussion has been to highlight the fact that membership in different group types, in different circumstances, could be a primary source of meaning and direction. Thus different group types might have the function of endowing group members with the relevant membership. As a result, the value and significance of group membership is not based on the type of group *per se*, but rather the function of the group in the lives of members. In order to avoid giving what might seem like an oversimplified account, let me now make some clarifications. If different types of groups in different possible worlds might potentially have memberships that are a primary source of meaning and direction for members, then two questions arise: (a) is there an unlimited range of such groups?; and (b) how do we recognize groups in which membership is a primary source of meaning and direction?

With regard to (a), different group types, hypothetically speaking, could have the function of endowing members with the relevant membership. We could imagine any group type from nations to aficionado clubs. But we know that membership in some groups tends to be a primary source of meaning and direction, whereas membership in other groups does not. We know that national memberships tend to be very significant, whereas membership in aficionado clubs does not often have the same degree of significance as national memberships. How do we know about these tendencies? With regard to (b), suppose that someone might be a member in two or more groups in which membership tends to be a primary source of meaning and direction, e.g., a religious group and a nation. How do we know whether those memberships are competing and conflicting sources of meaning and direction, or whether one of the memberships is indeed more significant than the other? The answer to these two questions is a matter of *empirical evidence*. If we want to inquire, for example, whether a particular membership is a primary source of meaning and direction, we must not begin by looking at the traits of the group or the group type *per se*. We must look at the function the group has in the lives of its members. Consider, for instance, the "Asian-American" group and identity. If we want to know the status of Asian-American membership, we will not get very far by looking at the group type—which could be thought of under some circumstances as an "ethnocultural" type. We must consider instead whether the group endows group members with the relevant membership or not. Accordingly, we will be able to find out whether membership in the Asian-American group is a primary source of meaning and direction or not. This is precisely the strategy I will be following with regard to Hispanic membership in subsequent chapters.

WHY MULTICULTURALISM?

I have challenged the notion that ethnocultural groups should be singled out as the preferred group type in which membership is a primary source of meaning and direction and is thus central to someone's identity. I have suggested instead that different group types, in different possible situations, might have the function of endowing members with such a membership. Now, if the claim is right that membership in different types of groups, and not just ethnocultural ones, can be of the relevant kind, there are three implications for Kymlicka's multicultural theory of group recognition. The implications I discuss are based on the premise that when membership in a certain group is a primary source of meaning and direction, the group, under some conditions, could potentially be accorded group-specific rights by the state. This premise is one that I have borrowed from Kymlicka himself.

The first implication is that different group types ought to be the potential recipients of public recognition, i.e., different group types could be potentially accorded group-specific rights. As we will see, however, the notion of publicly recognizing different group types is contrary to Kymlicka's theory. We must remember at this point that the primacy of ethnocultural membership is not in Kymlicka's view the only rationale for group recognition. Certain disadvantaged groups ought to be recognized and be granted rights because a society is based on principles of justice. But group recognition on grounds of justice assumes that membership in these groups has a special status—for why recognize disadvantaged groups unless membership in these groups is of a special kind?[29] Kymlicka does not believe that *all* disadvantaged groups should receive recognition. Drawing on an example I used in chapter two, take, for example, two groups: lawyers and musicians. Lawyers generally have greater access to a distributional good such as salaries than musicians do. So in a certain sense musicians are disadvantaged with regard to lawyers. Nonetheless, Kymlicka's multiculturalism does not contemplate musicians—presumably because membership in the group of musicians is not generally thought to be a primary source of meaning and direction.[30]

Let us grant that if membership in a disadvantaged ethnocultural group is indeed of the relevant kind, then it might be necessary to recognize the group and accommodate its needs. But now suppose that membership in a religious community, e.g., Muslims, is a primary source of meaning and direction for some group of Middle-Eastern immigrants to the U.S.[31] Let us also point out that the Muslim faith is indeed disadvantaged in comparison with the Anglo-Protestant majority in American society. Should the American state then specifically accommodate Muslims by recognizing group-specific rights in public life (e.g., celebrate Muslim holidays and allocate public funds for Muslim schools)? Given the presumed religious neutrality of the American state, the answer is negative. Kymlicka does indeed posit that since certain practices put Muslims at a disadvantage, certain provisions should be made to accommodate their needs. Groups like Muslims or Jews "are simply asking that their religious needs be taken into consideration in the same way that the needs of Christians have been."[32] One gets the sense, however, that with regard to the Canadian context Kymlicka construes these groups as ethnic ones—if that is not the case, I am not sure how religion then fits into his theory.[33]

If the criteria for public recognition and minority-group rights are relevant membership and disadvantage with regard to a majority group, then Kymlicka's theory is not wholly consistent. According to Kymlicka, ethnocultural membership is a primary source of meaning and direction. Additionally, when an ethnocultural minority is vulnerable to a majority society, the minority group ought to be recognized and protected by means of group-specific rights. Recognition and protection require the state to put aside any ethnocultural neutrality pretensions, and be in some measure "ethnoconscious."[34] But why should the state be ethnoconscious and not religious-conscious or social class-conscious—assuming that all these groups satisfy the criteria for public recognition and protection? It would seem that different group types, and not just ethnocultural ones, ought to be the potential recipients of public recognition.

Second, the view that ethnocultural groups always ought to be publicly recognized is put into question. Group types other than ethnocultural ones might have merits for recognition. But now a different question arises. Regardless of the merits of other group types, do ethnocultural groups *always* have merits for public recognition? Kymlicka's answer is presumably positive. Membership in ethnocultural groups is a precondition for self-respect, identity and being able to make meaningful choices.

Thus in the case of immigrant groups, for instance, Kymlicka's view is that

> we need to ensure that the common institutions in which immigrants are pressured to integrate provide the same degree of respect, recognition and accommodation of the identities and practices of immigrants as they traditionally have of the identities and practices of the majority group.[35]

Now, drawing on our earlier example, suppose that for a group of Middle Eastern immigrants to the U.S., membership in a religious group is a primary source of meaning and direction. The situation I have in mind requires that the state recognizes the Muslim identity of group members, which, as we saw, is not really contemplated in Kymlicka's view inasmuch as Muslims are construed as a *religious* group. Should the state, however, recognize the *Arab* identity of group members? A positive answer would seem to be plausible if "Arab" is construed ethnoculturally. But suppose that the Arab identity of the group at stake is of lesser value than its Muslim identity. If this is the case, the type of membership the state intends to recognize and protect, i.e., Arab, is not a primary source of meaning and direction for group members. And if membership is not of the relevant kind, this seems to be a case in which the ethnocultural identity of a group does not have enough merits for public recognition.

One might object that the religious identity of Arab immigrants is interwoven with their ethnocultural identity, a point that might be the case in Kymlicka's view. Thus, recognition of ethnocultural identity requires admitting overtly religious elements.[36] The observation, however, ignores the fact that the group of Arab immigrants is not coextensive with the group of Muslims—not all Arab immigrants, for instance, are Muslims and the group of Muslims is greater than the group of Arabs. Suppose the state recognizes the religious practices of Arabs on the basis that these practices are part of their ethnocultural identity. Still, non-Arab immigrants who happen to profess the Muslim faith are not entitled to public recognition because their religious identity is *not* attached to an ethnocultural membership. Note, however, that the last claim seems quite odd—for we would expect that if the state recognizes the religious practices of some Muslims, whether they are immigrants or not, it should then recognize the practices of all Muslims.

Let me explain the point differently. Two sets of people share the attribute of relevant membership in a religious group. Both sets, however, have a differential attribute: ethnocultural membership, i.e., one set consists of Arab immigrants and the other is Anglo American. Given that both sets have relevant memberships in a religious group, why then should recognition be extended to a certain set and not to the other one on the grounds of ethnocultural membership? If it is not clear that ethnocultural membership is a primary source of meaning and direction for the set of Arab immigrants, as opposed to Anglo Americans, I do not think there is a good way to answer the question.[37]

The third implication, and perhaps the most important one, is that given the variety of memberships that could potentially count as a primary source of meaning and direction, it is difficult to speak of a multicultural "model." Kymlicka's aim is to "clarify the basic building blocks of a liberal approach to minority rights."[38] These building blocks consist of cultural diversity *patterns* in Western liberal democracies. The patterns Kymlicka has in mind are minority nations and immigrants, which give rise to multinational or polyethnic states.[39] Although Kymlicka makes special mention of the Canadian case, e.g., aboriginal groups and the Quebecois, it is clear that his project is to develop a general multicultural theory for liberal democracies. One of the major themes in *Politics in the Vernacular*, for instance, is the general success of certain minority-rights patterns in multicultural societies.[40]

I suggested earlier that distinguishing groups and memberships that count as a primary source of meaning and direction is a matter of empirical evidence. Based on my previous discussion, I suspect that the empirical evidence in different societies is mixed—we could minimally count three group types: ethnocultural, religious, and social class. It seems to me that this observation casts doubts on Kymlicka's multicultural *model* for Western countries. If membership in different group types is a primary source of meaning and direction, different groups should ostensibly be recognized because of the value such groups have for their members. In other words, different group types should potentially be accorded group-specific rights. It is then difficult to speak of a uniform multicultural model across Western societies.

I have assumed for each of the implications above that groups could potentially be accorded group-specific rights by the state, under some conditions, when membership in these groups is a primary source of meaning and direction. If we take the assumption seriously, it would seem that we need a model of diversity that is more diverse than Kymlicka's model. But what if the assumption I have taken for granted is not entirely sound? Let us think for a moment what a more diverse model of diversity would entail. First, policy-makers would need to determine the group types in which membership is of the relevant kind.[41] Second, the degree of disadvantage of each group with regard to other groups will have to be determined. Third, assuming that there are several disadvantaged groups with relevant memberships, which ones should be accorded group-specific rights? Not all groups could be publicly recognized because then nation-building policies would not have much coherence, so some groups will be accorded rights whereas others will be left out.

These considerations would seem to make the task of the state very complicated. Is it really practical to expect for policy-makers to determine the group types in which membership is of the relevant kind? Should we also expect them to determine and define, under conditions of vagueness and group indeterminacy, which groups ought to be accorded group-specific rights? These are questions that come up whenever governments are involved in the task of classifying, collecting data and thus singling out particular groups for policy purposes. Focusing solely at this point on the prospects of a multicultural model, questions of this sort make me somewhat skeptical about group rights.

Kymlicka believes there is a growing consensus regarding group rights. According to Kymlicka, "liberal culturalism has arguably become the dominant position in the literature today, and most debates are about how to develop and refine the liberal culturalist position, rather than whether to accept it in the first place." Liberal culturalists believe that the state "must also adopt various group-specific rights or policies [in addition to individual civil and political rights] which are intended to recognize and accommodate the distinctive identities and needs of ethnocultural groups."[42] But I am not entirely convinced that we should accept multiculturalism and the group-rights paradigm instead of, say, the principle of neutrality. Given the skepticism I have expressed about the exclusive value of membership in ethnocultural groups, I believe that the matter is, to say the least, still an open one.[43]

CONCLUSION

In this chapter, I argued two points. First, ethnocultural membership should not be privileged as a primary source of meaning and direction. I accept Kymlicka's thesis that membership in some group type is a primary source of meaning and direction. But then I suggested, reacting against Kymlicka, that the type of membership that constitutes a primary source of meaning and direction is not always or necessarily confined to ethnocultural groups. Based on the first point, I also argued a second point. Kymlicka's model of group rights and diversity is not diverse enough for the sake of recognizing group types other than ethnocultural ones. If the rationale for the public recognition of groups hinges on the fact that membership in a group type is of a special kind, then the spectrum of group types that merit public recognition should be broader and include more than just ethnocultural groups. The corollary, as mentioned, is that

Kymlicka's model of diversity ought to be more diverse than what he contemplates. I incidentally suggested that the necessity for more diversity makes me skeptical about the prospects for coherent multicultural policies, a point that I will revisit in the final chapter.

In the remainder of the book, I will not focus on group rights or multiculturalism as such. In other words, I will not pursue the second point any further. My interest is rather to examine further the value of membership and then return to the rationale for group inclusion in the Standards for the Classification of Federal Data on Race and Ethnicity. For our immediate purposes, I will then turn to a discussion on membership and relevant groups in the next two chapters and explore what it means to have a relevant membership.

NOTES

1. Notice the shift in terminology in this chapter. I no longer speak of "ethnoracial" groups, but rather, following and respecting Kymlicka's terminology, I speak of national and ethnic minorities. This terminology will become clear throughout the chapter.

2. Will Kymlicka, *Multicultural Citizenship: A Liberal Theory of Minority Rights* (New York: Oxford University Press, 1995), 18.

3. Kymlicka, *Multicultural Citizenship*, 18.

4. Kymlicka, *Multicultural Citizenship*, 22–23; Will Kymlicka, *Liberalism, Community, and Culture* (New York: Oxford University Press, 1989), 135–57.

5. Kymlicka, *Multicultural Citizenship*, 19. For a discussion on the different kinds of "minority groups," see Will Kymlicka and Wayne Norman, "Citizenship in Culturally Diverse Societies: Issues, Contexts, Concepts," in *Citizenship in Diverse Societies*, eds. Will Kymlicka and Wayne Norman (New York: Oxford University Press, 2000), 18–24.

6. The meaning of "societal cultures" is explained in *Multicultural Citizenship*, 75–94.

7. He later calls them "accommodation rights." Will Kymlicka, *Politics in the Vernacular: Nationalism, Multiculturalism and Citizenship* (New York: Oxford University Press, 2001), 51.

8. Kymlicka, *Liberalism, Community, and Culture*, 90.

9. Kymlicka, *Liberalism, Community, and Culture*, 165.

10. Kymlicka, *Liberalism, Community, and Culture*, 151.

11. Kymlicka discusses this dilemma in *Liberalism, Community, and Culture*, 151–57.

12. Kymlicka, *Politics in the Vernacular*, 42.

13. Kymlicka, *Politics in the Vernacular*, 47.

14. Presumably, Kymlicka's own position, although he also seems to endorse the "identity" view.

15. Kymlicka, *Politics in the Vernacular*, 47.

16. Kymlicka, *Politics in the Vernacular*, 48.

17. Brian Walker, "Modernity and Cultural Vulnerability: Should Ethnicity Be Privileged," in *Theorizing Nationalism*, ed. Ronald Beiner (Albany: State University of New York Press, 1999), 145–46.

18. Walker, "Modernity and Cultural Vulnerability," 146.

19. Thomas Pogge, "Group Rights and Ethnicity," in *Ethnicity and Group Rights*, eds. Ian Shapiro and Will Kymlicka (New York: New York University Press, 1997), 200.

20. I will turn to a characterization of groups that have this function in chapter 6.

21. For an interesting and helpful discussion on the interrelation between religion and nationality, see Anthony Smith, *Chosen Peoples: Sacred Sources of National Identity* (New York: Oxford University Press, 2003).

22. Bill T. Arnold and Bryan E. Beyer, eds. *Readings from the Ancient Near East: Primary Sources for Old Testament Study* (Grand Rapids: Baker, 2002), 225.

23. For purposes of analytical consideration one can tend to be emphatic when distinguishing different types of groups, e.g., "national," "religious," "social class," etc. In reality, however, groups in which membership is a primary source of meaning and direction are generally highly complex and often difficult to categorize. I then agree with Steven Grosby when he points out that we may distinguish nationality from religion; but he then observes that these distinctions "vary historically and by civilization." "Nationality and Religion," in *Understanding Nationalism*, eds. Montserrat Guibernau and John Hutchinson (Malden, MA: Polity Press, 2001), 104.

24. Jacques Lizot, *Tales of the Yanomami: Daily Life in the Venezuelan Forest* (New York: Cambridge University Press, 1985), 2–3.

25. See Kymlicka, *Liberalism, Community, and Culture*, 136.

26. The two groups being compared in this example—Venezuela, a nation-state, and the Yanomami, an ethnic minority—are in some sense "cultural" groups. But we must remember that when multiculturalists speak of cultural groups, they often refer to minorities and not nation-states.

27. José Martí, "Our America," in *Latin American Philosophy for the 21st Century: The Human Condition, Values and the Search for Identity*, eds. Jorge J. E. Gracia and Elizabeth Millán-Zaibert (New York: Prometheus Books, 2004), 251.

28. In other words, communism did not fulfill its 1848 prediction that the common interests of the proletariat would supersede regional or national interests. See Karl Marx, "Manifesto of the Communist Party," in *The Portable Karl Marx* (New York, Penguin Books, 1983), 218.

29. According to Kymlicka, "if state institutions fail to recognize and respect people's culture and identity, the result can be serious damage to people's self-respect and sense of agency." Then he adds: "if we accept either or both of these points, then we can see minority rights not as unfair privileges or invidious forms of discrimination, but as compensation for unfair disadvantages, and so consistent with, and even required by, justice." Kymlicka, *Politics in the Vernacular*, 32–33. Note that minority rights are necessary not only because they compensate for certain disadvantages. They are rather necessary because they compensate for

disadvantages that arise when people's self-respect and sense of agency are damaged.

30. Kymlicka would also probably point out that the group of musicians does not have a societal culture or that being a musician is not a precondition for making meaningful choices.

31. According to Yvonne Haddad, "for Christians, Muslims, and Jews from the Middle East, one's religious affiliation determines one's identity. A person is born, grows up, and dies in a specific religious community." "Maintaining the Faith of our Fathers: Dilemmas of Religious Identity in the Christian and Muslim Arab-American Communities," in *The Development of Arab-American Identity*, ed. Ernest McCarus (Ann Arbor: University of Michigan Press, 1994), 65.

32. Will Kymlicka, *Finding Our Way: Renegotiating Ethnocultural Relations in Canada* (Ontario: Oxford University Press, 1998), 47.

33. He claims that the idea that liberal-democratic states "are ethnoculturally neutral is manifestly false." But "the religion model is altogether misleading as an account of the relationship between the liberal-democratic state and ethnocultural groups." The reason is presumably because the state should be neutral with regard to religion, but not with regard to ethnocultural groups. Kymlicka, *Politics in the Vernacular*, 23–25.

34. Kymlicka, *Politics in the Vernacular*, 32.

35. Kymlicka, *Politics in the Vernacular*, 30.

36. I am not sure if Kymlicka would endorse this connection or not. He takes pains to point out that societal cultures are not distinguished by religious elements. He says, for instance: "I call it a *societal* culture to emphasize that it involves a common language and social institutions, rather than common religious beliefs, family customs, or personal lifestyles" (original emphasis). Kymlicka, *Politics in the Vernacular*, 25.

37. The state could also find itself in the dangerous business of judging and creating group-type hierarchies. On this point, see Thomas Pogge's helpful discussion about equality and group value. "Accommodation Rights for Hispanics in the United States," in *Language Rights and Political Theory*, eds. Will Kymlicka and Alan Patten (New York: Oxford University Press, 2003), 109.

38. Kymlicka, *Multicultural Citizenship*, 2.

39. Kymlicka, *Multicultural Citizenship*, 11–17.

40. The aim to provide a general theory becomes evident in Kymlicka's attempt to answer his critics. One of the criticisms against Kymlicka's minority rights theory is that too much weight is put on two paradigmatic cases: minority nations and immigrants—who are generally legal immigrants. Kymlicka acknowledges that several groups are left out in his theory, most notably African Americans, because they do not fit any of the paradigmatic cases (see Kymlicka, *Multicultural Citizenship*, 24, and Kymlicka, *Politics in the Vernacular*, 56). Nonetheless, he points out that "the fact remains that immigrants and national minorities form the most common types of ethnocultural pluralism in Western democracies." Kymlicka, *Politics in the Vernacular*, 57. Moreover, "insofar as secure membership in a viable societal culture is a precondition for the sort of freedom and equality that liberalism aspires to, then the immigrant/national minority models are worth consider-

ing, even if this would require both the majority and minority to rethink their self-identities." Kymlicka, *Politics in the Vernacular*, 58.

41. I am assuming for the sake of argument that there are group types such that membership is always a primary source of meaning and direction for most group members. But this picture can get somewhat complicated. Is Jewish membership, for instance, of the relevant kind? The answer will vary for different people.

42. Kymlicka, *Politics in the Vernacular*, 42.

43. For another critique of Kymlicka's views, and multiculturalism in general, see Brian Barry, *Culture and Equality: An Egalitarian Critique of Multiculturalism* (Cambridge, MA: Harvard University Press, 2002), particularly 308–17. Thomas Pogge also critiques Kymlicka's theory as it may be applied to Hispanics. See "Accommodation Rights for Hispanics."

5

✛

Identity and Basic Membership

I have talked so far about membership and identity. I have made claims about relevant membership as the sort of membership that is central to someone's identity. More specifically, I argued in the previous chapter that membership could be a primary source of meaning and direction in different group types. We now need to examine further membership and identity. The question that arises is this: if membership in different group types could be a primary source of meaning and direction, when is membership of the relevant kind? In other words, what kind of membership is central to members' identities and under what conditions?

By not focusing on group types but rather the structure of identity and groups in which membership is relevant, I hope to circumvent the pitfall of assumptions based simply on how a group is typified.[1] As I have suggested, asking whether a group is ethnic or racial for purposes of knowing whether the group is a significant source of identity is not the most productive route. What we need to know is whether the group has the function of endowing members with relevant memberships. Thus, we need to examine membership and the conditions of groups in which membership is relevant. I will begin this chapter with a discussion on the general meaning of identity. In the second section, I will introduce and discuss the notion of *basic membership* and lay out the conditions under which membership is central to someone's identity. Finally, in the third section, a few remarks about the value of membership will be made.

WHAT DOES IT MEAN TO HAVE AN IDENTITY?

In order to speak of "identity," we must know what is meant by the term. We speak of our identities as something highly significant for personhood, but what does it mean for a person to have an identity? Let me first suggest that to have an identity is to have a certain understanding of who I am, which entails a certain grasp of the traits that characterize me as a human being. I may characterize myself as a baseball fan, a clever person, a Jamaican, an opera lover, a Muslim, or a high school student; and in such an act of characterization, I am articulating self-understanding. When I am able to characterize who I am, and thus show a degree of self-understanding, I may be said to have an identity.[2]

My first point implies a second characteristic of identity that must be made explicit. We have seen that I show self-understanding by characterizing myself: I am an opera lover, a Buddhist, an office manager, a football fan, an athlete, etc. Note that characterization entails, for the most part, association with and membership in a group. The understanding of who I am is often relational, namely, connected with a set of people.[3] For instance, in characterizing myself as an athlete I am saying that I belong to the set of athletes, which means that I have certain features in common with other athletes.[4] Within the set of athletes, I may in turn be a member of the subset of soccer players. Even as a soccer player, I could be a member of the subset of goalkeepers, etc. What I wish to illustrate is that the characterization of who I am, i.e., self-understanding, generally entails group membership. The reason for establishing this connection between identity and group membership is that the self arises by internalizing what Mead calls "the generalized other."—i.e., organized communities or social groups to which individuals belong. In developing a sense of identity, it is not sufficient for individuals to take attitudes from other individuals. People must also take the attitudes of other individuals toward one another "as members of an organized society or social group." And when individuals internalize these "general others," "the social process influences the behavior of the individuals involved in it, and carrying it on."[5]

It is then the case that descriptions of who I am will commonly join me to a set or class of people,[6] and thus the understanding of who I am is often coupled with membership. As Mead observes, the self-conscious individual "takes or assumes the organized social attitudes of the given social group or community (or of some one section thereof) to which he belongs."[7] The main point is that self-understanding is tied with groups. Such a connection highlights the fact that the collective dimension is an integral part of the human experience.[8] What does it mean then for a person to have an identity? I have so far pointed out two aspects of identity-bearing: *self-understanding* and *group membership*. To have an identity is to possess an understanding of who I am, indicated by the sort of characterization that makes me a member of a group.

In order to clarify my view of identity, let me make a distinction between the *phenomenon* and the *vocabulary* of identity. Truly, the vocabulary of "identity" is relatively new in human history and seemingly unique to the modern world. The ways in which modern people are able to think in and formulate detailed accounts of who they are and how they view themselves, seem to be absent in, for example, some premodern societies.[9] One might therefore be inclined to suggest that the phenomenon of identity is a modern one. I wish to suggest, however, that it is possible to speak of identities in premodern and nonmodern societies, which is why it is essential to draw a distinction between the phenomenon and the vocabulary.[10]

It may be the case that a member of the Yanomami[11] tribe in the Amazon, a non-modern community, does not readily give an account of his or her identity as a Yanomami. It would be wrong to say, however, that the Yanomami does not possess a certain degree or capacity for self-understanding that makes her a member of a group. Suppose that I, a Yanomami, am able to characterize myself as someone who believes in certain myths and carries out tasks such as parenting, fishing, and providing for my community, in a way that is similar to what other people around me do. Imagine, for instance, that my name is *Ebrëwë*, living in a community by the name of "Yanomami" which is surrounded by objects described as *waima, tokori, shitibori, hoko* (types of tress) and *kirakirami, kōbari, kreōmri* (types of birds), etc. There are also other types of invisible objects that go by names such as *hekura, bore koko* and *hera*.[12] I, along with other men of my group, hunt wild pigs according to certain rituals and customs.[13] Like other people in my group, I believe that our ancestors were at one time immortal, but because they stole the fire from Caiman, we ceased to be immortal. Now after death my *bei kë mī amo* (soul) will leave my body and "rise along the ropes of the hammocks and climb up the supporting posts of the shelter to go to live on the celestial disk."[14]

In characterizing myself, I show an understanding of who I am. My community is known as the "Yanomami" and so my self-understanding entails being a member of the Yanomami. I presumably view myself and the world through the lens of my membership in the Yanomami community. Note that, in our example, I characterize myself and thus show self-understanding, which connects me with the Yanomamis. I may not possess the vocabulary of "identity," but according to the phenomenon described I may be said to have an identity.

The phenomenon of identity I have described must also be distinguished from the vocabulary of identity in another respect. The phenomenon I have in mind is different from what goes on in identity politics or the politics of difference and recognition. On my view, identity simply means that I see who I am, the world and my place in it, through the lens of a worldview that makes me a member of a group. This phenomenon is to be distinguished from the vocabulary of identity in identity politics.[15] In the framework of the politics of difference, identity means that I—as, say, a member of an "ethnic" group in modern American society—am fully aware of certain features that distinguish me and the group to which I belong, and am hence able, for example, to demand political recognition for those features.[16] The vocabulary of "identity-value" and "distinctiveness" is conducive to demands of difference-recognition. Here, one sees group members "insisting on their value as a group and on the solidarity of its members" and thus demanding "some form of public recognition."[17] The phenomenon of identity I have described, however, is not necessarily related with the politics of difference and recognition.

In order to distinguish the phenomenon from the vocabulary of identity politics, let us make a distinction between *identity as self-understanding* and *political identity-awareness*. The first type of identity requires self-understanding, without necessarily leading to political demands of recognition. The second type of identity entails a strong awareness of the distinctiveness of my features, which may lead to the demand of public recognition. The Yanomami has an identity, in that he or she possesses self-understanding; but the Yanomami may not necessarily have an identity if we require that he or she be strongly aware of his or her Yanomami distinctiveness and thus be in a position to demand public recognition. The point is that self-understanding is different from a politically laden deep consciousness and articulation of "Yanomami identity."[18] In conclusion, human beings, given their cognitive complexity, are able to characterize themselves and as such show self-understanding. Such a self-understanding makes them members of a group. People may not be deeply aware of their identity—in the way that many moderns citizens are—but they possess *self-understanding* and group membership, which is all that is required for my account of identity.

BASIC MEMBERSHIP

Now that we have discussed identity we can move on to examine the conditions under which membership is *central* to members' identities. Many memberships could be bundled up together in order to give me a sense of who I am. My identity, for instance, finds its source in the fact that I am a firefighter, a Mennonite who grew up in rural Pennsylvania, I like car racing and happen to also enjoy gardening. I may also be an atheist medical doctor with a high income who does not care about my Italian descent, and who supports the war in Iraq for patriotic reasons. All those circumstances make me a member in different kinds of groups and come together when I characterize who I am. Human beings are members in many group types, but not all memberships have an equal status—some memberships will be more significant than others for determining my own identity. Whereas some memberships will be a primary source of meaning and direction and thus central to my identity, some other memberships will be less relevant. What I want to do now is isolate the sort of membership that is central to my identity and query when this might be the case.

Let me now introduce the notion of *basic membership*. Briefly, membership is basic when certain traits that make someone a member of a particular group are essential to her self-understanding. Suppose it were virtually impossible for me to characterize myself as anything other than an Irishman, a Roman Catholic or a Communist because the traits that are essential to my own self-understanding make me a member in any of those groups. Then my memberships in the Irish nation, the Catholic Church and the Communist Party are said to be basic. Notice that basic membership has two components: (a) certain traits are essential to my own self-understanding and (b) these traits make me a member of a particular group. The second component entails conscious identification with the group. So it is not only the case that the traits that are essential to my self-understanding are associated with and make me a member of a group; it is also the case that I view myself as a member of the group.

Keeping these two components together is important because otherwise we will miss the full picture of basic membership. If we separate these two elements from each other, we will end up with two incomplete pictures. First, one might simply think of traits that are essential to someone's self-understanding. It is necessary to see, however, that oftentimes these traits derive from and are associated with a particular group. And so the traits that are essential to someone's self-understanding are generally traits that presumably make her a member of such a particular group. It is important to incidentally mention the following point: the insistence that someone is a member of a *particular* group is very intentional. A trait that is essential to someone's self-understanding could potentially make her a member of a very general group, e.g., the group of English speakers or human beings. But this is not what I refer to as basic membership. Membership is basic when certain essential traits make someone a member of a particular group, e.g., Americans or Australians. I will turn to the discussion of particular or relevant groups in the following chapter. It is sufficient simply to say here that particular groups are those that are distinguished and individuated on the basis of certain criteria. Additionally, in many of the cases I have in mind this kind of group individuation has a significant political component, i.e., groups are individuated by states or political units.

Second, one might think that being a member in a particular group might be essential to a member's self-understanding. But this is not always the case. Think, for example, of nationality. In many situations, nationality will be the type of membership containing traits that are essential to a member's self-understanding.[19] Imagine a case, however, in which someone is born in France, but is brought up in a very strong Muslim setting, which isolates her to a significant extent from French mainstream society. In this case, most of the traits that are essential to her self-understanding derive from and are associated with the Muslim faith and not the French nation. So despite being a French citizen, one can assume that her national membership is not basic—or at least not to the same degree that her Muslim membership is—for the traits that are essential to her self-understanding are not the ones that make her a member of the French nation. Another way of expressing the point is this: membership is basic if and only if group traits are essential to a member's self-understanding.

When I say that certain traits are essential to someone's self-understanding, I am drawing on the Aristotelian and medieval distinction between essential and accidental properties—a distinction that will become clearer when I discuss nonbasic memberships below. In Aristotelian terms, necessary is "that without which, as a condition, a thing cannot live; e.g., breathing and food are necessary for an animal; for it is incapable of existing without these."[20] An accident, in contrast, is "that which attaches to something and can be truly asserted, but neither of necessity nor usually."[21] I apply the distinction between essential (or necessary) and accidental traits to the self-understanding. Notice that my claim is that whereas some traits are essential to someone's self-understanding, others are not. As we will see below, I do speak of certain factual tendencies, but I stay away from prescribing specific essential traits. The point is significant because I do not think that certain traits are inherently, by virtue of the traits themselves, essential to someone's self-understanding. So while I speak of essential traits, different traits will be essential to different people's self-understandings and change under circumstances in which different ascriptive qualities are internalized.[22] I will come back to this point below.

Note also that the sorts of traits I call essential to the self-understanding are conditioned by varying circumstances. The view I am outlining then is not necessarily a *primordialist* one. Primordialism is the view that nations or cultural groups precede and are above individuals.[23] So there is something primordial about the group and its own characteristics, which will remain independently of individual members.[24] In my account, certain traits are essential to someone's self-understanding, making her a member of a particular group. But essential traits for people's self-understanding do not entail essential group traits. In my account, essential traits for the self-understanding allow for different particular group configurations. So in my subjective view of essential traits, group identities are contingent upon group configuration.[25]

Now that I have briefly explained basic membership, I will flesh out the notion with some examples. Let me begin by mentioning two traits that are likely, as a matter of factual tendency, to be essential to someone's self-understanding: language and birthplace. First, consider language. The language I speak (with a certain accent) as my native tongue could generally said to be one of the core properties for the depiction of who I am. If I did not speak the language I do, I would probably not be the same person I am now. Imagine I spoke Italian or English—as my first and native language—instead of, say, Spanish. My self-understanding would be different than what it currently is. Native language then is a trait that is likely to be essential to someone's self-understanding.

In order to reinforce the claim that language is generally essential to someone's self-understanding, let me turn for a moment to a discussion about the relationship between language and culture. In making a case for linguistic self-defense, George Fletcher points out that language is closely related with culture.[26] I am not concerned with his case for linguistic self-defense or the direction in which he takes his discussion. I simply want to use one of his arguments in order to highlight the significance of language for cultures, and more specifically the self-understandings of culture's members. Fletcher devises a thought-experiment in which Germans during World War II initiate a campaign called "operation Babelosa." The idea is that Germans abandon their efforts to physically conquer England and instead design a strategy whereby the English language is transformed into German. Accordingly, all means of communication, telephone, radio, typesetters, etc., are programmed so that when ideas are expressed in English the output is changed into German. The end result is that this subterfuge will force the English-speaking culture to adopt the German language in order to make communication possible.

If the English language is not essential to the maintenance of English culture, the linguistic transformation described in the thought-experiment will not be a casus belli. If, in contrast, the English language is essential to the maintenance of English culture, "then the imagined substitution of German for English would arguably be as serious a form of aggression as a physical invasion." And as a result, the English will have as much of a right to go to war for their language as they would "for the flowered fields of Wiltshire or the white Cliffs of Dover."[27] The conclusion in this thought-experiment is that, given the violation of linguistic sovereignty, the English presumably have a right to self-defense. And the reason why the English have such a right to self-defense is because language is indeed essential to the maintenance of English culture. The insight in the thought-experiment that interests us at this point has to do with language being essential to the maintenance of a culture. If English culture were not, for example, English-speaking—it would be German-speaking instead—it would not be English culture. This is presumably true of many cultures: language is essential to their collective self-understanding. It is also generally true of individuals. Everyone speaks a language as a native-speaker. These languages often make us who we are. If we spoke a different native language than the one we do, we would probably be a different person. Thus native languages are an essential trait of who we are. The range might indeed be expanded for those who speak more than one language, even if it is not at the full-fluency level. But note that my point is simply that language is, generally speaking, an essential trait for my self-understanding—whether I speak one or many.

Consider, likewise, a trait such as birthplace. For example, one of the traits by which I characterize myself is that of being born in a particular place. Here we must remember that birthplaces are often "homelands." Birthplaces are not only the place where someone is born, but they are also places representing a sense of belonging. Imagine, for instance, that I was born in India or Australia, instead of my homeland. In this case, the course of events would have made my self-understanding different than what it currently is and thus I would be a different person. Homelands are significant because of a phenomenon that Anthony Smith describes as the "territorialization of memory." The term refers "to a process by which particular places evoke a series of memories, handed down through the generations, and it summarizes a tendency to root memories in persons and events in particular places and through them create a field or zone of powerful and peculiar attachments."[28] In short, homelands are symbolic territories that create strong attachments.

Another thought-experiment will help us see the significance of homelands. Suppose that we take two cultures, American and English, and exchange their respective territories. In such an exchange, the key symbols and events of American culture become the House of Parliament, the Tower of London, the Battle of Hastings, etc. Similarly, the key symbols and events of English culture become the Capitol and White House, the Washington Memorial, the Civil War, etc. But there is something odd about such an exchange, for all these symbols and events (which are territorially confined) are associated with a particular culture. So American and English cultures would not be what they are if they did not have their respective symbols and events in their own territories. In our thought-experiment, territory is essential to collective self-understanding. Something similar occurs with individuals. Everyone has a certain birthplace and homeland. We generally have strong attachments to these places because they make us who we are. If we had a different birthplace and homeland, we would probably be a different person. Thus birthplace and homeland are generally an essential trait of who we are. As suggested with regard to language, the sense of homeland can also be more complicated if I, say, am born in a certain place, but then move to another country. But even supposing that the place, or places, to which I have a strong attachment is not my homeland, the point is that I will still be attached to places with symbolic meanings that make me who I am.

Notice now that the two traits I have discussed so far, language and birthplace, derive from and are associated with a particular group—or in the case of some people, a variety of groups. So if I possess traits of this sort, they will probably make me a member of a particular group. Take, for example, Argentina: it is a group that speaks Spanish and comprises a geographical region in the South Cone. It is then the case that the property of speaking Spanish (with an Argentinean accent) and being born in the territory known as "Argentina," make me a member in the Argentinean group. In my example, membership in the Argentinean group is basic for two reasons. The first reason is that for me to be the person I am, I must be someone who, in my example, speaks a certain language and has a certain birthplace—or attachment to a territorialized community. In other words, these traits are essential to my self-understanding. Second, the traits that are essential to my self-understanding derive from and are associated with the Argentinean group, making me a member of this group. Putting these two reasons together, we can see that Argentinean traits are essential to my self-understanding and thus my Argentinean membership is basic. Naturally, for people who, as I said before, speak several languages or feel attached to different territorialized communities, we may speak of various basic memberships with regard to linguistic and territorialized groups. One of these memberships may be dominant or a variety of memberships may compete against one another.

Basic membership can be contrasted with the kind of membership entailing traits that are not essential to someone's self-understanding, i.e., accidental traits. This contrast will help us to understand more clearly what basic membership is. Suppose I characterize myself as someone who enjoys reading history, practices psychology and votes Democrat on every election. Suppose further that I might obtain the traits I have just mentioned without significantly affecting the sense of who I am. These traits may change—I may stop reading history, change careers, or vote Republican—without significantly altering my self-understanding. The traits I have in mind may be very significant to me, but they are not essential to my self-understanding. Given that these traits are not essential to my self-understanding, I may lose my membership in the History Book Club, the American Psychological Association or the Democratic Party without significantly altering the sense of who I am. So the memberships just mentioned may indeed fluctuate without a significant impact on my self-understanding. This kind of membership is nonbasic.

My discussion so far might make it seem like there are clear-cut categories and distinctions: essential and nonessential traits; basic and nonbasic memberships. This is true in a sense, but it can also be misleading. At this point, two complexities in the notion of basic membership are worth highlighting. First, a point underlying my discussion (one that I will bring up in other occasions) is that the traits that are essential to someone's self-understanding are often highly imprecise. To some, for instance, having a strong sense of nationality is intimately coupled with membership in a political party. It is often very hard to be precise about which traits are essential to someone's self-understanding and which are not. All that must be granted in my discussion, however, is that some traits are indeed essential for defining who I am, whereas others are not. I think that there are significant generalities with regard to essential traits (e.g., nonvoluntarily acquired traits such as language and birthplace), but I do not wish to focus on traits per se. What I wish to focus on is the fact that there are essential and nonessential traits—whatever they may be—for someone's self-understanding. I will return to this point below when I discuss nonvoluntarily acquired traits.

The second complexity is that basic membership admits of degrees. I clarified before that people may have more than one basic membership even with regard to groups that are distinguished by criteria such as language and territory. Let me emphasize that people tend to have many basic memberships. The fact of the matter is that people have essential traits of self-understanding that make them members in different groups. Among the traits that are essential to someone's self-understanding, one may find traits that make her a member in three different groups: an Argentinean, a Jew, and a Communist. All three memberships are basic. But note also that despite the variety of basic memberships, one of these memberships may have a higher degree of significance in various contexts and circumstances. In other words, several memberships may be basic; but among these, one membership, in a certain context, may have a higher degree of basicness than the other basic memberships. Suppose that three different memberships are basic, which means that certain traits that are essential to someone's self-understanding make her a member in these three groups. Hypothetically speaking, in context A, the person has nine essential traits that make her a member of the first group. In the same context, she has seven essential traits making her a member of the second group; and, finally, six essential traits for the third group. All three memberships are basic, but, in context A at least, the first membership is more basic than the second and third one. The number of traits may of course vary in context B. Basic membership then, when compared with other basic memberships, may have degrees of basicness. Another way of stating the point is by saying that basic memberships can be ranked. I will come back to this point in chapter seven when we compare national and Hispanic memberships.

I said above that the traits which are essential to someone's self-understanding are often imprecise. I also suggested, however, that certain types of traits are, as a matter of general tendency, essential to people's self-understanding (e.g., language and homeland). If this is right, the question is: what types of traits are generally essential to group members' self-understanding?[29] Let us make a distinction between *nonconsensual* and *consensual* markers of personhood. The first cannot be changed because I did not have an initial choice as to whether I should acquire a certain marker or not.[30] I am born and raised in a milieu, nonvoluntarily absorbing a set of traits that are very hard to change and that also essentially define who I am. By way of illustration we could think of someone who is born and brought up in England, and thus acquires a series of traits and attachments that essentially define who she is. She is someone whose native tongue is English, has British citizenship and is subject to British government and law, and participates in the English way of life. These nonvoluntarily acquired markers will presumably be essential to her self-understanding. So she will view herself as an Englishwoman in a way that makes her English membership basic.

Consensual markers, in contrast, are the result of choice. I may decide to learn a new language, become a Buddhist, learn to play football, and identify myself with my Irish grandparents. Strictly speaking, I did not decide to have Irish grandparents, but neither did I have a choice when they decided to migrate to the U.S., where I was born and raised. So, in this case my American membership is nonvoluntary, whereas identifying with my Irish background is optional. The main point about consensual markers is that they can be altered without significantly modifying the sense of who I am. So, many consensual markers are nonessential traits of self-understanding. The reason why consensual markers may vary without significantly altering my essential traits of self-understanding has to do with the fact that these markers are the result of choice.

The point I am trying to make needs to be explained further. I do not wish to suggest that all nonconsensual markers lead to essential traits or that consensual markers do not. Strictly speaking, nonconsensual markers alone are not enough to explain basic membership, since those markers need to become part of my self-understanding and thus I—and other members of the group to which I belong—must in some respect be aware of and care about them. Let me emphasize that even those elements that I have not chosen, which become essential traits of my self-understanding, must be associated with beliefs and social conceptions in order to become essential traits of my own and other group members' self-understanding. The suggestion is simply that when characterizing myself in a way that expresses traits, which are essential to my self-understanding, many of those traits will be tied to elements that I have not chosen and am not likely to be able to change, easily or at all.

Think now about the complexities of basic membership I mentioned earlier. Consider how memberships that are acquired voluntarily become very important to some people. My suggestion, however, is that nonvoluntarily acquired traits are more stable because they are harder (and sometimes impossible) to change, and thus many of these traits tend to be essential for defining who I am.[31] I can convert to Hinduism—or any other religion—but also in the midst of a disappointment, stop professing Hinduism and go back to "who I was before." Let me incidentally mention that using religious examples can be misleading, for religion is not always a matter of choice. Religion may, as a matter of fact, be in some sense nonvoluntarily absorbed. Religion is a matter of conscious decision, but I did not decide to be born into a Jewish family. So if my family practices the rituals and teachings of the Jewish religion, the world-view conveyed by such rituals and teachings will be absorbed nonvoluntarily. When religion is in some sense nonvoluntarily absorbed—meaning that one grows up within a certain religious environment—it often becomes a very powerful source for self-understanding.

Returning to voluntary memberships, I can choose, for example, to describe myself as an "Italian American." But I could also drop the label without much impact on the features that are generally indispensable for my self-understanding. In contrast, my first language, family members and birthplace are traits I did not choose and, moreover, I cannot alter. Accordingly, any definition describing the essentially constitutive elements of who I am would generally tend to include traits such as language, kinship and birthplace. In other words, my self-understanding is often bound with the elements I cannot alter; and thus those elements are essential to the definition of who I am.

It is important to emphasize here a point that was made earlier. We must be careful and avoid making clear-cut distinctions because the categories are not always clear. Note that I speak in terms of tendencies and generalities, for the distinction between nonvoluntarily acquired traits and those memberships that are voluntarily acquired is not always easy to point out in precise terms. Donald Horowitz reminds us that it is true that certain memberships (e.g., ethnic) are not chosen but given. Nonetheless, both "principles of membership—birth and choice—are capable of fictive elements."[32] It is also important to emphasize that I am not implying any type of determinism when I speak about nonvoluntarily acquired traits. If such was the implication, I would be committing what might be described as the "culturalist fallacy." This fallacy consists in the belief that a group *determines* who we are, and thus precludes the possibility of significant personal change.[33] I am only speaking here about general tendencies with regard to necessary traits for someone's self-understanding —not cultural determinism.

Let me go back at this time to an earlier point about identity groups, since a discussion on this topic will shed light on my understanding about the significance of nonvoluntarily acquired traits. One might think that nonconsensual markers of personhood make people members of the identity groups in a multicultural society. This could indeed be the case, but not necessarily. Discussing the relationship between certain types of identity groups and nonconsensual markers will help us to see more clearly what nonconsensual markers are and how they are related to basic membership. The sorts of traits we sometimes associate with "ethnic groups" are not always nonconsensual markers. Think for example of "Irish-American identity" in the multicultural context of American society. In a study on the dynamics of "ethnic" identity within groups of European extraction in America, Mary Waters describes a kind of identity that is voluntary and thus selective. So, for instance, "you can choose those aspects of being Irish that appeal to you and discard those that do not."[34] As Waters observes, Irish-American identity (or identities like Polish American and Italian American) may be, and is in fact, meaningful to people. Nevertheless, despite being valuable, the identities she describes are not (for the most part), due to their voluntary and selective nature, the basis for nonconsensual markers of personhood.

Not surprisingly, the identities Waters describes are not, generally speaking, essential to someone's self-understanding. I can choose to apply the label of "Irish American" (with its selective characteristics) to portray myself, but I could also choose to discard the label. In this sense, my Irish-American identity, despite its potential personal significance, is not essential for characterizing who I am.[35] In other words, my Irish-American membership may be put aside without significantly altering the essential traits for personal self-understanding. As a consequence, Irish-American traits are nonessential and thus Irish-American membership is nonbasic.

THE VALUE OF BASIC MEMBERSHIP

When membership is basic it is presumably valuable. Here the following two questions arise. First, in what ways is membership valuable? And second, why is basic membership valuable? In order to address the first question, I will return to points discussed in the previous chapter, turning again to Will Kymlicka, and suggest that membership is, first, instrumentally valuable and, second, the value of membership derives from identity. One of Kymlicka's contributions to contemporary political thought has been to establish the connection, which John Rawls and the liberal tradition do not deal with in detail, between group membership and the primary goods of people.[36] According to Kymlicka, "if we view cultural membership as a primary good within Rawls' scheme of justice, then it is important to remember that it is a good in its capacity of providing meaningful options for us, and aiding our ability to judge for ourselves the value of our life-plans."[37] Note that, for Kymlicka, cultural membership is important because it provides individuals with a "context of choice."

In establishing a warranted relationship between group membership and individual choice, Kymlicka also reacts against Michael Walzer's view of group membership. According to Walzer "the primary good that we distribute to one another is membership in some human community."[38] Note that for Walzer membership is a good in itself, or in the words of Kymlicka: "the theoretical framework Walzer employs seems to make cultural membership the foundational value."[39] Whereas for Walzer cultural membership seems to have some sort of *intrinsic* value, Kymlicka believes that cultural membership is *instrumentally* valuable because it points to a context of choice.[40]

Walzer claims, for instance, that "the survival and flourishing of the groups depends largely upon the vitality of their centers,"[41] but one is left wondering why such is the case. What is the group's "center" and what is so important about it? Why should we think that certain groups ought to survive or flourish? Why is group membership highly significant? It seems to me that groups or cultures are not intrinsically valuable. If that is indeed Walzer's suggestion, he does not seem to go far enough. Cultures and groups might be highly valuable, but we must go further than Walzer in inquiring about the value of groups and membership. Kymlicka's instrumental approach seems more promising. But here we must point out two different strands in Kymlicka's view. I already mentioned the first strand: the value of group membership is connected with the "context of choice." Thus group membership is valuable because our "range of options is determined by our cultural heritage."[42] The second strand has to do with "identity," or a sense of who I am. Accordingly, "someone's upbringing isn't something that can just be erased; it is, and will remain, a constitutive part of who that person is. Cultural membership affects our very sense of personal identity and capacity."[43] This type of membership is what I have described as basic membership.

It is not always clear how the two strands interact with each other in Kymlicka's view of membership. Regardless of the interconnection between both strands, I think that the importance of the context of choice must certainly be acknowledged. Nonetheless, understanding who we are seems to be a more fundamental matter than having choices. The reason for this last point is that self-understanding is a precondition for the possibility of making choices. We can indeed imagine coercive situations, legitimate or not, in which self-understanding is not conducive to choices. Coercive circumstances could arise when the expression of values and beliefs is legally forbidden in a particular society. But these circumstances could also be more subtle. Think of a situation in which the coercive mechanisms of family upbringing, deeply and successfully internalized, preclude the possibility of marrying someone who is not from the same culture. The point is that there seem to be circumstances in which self-understanding is not conducive to choices—whether these circumstances are legitimate or not is beside my current point. The insights just mentioned lead me to think that the value of membership derives from group members having a sense of who they are—namely, an identity. I would then suggest that the instrumental case for the value of membership is better made when emphasizing "identity"—which, again, does not necessarily diminish "choice," but the emphasis should lie on "identity."

I will now turn to the second question. I have made the claim that certain types of memberships are a primary source of meaning and direction. These memberships are central to members' identities, which is also to say that they are basic. These memberships are presumably highly significant and so I have also made claims about the value of membership. I have argued that the case for the value of membership is best made when looking at membership instrumentally and emphasizing identity. But we have still not answered a more fundamental question: why is membership valuable? Now, we clearly do not have just any type of membership in mind. We have in mind the type of membership that is central to someone's identity, i.e., basic membership. So the question we need to address is really this one: why is basic membership, the type of membership that is central to someone's identity, valuable?

Basic membership is often highly valuable to group members because it significantly contributes toward members' well-being. The essential traits by which group members characterize themselves give each individual a sense of who he or she is. Such a sense is often a vital condition for personal well-being. If we posit that conditions of this sort are highly valuable because they contribute toward well-being, we can then say that basic membership is highly valuable. Given the value of basic membership, it is no surprise that situations of tyranny often entail attacking the characteristic traits of basic membership in the oppressed group. Consider measures such as forbidding the religious or social practices of enslaved or oppressed groups. For instance, African slaves brought to America were not allowed to practice their ancestral religions. In another example, the Turkish government banned the use of Kurdish until 1991—although expressions of Kurdish culture are still deemed to have a separatist purpose. These kinds of measures typically have the effect of subjugating a particular group by curtailing expressions of basic membership and hampering the well being of oppressed group members.

CONCLUSION

This chapter has focused on membership. What kind of membership is central to someone's identity? To answer the question, we first need to have an idea of what identity is. I characterized the phenomenon of identity on the basis of two components: self-understanding and group membership. According to my account, to have an identity is to possess self-understanding, which generally makes someone a member of a group. I then introduced the notion of basic membership, which gets to the heart of the matter. Here I argued that some traits are essential to someone's self-understanding, and these essential traits make her a member of a group. When this is the case, membership in a group is said to be basic. I furthermore suggested that the traits, which are essential to someone's self-understanding, are oftentimes nonvoluntarily acquired. So, some nonvoluntary traits will have a propensity to be basic. The type of membership I discussed is presumably very significant. Thus my discussion of membership would not be complete without addressing the importance of membership. In the final section of the chapter I made two points. First, in the context of Kymlicka's views, membership is valuable because it gives members an identity, which means that the value of membership is instrumental. Second, Basic membership is highly valuable because it significantly contributes toward well-being.

NOTES

1. I agree with Kwame Anthony Appiah when he says that "one reasonable ground for suspicion of much contemporary multicultural talk is that the conceptions of collective identity they presuppose are indeed remarkable unsubtle in their understandings of the processes by which identities, both individual and

collective, develop." *The Ethics of Identity* (Princeton: Princeton University Press, 2005), 107.

2. Human beings are capable of self-understanding because of their level of cognitive complexity. I take it then that trees, ants, and dogs do not have identities. Since they do not possess the cognitive complexity necessary for developing self-understanding, it is not possible to say that they have identities in the same sense that human beings do.

3. For relevant literature on the way I treat the connection between self-understanding and self-knowledge with groups, see Donald Davidson, *Subjective, Intersubjective, Objective* (New York: Oxford University Press, 2001), 205–20; Anthony Giddens, *The Constitution of Society: Outline of the Theory of Structuration* (Berkeley and Los Angeles: University of California Press, 1984), 41–92; and G.H. Mead *Mind, Self and Society: From the Standpoint of a Social Behaviorist* (Chicago: University of Chicago Press, 1967).

4. Properly speaking, identity consists of having traits in common with other members of the group. I belong to a group and thus derive an identity from such a group because of traits that, in some respects, make me identical with other members.

5. Mead, *Mind, Self and Society*, 155.

6. The exception, of course, is belonging to a set with only one member: the father of Mary, or the Fire Chief of Boston. But even in this case one may point out that the connection is with a broader set, i.e., the set of fathers or Fire Chiefs.

7. Mead, *Mind, Self and Society*, 156.

8. In a Meadean fashion, Jorge Larraín Ibañez puts the point this way: ". . . identity, in a personal sense, is something that the individual presents to the others and that the others present to his or her. The self presupposes the prior existence of the group and its evaluation of it. The meaning of identity responds not so much to the question 'who am I?' or 'what would I like to be?' as to the question 'who am I in the eyes of the others?'" "The Concept of Identity," in *National Identities and Sociopolitical Changes in Latin America*, eds. Mercedes F. Durán-Cogan and Antonio Goméz-Moriana (New York: Routledge, 2001), 8–9.

9. For an interesting discussion on this point, see Charles Taylor, "The Politics of Recognition," in *Multiculturalism: Examining the Politics of Recognition*, ed. Amy Gutmann (Princeton: Princeton University Press, 1994), 26–31.

10. I follow Taylor's insight when he says that "in premodern times, people didn't speak of 'identity' and 'recognition'—not because people didn't have (what we call) identities, or because these didn't depend on recognition, but rather because they were then too unproblematic to be thematized as such." "Politics of Recognition," 35.

11. In using this example, I draw from Jacques Lizot's well-known ethnographic study, presented in a narrative form, first published in 1976, *Tales of the Yanomami: Daily Life in the Venezuelan Forest* (New York: Cambridge University Press, 1985).

12. For a glossary of words and proper pronunciation for the transliteration, see Lizot, *Tales of the Yanomami*, 190–96.

13. Lizot, See *Tales of the Yanomami*, 144–52.

14. Lizot, *Tales of the Yanomami*, 26.

15. See Todd Gitlin's interesting discussion on identity politics in the U.S., "The Rise of Identity Politics," *Dissent*, 40 (1993): 172–77.

16. For a discussion on how liberal democracies took a step from what David Miller calls the politics of inclusion to the politics of recognition, see "Group Identities, National Identities and Democratic Politics," in *Citizenship and National Identity* (Cambridge: Polity Press, 2000), 67–69.

17. Michael Walzer, *What it Means to Be an American: Essays on the American Experience* (New York: Marsilio Publishers, 1996), 4.

18. On this point, see Jeremy Waldron's interesting discussion about cultural identity and the requirements of authenticity and self-consciousness. "Cultural Identity and Civic Responsibility," in *Citizenship in Diverse Societies*, eds. Will Kymlicka and Wayne Norman (New York: Oxford University Press, 2000), 168–69.

19. Nationality is not inherently significant, although in many cases it does play a commanding role in people's identities—which, as we will see later on, tends to be the case in Latin America. But any role nationality might play is contingent upon circumstances that may change. Nationality then might be an instance of "national identification" (dominant), "complex identification" (compatible with other sources), or a nonobject of identification. For the distinction between national and complex identifications, see Jeff McMahan, "The Limits of National Partiality," in *The Morality of Nationalism*, eds. Robert McKim and Jeff McMahan (New York: Oxford University Press, 1997), 121.

20. *Metaphysics*, 1015a, 20–25. Strictly speaking, "necessity" and "essence" are not the same, but the difference is not relevant for my purposes and so I use "necessary" and "essential" interchangeably. I quote from the text edited by Richard McKeon, *The Basic Works of Aristotle* (New York: Random House, 1941).

21. *Metaphysics*, 1025a, 10–15.

22. On internalizing traits that become essential to someone's self-understanding, see Jean Paul Sartre *Anti-Semite and Jew: An Exploration of the Ethiology of Hate* (New York: Schocken Books, 1995 [1948]), 67–75; and Appiah, *The Ethics of Identity*, 65–70.

23. Primordialism is also related to what Rogers Brubaker calls "groupism" in the study of ethnic groups and nationalism. Groupism is "the social ontology that leads us to talk and write about ethnic groups and nations as real entities, as communities, as substantial, enduring, internally homogeneous and externally bounded communities." "Myths and Misconceptions in the Study of Nationalism," *The State of the Nation: Ernest Gellner and the Theory of Nationalism*, ed. John A. Hall (Cambridge: Cambridge University Press, 1998), 292.

24. See Anthony D. Smith, *Nationalism: Theory, Ideology, History* (Malden, MA: Polity Press, 2001), 51–54.

25. On the point of how group configurations change, see Anthony D. Smith's discussion on ethnic identity-formation. *National Identity* (Reno: University of Nevada Press, 1991), 23–26.

26. George Fletcher, "The Case for Linguistic Self-Defense," in *The Morality of Nationalism*, 326.

27. Fletcher, "The Case for Linguistic Self-Defense," 326. Further on, he expresses the point this way: "The history of any people is tied to its language. The narrative of the people unfolds in legends, historical events, poetic renditions of

key moments, slogans that never die, great oratory, and, of course, legal phrases that define a culture's sense of justice." 332.

28. Anthony Smith, *Chosen Peoples: Sacred Sources of National Identity* (New York: Oxford University Press, 2003), 134.

29. Here I elaborate on the insight by Avishai Margalit and Joseph Raz. They comment that "although accomplishments play their role in people's sense of their own identity, it would seem that at the most fundamental level our sense of our own identity depends on [nonvoluntary] criteria of belonging rather than on those of accomplishment. Secure identification at that level is particularly important to one's well-being." "National Self-determination," in *Ethics and the Public Domain: Essays in the Morality of Law and Politics*, Joseph Raz (New York: Oxford University Press, 1994), 117.

30. Not all unalterable markers are nonvoluntarily acquired. I can, for instance, choose to put a tattoo on my arm: a situation that then becomes unalterable, despite being a matter of choice.

31. Nenad Miscevic provides an account that places less value on involuntary traits for the sense of personhood and focuses on endorsement. "Is National Identity Essential for Personal Identity," in *Nationalism and Ethnic Conflict: Philosophical Perspectives*, ed. Nenad Miscevic (Chicago and La Salle: Open Court, 2000), 250–56. I agree with her claim that national identity is one form of identity among many, but I think her account is flawed for two reasons. First, she contrasts nonvoluntary traits—constitutive of what I call basic memberships as a matter of propensity—with national belonging and endorsement. But the significance of national identification by way of consent does not preclude that nations might be a source of nonvoluntary traits. National identification might be produced by, and derive its value from, a mixture of nonvoluntary traits and voluntary decisions. Second, she confines nonvoluntary traits to *nations*. Note, however, that although nonvoluntary markers are often attached to nations, this need not necessarily be the case. Nonvoluntary markers, as related to basic membership, are part of a group function, and not necessarily a group type, e.g., nations. Moreover, even when nations are the source of nonvoluntary traits that become part of someone's basic membership, nations are not the only source of basic memberships.

32. Donald Horowitz, *Ethnic Groups in Conflict* (Berkeley and Los Angeles: University of California Press, 1985), 55–56.

33. See the discussion by Bhikhu Parekh for a description of this fallacy. *Rethinking Multiculturalism: Cultural Diversity and Political Theory* (Cambridge, MA: Harvard University Press, 2002), 76–79.

34. Mary C. Waters, *Ethnic Options: Choosing Identities in America* (Berkeley and Los Angeles: University of California Press, 1990), 115.

35. The type of "ethnic" identity Waters examines, apart from being a matter of choice, does not have much relevance for everyday life: "it does not, for the most part, limit choice of marriage partner. . . . It does not determine where you will live, who your friends will be, what job you will have. . . ." Waters, *Ethnic Options*, 147. Nonvoluntary markers of personhood, in contrast, will presumably determine to a larger extent where I work or who I marry. For instance, I would not ordinarily work in a particular setting or marry someone without knowing the language in which business is conducted or my spouse speaks.

36. See chapters 7, 8, and 9 of Will Kymlicka, *Liberalism, Community, and Culture* (New York: Oxford University Press, 1989).
37. Kymlicka, *Liberalism, Community, and Culture*, 166.
38. Michael Walzer, *Spheres of Justice: A Defense of Pluralism and Equality* (New York: Basic Books, 1983), 31.
39. Kymlicka, *Liberalism, Community, and Culture*, 221.
40. For varieties of intrinsic and instrumental value arguments, see Margaret Moore, "Nationalist Arguments, Ambivalent Conclusions," in *Nationalism and Ethnic Conflict*, 177–90.
41. Walzer, *What it means to be an American*, 74.
42. Kymlicka, *Liberalism, Community, and Culture*, 165.
43. Kymlicka, *Liberalism, Community, and Culture*, 175.

6

✢

The Conditions of Relevant Groups

I have discussed membership. In this chapter, I will turn to groups. I have claimed that the value and significance of group membership is not based on the type of group *per se*, but rather on the function of the group in the lives of members. If we posit that certain groups have the function of endowing group members with the type of membership that is central to members' identities, i.e., basic membership, one of the questions we need to address is, how do we characterize groups that have the function at stake? Following my strategy of not focusing on group types as such (e.g., *cultural* or *national* groups) to determine when membership is significant, I will turn instead to the conditions that groups of this sort tend to satisfy.[1] In this chapter, I suggest that the groups I have in mind generally satisfy three conditions: first, the condition of *relevant identification*; second, the condition of *differentiation*; and, third, the condition of *intrinsic identification*. These conditions will help us to understand later on the nature of the Hispanic group and whether it has the function at stake or not.

RELEVANT IDENTIFICATION

Let me begin with a basic fact about groups and societies: they are first and foremost interactive. People belonging to the same group interact with one another. There is a process of socialization by which people develop and learn languages, habits, myths, values, and maps of meaning. These elements are not absorbed in a solitary way, but rather in the context of social interaction.[2] In large groups such as nations, for example, the process of socialization does not mean that I necessarily interact with *all* the members of the group, since the size of the group may make it literally impossible to even personally *see* all other co-members. Nations, for example, are kinds of groups that Benedict Anderson describes as "imagined communities." Communities of this sort are imagined because group members "will never know most of their fellow-members, meet them, or even hear of them, yet in the mind of each lives the image of their communion."[3]

We have then two levels of membership in groups such as nations: *immediate* and *extended*. I am an immediate member of a given group, e.g., a family, and also an extended member of another group, e.g., a nation. I grow up in the setting of a given family and circle of friends and acquaintances most of whom are presumably members of a larger group. There is an immediate sphere of interaction that is part of a larger and indirect sphere of interaction. Now, it is important to highlight that the former is oftentimes part of the latter. So, for instance, my family is, in fact, part of a nation, and thus being a member of my family also makes me a member of such a nation. One could also put the matter in terms of coextensive membership. I am part of a subset of the whole set. Being a member of the subset is generally coextensive with being a member of the whole set. Thus if I immediately interact with people in subset A, which would make me a member of such a subset, I will also be a member of the larger set A*. A question here is: what is the criterion whereby large and imagined communities of this sort are individuated and unified? This question arises in the debate between modernists and ethnosymbolists, to which I will return below. Although the modernist account has been criticized for not putting enough emphasis on collective bonds and common attributes, a point I will make later on, I tend to agree with the modernist's claim that individuation and unification of this kind is generated and reinforced by the political factor, e.g., states.[4]

Note that the group in which I interact as an immediate and also an extended member generally has a limited number of members. What I mean by limited membership is that not every single human being is, in fact, a member of my extended group. So, for instance, not every human being living at the present moment is a fellow national. The sort of imagined community I am now describing is then a partial portion of the whole living human community at a certain point in time. The set to which I belong is a community with a limited number of members drawn from the universe of "humanity." In other words, I am a member of a group that comprises only *some* human beings who presumably have a great deal in common. So some people will be members of my group, whereas others will not be members. I will have a great deal in common with, say, fellow nationals—since we speak the same language and have similar habits—whereas other people who are not members of my same nation will be foreign to me.

Given that group members interact with one another, they will learn to recognize fellow members. Similarly, mutual recognition between group members is what often makes interaction possible. Interaction between group members is both a cause and a consequence of recognition, by which I mean not political recognition, but rather the possibility of distinguishing fellow members of a group on the basis of mutually shared attributes. So when we think of interaction between group members we must also think of social recognition. Recognition of fellow members, of course, makes it possible to also recognize nonmembers of a group. If I can recognize those who belong to my group, it is because I can also recognize those who do not. At the moment, however, I am not concerned with recognition of nonmembers, but rather recognition of fellow members.

When fellow members of a group recognize each other, what is it that they are able to recognize? It is generally the markers of the social settings to which all members of the same group belong. When coming across a fellow member of my group, I can recognize such a member because of the social markers she displays. My point is best illustrated with an example of two tourists in a foreign land. If I am a Spanish citizen from Madrid on vacation in Hawaii and come across a fellow Spanish citizen from Madrid, I will most likely be able to recognize her due to a set of social markers. Suppose I see her wearing a *Real Madrid* jersey, and immediately wonder about the reason why she would want to wear the jersey. I engage her in a conversation and immediately detect a *Madrileño* accent, pretty much like mine. I learn that she was brought up in Madrid under a school system that I can immediately recognize— presumably she has, among many other things, read excerpts of the Spanish classics, Miguel de Cervantes, Francisco de Quevedo, Pio Baroja, etc., played games that are also familiar to me, and has gone on field trips to places that I know.[5] I notice we communicate using similar jargon and have a peculiar picaresque sense of humor that we can both understand. Someone who is not acquainted with our realm of references could probably not understand our jokes (even if such a person spoke our language). It might certainly be the case that members from the group run into each other in a tourist situation and immediately block the possibility of interaction—since co-nationals are embarrassing or the purpose of traveling is, say, to interact with people different than oneself, not co-nationals. My main claim, however, still holds true: whereas I engage or reject someone occurs on the basis of markers that are readily recognizable.

I have so far made the following points: (a) human beings interact with people in their groups; (b) these groups generally have a limited number of members; (c) human beings are able to interact with people in their groups because they can recognize each other; and (d) recognition is based on social markers. From these four points, it follows that groups and members are *identifiable*.[6] In the process of interaction, group members can discriminate members from nonmembers by recognizing certain social markers in fellow members, and such process of discrimination by recognition means that groups and their members are identifiable. Note first that groups are identifiable by virtue of their particular properties. I can say, for example, that the American group is distinguished by certain properties such as a tradition of liberty and democracy, the practice of certain sports such as baseball and football, a geopolitical affiliation, and a language, i.e., American English. What we need to see is that a set of particular properties make it possible for us to speak of a group that can be identified as "American." Note also, in the second place, that group members can be identified according to certain properties.[7] Think, for instance, of the fact that a graduate from a certain college can be identified by a graduation ring on her finger or by expressing her preferences on basketball college teams. I can also recognize someone who shops in the same grocery store where I do by noticing the bags he happens to use for his garbage. There are equally a huge number of markers that would allow me to potentially recognize people who drink coffee in the same coffee shop where I do, support the same political party I do, share my musical preferences for a particular band and use the same company I do for their cell phone service.

We are not concerned, however, with the possibility of identification through all those kinds of properties. We are concerned instead with identification under some condition, i.e., by virtue of a certain kind of property that creates a certain kind of group configuration. The condition of identification must be such that it says something relevant about the members we identify.[8] We are not interested in identifying the group of people on the basis of attributes that do not express in a meaningful way who they are. If that is the case, what is then the specific condition of identification? Let us think here of two different situations. In the first hypothetical situation, mentioned above, I come across a fellow Spanish citizen while on vacation that I am able to recognize because of her jersey, accent, school education and characteristic sense of humor. In the second situation, I recognize someone who graduated from my same college, e.g., University of Maryland, by detecting the ring on his finger and his basketball college team preferences. Now combine the properties in each situation and we produce an inventory with the following properties: (i) possessing Spanish citizenship (ii) wearing a jersey; (iii) speaking a language (with a certain accent); (iv) attending a particular school; (v) having a characteristic sense of humor; (vi) wearing a ring; and (vii) preferring a specific basketball team.

Note that a distinction between properties can be made. Some properties are more significant to someone's identity than others. In fact, some properties will be essential to someone's self-understanding, whereas others will not be so. Let us say that there is a continuum in which one end represents "essential properties for self-understanding," and the other end "nonessential properties for self-understanding." Along the continuum, we can place all the properties mentioned above.

Property (i) is essential to the self-understanding of most people. Having a particular citizenship often defines where we come from, who we are and what we believe. Property (ii) does not strike me as the kind of property that would be essential to someone's self-understanding. The sense of who I am is not linked in any significant sense to whether I wear a particular jersey or not. Property (iii) does often seem to be essential to someone's self-understanding. As we saw in the previous chapter, languages often define who we are, for we would probably be different people if we did not speak our native language, or any other language that we have adopted at the level of a certain degree of fluency. Property (iv) could be very significant and even perhaps essential to someone's self-understanding. Nonetheless, I do not think it has, generally speaking, the same level of significance as property (i) or (iii). Property (v) is a difficult one. I do not think that having a characteristic sense of humor is essential to someone's self-understanding, but it could be for some people. Property (vi) is nonessential. Wearing a ring is like wearing a jersey: the property can be altered without significantly altering our self-understanding. Finally, property (vii) may be very significant to some people, but I doubt that the preference of sports teams is essential to the self-understanding of many people. Preference of sports teams can indeed be a manifestation of national or regional attachments. If this is the case, then we must look not at the preference of a team as such, but rather the attachment underlying such a preference.

To see what can be derived from this discussion, four elements must now be highlighted. First, as we just saw, there are different kinds of properties. An inventory of the properties in our examples shows that some are generally essential to someone's self-understanding, whereas others are not. The purpose is not to classify all the properties in a clear manner, but rather to show that different properties have degrees of significance for someone's self-understanding, ranging from essential to nonessential. I have talked about properties classifying them as essential or nonessential, but the main point, as I mentioned previously is not whether a particular property per se is essential or not, but rather that certain properties will be essential for someone's self-understanding and others will not. Second, the properties we have surveyed are properties that make someone a member of a particular group. In our examples, those groups were the Spanish nation and the group of Maryland graduates. Third, members of each group can be identified on the basis of the properties we discussed. The point, which should be obvious by now, is that I recognize a fellow national or graduate on the basis of identifiable properties. Fourth, the balance of properties in the situations we discussed is asymmetrical. As a matter of tendency, we notice that there are more properties closer to the end of "essential for self-understanding" in the national group than in the group of college graduates.

We now have all the elements for arguing two points. First, since properties make identification possible, group members can be identified according to different types of properties. More specifically, we can identify members of two different groups on the basis of two types of properties: those that are essential for members' self-understandings and those that are not. As we saw in our examples, the balance of properties shows that national members are identified according to properties that tend to be essential for a member's self-understanding. In contrast, graduates are identified according to properties that, on balance, are not essential for the self-understanding of a group member.

From this first point follows a second one. We can identify members according to properties that make their membership basic and properties that do not have this tendency. If we posit that membership is basic when properties are essential to members' self-understandings, we can see that membership in the national group is basic, whereas membership in the group of graduates is not. Or, at the very least, even if properties for members' self-understandings in the two groups are basic, we have to take into account degrees of basicness. Incidentally, I am assuming here that members are indeed identified on the basis of properties that are essential to their self-understanding. Let me clarify, however, that this process of identification is not always the case: in some cases members of a group in which membership is basic may be identified on the basis of non-essential properties. For example, I look at someone's weight and conclude that they are from a certain country. Still, I would suggest that in cases such as these the properties whereby someone is identified as a member of, say, a country are not inherently connected with relevant membership in that particular group. As I mentioned earlier, one may identify members of any given group—e.g., humankind—in many different ways—the property of not being non-human. But, as also previously indicated, it is necessary to emphasize that we are interested in the type of identification that says something relevant about who members of a group are by virtue of properties that create a certain kind of group configuration.

Returning to the comparison between members of the national group and those in the group of graduates, one might indeed object that the two memberships could be basic given that traits from either membership may be essential to someone's self-understanding. Even if this is true, note that according to the balance of essential properties in the example, national membership will be more basic than membership in the group of college graduates. For the sake of simplification and clarity in the argument, let us then say that one membership is basic, whereas the other is not. In setting up the argument, I picked two groups—nation and college graduates—to give an example that is likely to generate a clear contrast. But comparisons between other groups will undoubtedly be more complex. Suppose we compare a national and a religious group, assuming that membership in the two groups is identifiable on the basis of group attributes that do not necessarily overlap with each other. If we posit that memberships in the two groups have a high degree of basicness, comparisons can get complicated. Memberships might, in fact, compete against one another and, as I have suggested before, produce different outcomes in different situations.

I began my discussion by saying that we are not concerned with identification of groups and memberships as such. Instead, we are interested in identification under a certain pertinent condition. The question is: when are group and membership identification relevant? We can now answer this question. Identification is relevant when we are able to distinguish the sorts of properties that make membership in a particular group basic. In other words, relevant identification is done on the basis of properties that are essential to the self-understanding of members in a particular group. This condition is the first step for characterizing the kinds of groups we are interested in. If this were the only condition, our understanding of groups would be rather limited, especially taking into account that the claim so far has been somewhat circular—membership in certain groups is basic, and those groups are identified on the basis of basic membership. We must then move a step further and examine what is precisely the quality that distinguishes the groups we are interested in.

DIFFERENTIATION

We know that relevant identification singles out properties that constitute basic membership in particular groups. Attention now needs to be drawn to the fact that groups are differentiated from each other, which is what makes identification of groups and members possible. Highlighting this fact, I will now argue that basic membership is necessarily connected with the difference-sensitive attributes of groups.

I will begin the discussion with some general remarks about group description. Imagine three groups of people, farmers, Jews and Argentineans. In attempting to describe farmers we can say that they are people who normally have families, believe in a deity, and ingest food. Likewise, we describe Jews as people who normally have families, believe in a deity, and ingest food. Lastly, we describe Argentineans in the same manner. This mode of describing has two characteristics. First, the descriptions are so broad that *differences* among groups are not evident. Second, the description of these three groups is probably accurate, but it is so broad that it does not really say much about the *meaningful* features of groups or group members. One could, however, describe, say, Argentineans by pointing to features that make them different from other groups and are also meaningful to Argentineans. Let us say that Argentineans are the people living in a particular geopolitical sector who happen to have a history and a culture. They generally accept the institution of monogamous marriage, mostly profess the Roman Catholic or Lutheran faiths, like to eat beef and *churrasco*, speak Spanish (with a certain accent) and like to watch soccer.

Argentineans will perhaps have some of these elements in common with the group of Jews and farmers; for example, monogamous marriage and Spanish. We can perhaps also think of someone who is a member in all three groups, i.e., a Jewish farmer who incidentally happens to be an Argentinean. But despite the fact that all three groups might have features in common or that someone might be a member in all three groups, note the following: all three groups are *different* from each other. The group of Argentineans is not the group of Jews or farmers, although they may overlap in some respects.[9] Note also that some of the properties by virtue of which Argentineans, or members of the other two groups, will characterize themselves are meaningful to the point of being properties which are essential to their self-understandings. Looking simply at the case of Argentinean membership, an Argentinean will probably characterize herself as someone who was born in Argentina, speaks Spanish, has certain dietary customs (e.g., eats beef and *churrasco*), professes or has an affinity with a certain monotheistic religion (e.g., Christianity) and the moral outlook that originates from that religion, etc. We can reasonably think of some of these traits as being essential to her self-understanding, thus making her Argentinean membership basic.

What I wish to propose now is that there is a necessary connection between differences among groups and properties that are essential for the self-understandings of group members. Put differently, only groups that are distinguished by way of exclusion and contrast are likely to be the sort of group in which basic membership is possible. Let me explain my thesis more formally. Imagine a group Ga impossible to distinguish from groups Gb, Gc, or Gd. Ga is so broad that it would be impossible to indicate the exclusive traits that all the members of Ga have in common, and that distinguish Ga from Gb, Gc, or Gd. In other words, Ga would be indiscernible. Now suppose that we are able to characterize Ga according to traits that all members of Ga have in common and separate the group from Gb, Gc, or Gd. In this case, Ga would be discernable.

Note that for a group to have the *status of discernibility* two circumstances must be true. First, group members have traits in common. Second, the traits that group members have in common are such that they make the group distinguishable from other groups. My contention is now the following. If Ga is indiscernible, it is not likely to be the kind of group that endows members with basic membership, i.e., generate the sorts of properties that are essential to the self-understandings of group members. If, in contrast, Ga is discernible, it could possibly be the kind of group that endows members with basic membership. I have said that discernible groups may endow members with basic membership. Let me be more precise with regard to this statement. Not all discernible groups give rise to basic memberships, but all basic memberships tend to stem from discernible groups. In other words, the status of discernibility is a necessary, yet not a sufficient, condition for basic membership.[10]

The reason for the necessary connection between discernibility and basic membership is ultimately a factual one. As a matter of fact, particular groups have a sense of "us" based on difference-sensitive attributes. This means that groups can be divided between *us-type* and *them-type* groups. The properties that are essential for the self-understandings of group members are evidently not properties of them-type groups, but rather properties of us-type groups. In other words, the properties that create the sense of "us" in a particular group are also the ones that could possibly make membership in the group basic. Note first that human beings are members of groups that give them a sense of "us." The substance of the "us" is what Harold Isaacs, paraphrasing a term by Francis Bacon, describes as the "idols of the tribe." Different groups have different idols and so humanity consists of a composite of us-type groups, which are always set in contrast with other them-type groups. Isaacs expresses his view by discussing the idols (or what he also calls "holdings") that shape human identity—namely, birthplace, names, languages, history and origins, religion, and nationality. He comments that:

> How [the holdings] are seen and celebrated has provided the substance of most of what we know as history, mythology, folklore, art, literature, religious beliefs and practices. How the holdings of others are seen has provided most of the unending grimness of the we-they confrontation in human experience. Raised high or held low, these are the idols of all our tribes.[11]

These groups might also be thought of as what Michael Walzer calls "thick cultures." He observes, for instance, that "the crucial commonality of the human race is particularism: we participate, all of us, in thick cultures that are our own."[12] I mention incidentally that the claim that people belong to thick cultures, does not necessarily lead us to primordialist commitments.[13] The claim is quite compatible with instrumentalist accounts of group identification, according to which members identify with a particular group because it is in their best interest to do so.[14]

Also note, in the second place, that given the quality of differentiation, the properties that are essential to the self-understandings of group members are explicitly not properties of them-type groups, but rather properties of us-type groups, of groups they call "their own."[15] Why is that the case? Note, in the third place, that us-type groups are characterized directly with reference to them-type groups. In an extreme form, we may see the logic of total exclusion at work here. In an illuminating study, Jean Paul Sartre shows how Jewish identity and anti-Semitism emerged due to a process of configuration in which Jewish membership was differentiated from and no longer compatible with French identity. According to such configuration, Jews were defined with reference to the French, so that membership in the first group precludes the possibility of belonging to the second one. Sartre comments that, in this dynamic, the French have access to a set of authentic values and principles by virtue of their Frenchness and thus:

> ... an attempt is made to persuade [the Jew] that the true sense of things must always escape him; there is formed around him an impalpable atmosphere, which is the genuine France, with its genuine values, its genuine tact, its genuine morality, and he has no part in it.[16]

The argument is that membership in group G, by virtue of membership itself, entails attachment to the principles and values of G. This attachment is not available to members of group G*, who are necessarily nonmembers of G, and thus members of G* will never be able to appreciate the genuine principles and values of G. For our purposes, I want to highlight the rigid differentiation that exists between G and G*, where G is defined in contrast with G*.

Even without these forms of complete exclusion, human beings belong to what Walzer calls thick cultures, which are particular and are thus distinguishable from and contrasted with other cultures that are not "our own." Not everybody has the same set of properties: not everyone is born in the same place, speaks the same language, and shares the same social practices and worldview. The point about the quality of contrast between groups is a clear one. If I am born and raised a Protestant in Northern Ireland I will then be distinguishable by a set of recognizable group markers that separate me from a foreign group, namely, Catholics. Similarly, if I am born and reared in Quebec I will also possess recognizable traits that differentiate me from other Anglo-Canadians. In another instance, I am born an African American and so given a set of markers, I will be a member of a particular group, which separates me from other "racial" groups in American society.[17] What we see in these situations is that there are us-type groups that are different from and defined in contrast with other them-type groups.[18]

We are now able to see more clearly the necessary connection between group discernibility and basic membership. The properties that will be essential to the self-understanding of, say, the Protestant in Northern Ireland will be those of his group, characterized by a set of common traits, and not those of, say, the Catholic group. Something similar occurs with Quebecois and Anglo Canadians, and African Americans and other racial groups. The fact is that certain groups are explicitly different from and contrast with other groups. Given such a differentiation and contrast, I can only find properties that will be essential to my self-understanding in the particular group configuration in which I happen to be placed, with its own common characteristics, and which is defined explicitly in contrast with other groups.

By way of afterthought, let me remind us of a point that was made in the previous chapter with regard to clear-cut distinctions. What I wish to highlight now is that us-type groups are not always easy to distinguish from them-type groups, even in situations in which you have extreme forms of exclusion as illustrated by the case of anti-Semitism above. I will mention two complexities here. First, groups are not easy to individuate. Second, all groups are generally an overlapping structure of many other us-type groups. With regard to the first point, attention must be drawn to an assumption that underlies the way in which we commonly refer to some types of groups. Such an assumption is pervasive in our ordinary language or common speech.

In speaking about groups, or a particular group, it may sound like one might be referring to group *units*. Such an impression could in fact be misleading because groups are not always easy to *individuate* or even characterize. Groups are indeed not only dynamic, but also complex phenomena. Nevertheless, as suggested above there are, in fact, properties that make it possible to identify groups at a certain point in time and thus differentiate them from other groups. We see then that, on the one hand, groups are sometimes difficult to individuate, i.e., to single out as precise units. Even when a group may be individuated at a formal level, say, by a political unit, the question still may be what the core traits are whereby it is possible to individuate the group. On the other hand, however, groups can indeed be identified—namely, particular groups can be distinguished from other groups due to a cluster of properties that group members have in common and which differentiated them from others. The distinction I am making is between *individuating* and *identifying* groups. The upshot is that groups are often complex phenomena and are thus sometimes difficult to individuate. Groups are not always distinguishable *units*. By the same token, however, one may say that there are a number of traits and properties that presumably allow us to identify certain types of groups. Otherwise, the notions of "group" and "group identity" would not make much sense.[19]

Let me turn here to the second complexity about groups mentioned above. Groups tend to consist of an overlapping structure of many other us-type groups. Consider, for example, a nation as an instance of an us-type group. But here we think immediately of regional and cultural groups within nations. Think, for example, of the fact that that there are several us-type groups within a nation and these groups can be construed in different ways. An instance of what I have in mind now is expressed by Neal Ascherson by raising the question about European unity. He asks: How European can or will we be? And he comments that:

> to reach any answers several assumptions have to be made about this question. And the first assumption is that 'we' can be interpreted in several ways, leading to several divergent conclusions. 'We' may denote the inhabitants of Britain, or of the United Kingdom. On the other hand, it could also stand for the English, the Scots, the Welsh, the people of Northern Ireland and the populations of the various autonomous small islands in the archipelago.[20]

But let me now stick to a simple and more fundamental point: us-type groups are overlapping structures of other us-type groups. Think again of a nation as an us-type group and all other us-type groups within the national group.

By way of illustration, in the Venezuelan nation there are several distinct groups, e.g., *Costeño* (born on the coast), *Maracucho* (born in Maracaibo), *Andino* (born in the Andes), *Isleño* (born in one of the islands). Members of those groups can usually be identified by different accents and regional idioms, food habits, personality traits (*Maracuchos* are extrovert and *Andinos* are introvert), skin complexion (those born on the coast tend to have a darker complexion than those born in the Andes), etc. These regional groups are often instantiations of us-type groups that happen to be embedded within an overarching national us-type group.

Given this complex structure of embedded us-type groups an interesting question arises. Despite their differences, do all these groups have a strong enough sense of national commonality to bind them together?

There is obviously an us-type national group and an us-type regional group. But imagine that the *Maracuchos* attempted to secede from the rest of the country—a theme expressed in popular jokes due to the fact that Maracaibo has the largest oil reserve in the country. Or suppose that the tension between regional groups began to escalate beyond the point of reconciliation. In such instances of conflict, one can often see one of the us-type groups prevailing over the others. We can think of conflict with regard to many us-type groups embedded in other us-type groups. Using the Venezuelan example again, one could think of social classes—the "rich" and the "poor"—instead of thinking about regional groups. One can see in a country such as Venezuela, as well as other Latin American countries, how the tension between these two us-type groups is always on the verge of exploding. My general point is that people belong to several us-type groups—e.g., nations, fraternities, alliances, social classes, families, etc.—and all these us-type groups are often embedded within each other. Us-type membership is then multidimensional.

Now, this general point has important implications for the significance of groups and memberships. Given the reality of embedded us-type groups, when we look at the significance of us-type groups, what we need to examine is not so much the different us-type groups to which someone belongs. We know for a fact that people have different layers of membership in different (and sometimes conflicting) us-type groups. The question is rather this: at what level and in what contexts do we generally find the *primary* sense of "us"—the one that tends to override and overpower all other us-type group memberships in a certain situation? Given the modal framework I presented in chapter 4, I suspect that the answer to that question will vary for different groups and circumstances. Under some conditions, the primary us-type group for some people might be the nation; for others a religious us-type group; yet others will find their primary sense of "us" in their tribal group or clan. The overlaying dimensions of membership are highly complex. What does seem to be the case in many instances, however, is that some of the memberships in us-type groups are a primary source of meaning and direction, and thus could have the potential for overriding other memberships in some specific situations.

INTRINSIC IDENTIFICATION

When we think of groups and identification several questions arise: How are groups identified? Who or what defines and determines the cluster of properties that distinguishes a certain group? Similarly, how does group identity emerge? Is such a process a fortuitous and spontaneous one, or is it primarily intentional? Is it possible to misidentify a group, i.e., furnish properties that a group does not really possess? Groups can presumably be identified in different ways. We can speak for example of people coming from the Asian continent as "Asians." But is the identification of people from Asia as "Asians" necessarily relevant *to them*?

I can presumably characterize groups from two points of views. I can characterize my own group, the one to which I belong, and I can also characterize other groups, those groups to which I do not belong. When I characterize my own group I will express those properties that are meaningful to me and other members of the group. Hence my characterization of the group will be meaningful. In contrast, when I characterize other groups, without much knowledge of the group, I may do it in a way that is either irrelevant or meaningless *to them*. An example will help us to appreciate the contrast I have just described. The description and studies of Bali culture by the anthropologist Clifford Geertz are well known.[21] Geertz's sense of cultural practices, as an observer who identifies and codifies the way of life of the Bali people, is different from the sense such practices might have from the perspective of a Bali native. The native, who is the object of study, may not necessarily be interested in identifying or codifying his or her culture in the same way as Geertz. In fact, Geertz's identification of Bali culture may be utterly irrelevant and meaningless to the native, who would perhaps identify his or her culture in a different way.

Notice in our example how there are two possible ways in which the Bali culture may be identified: from the *inside* and from the *outside*. A group is identified from the inside when the person who identifies the culture is deeply immersed in the cluster of experiences, narratives and myths of such a group. In contrast a group is identified from the outside when one is not an agent, but rather an observer, attempting to identify the group; or rather someone who is not deeply immersed in the cluster of experiences, narratives and myths of the group.

My contention is that the identification of groups is meaningful when it is done by its members, i.e., from the inside. Members of groups can characterize the narratives, myths, values and practices that give meaning and direction to their lives. They are able to characterize these traits because they are immersed in them. Since members are immersed in the properties that are essential to their self-understanding, they are in a position to identify those properties in a meaningful way. But when is one immersed in a group in a significant manner? Presumably, an anthropologist can study and observe a culture as much as he can and in this sense be immersed in it. He can even live within the culture for a number of years and behave as if he were a member. Such an immersion would not be relevant, since the traits of the culture would presumably not be the ones that are essential to his self-understanding. Suppose, however, that the traits of the culture he studies are indeed essential to his self-understanding. In this case he would be inside the culture. He may be studying his own culture or perhaps becomes "naturalized" in a different culture. When the latter situation is the case, the anthropologist or anyone who might have been formerly in the outside could be said to be immersed within the group in a significant manner. The upshot of the discussion is that the act of identifying a particular group is generally meaningful when it is done by people whose membership in the group is basic. In other words, group identification is meaningful and relevant when it is done from inside the group.

Nonetheless, a question now arises: can identification from outside a group ever be meaningful and relevant? The question is an important one because that has often been the case with regard to the historical origin of modern national identities. States, in conjunction with nationalists, have been one of the factors shaping, configuring and codifying cultural groups in terms of national identities. The process of national identification has not generally been a spontaneous one, but rather one that stems from states and nationalist ideologists. It is then the case that nationalities consist of groups whose identities have been formed and defined from the outside. National identities have not been generally characterized—at least initially—by members of cultural groups, but rather by states and nationalist ideologues. As an instance of what I am now describing, we can think of Eugen Weber's examination of the historical process that turned "peasants" into "French citizens."[22]

I have suggested above that group identification is meaningful and relevant when it is done from inside a group, i.e., by group members. Does that mean then that national identity, a kind of identity shaped by states and nationalists, who could very well be shaping the identity of the group from the outside, is meaningless or irrelevant? In order to properly answer this question we must very briefly examine the process by which modern national identities have historically emerged.

There is a debate among historians regarding the historical emergence of the nation, with its respective identity. The question is whether the nation is a feature of the modern era or if there are important antecedents that would allow us to speak of "nations" before the birth of the modern world. There are roughly two camps on the topic. The *modernists*[23] believe that the nation could only arise in the social and cultural configuration of modernity. The modernists characterize the nation as an "invented tradition" (Hobsbawm), an "imagined community" (Anderson), or a phenomenon that arises due to the operation of intellectual elites (Kedourie) or the needs of industrial society (Gellner). The conundrum for the modernists is that nations seem to be more than fabrications or conceptual constructions of elites or political systems.[24] Some elite leaders might declare that a people now become a "nation," but that does not mean that the newly prescribed "national identity" becomes a reality for everyone. As an illustration of this type of situation, consider the numerous groups in the African continent that can hardly identify themselves with the "national" structures set up by former colonial powers. If nations are not merely the fabrication of elites or political units, what is it that makes nations and national identity possible? Likewise, how do we describe the notions, sentiments and collective symbols by which masses that identify themselves with a particular nation are mobilized? In addressing the latter question, we find the second camp in the debate on the emergence of nations. *Ethnosymbolists* or *premodernists*[25] claim that modern nations have an "ethnic core." Given such a core, nations are, in fact, very old communities. Hence the modern nation is simply the development of political institutions that entail a preexisting element, i.e., an ethnic core.[26] The ethnosymbolists, however, often seem not to take fully into account the major political dimension of ethnic and national identity.[27] If political units (e.g., states) do, in fact, play a role in the formation of national and ethnic identity, then the ethnosymbolists need to explain how such identities are possible before the emergence of the modern nation-state.

An interesting notion proposed by Eric Hobsbawm in an attempt to address the complexity of national identity, in some sense "invented" and yet in a different sense "preexistent," is that of *proto-nation*.[28] A proto-nation is a pre-political community, or set of communities, bound by feelings of collective belonging or some degree of affinity. One of the benefits of the notion just mentioned is that we are able to make a distinction between *nations* and *proto-nations*. Nations are the phenomena modernists attempt to describe. Proto-nations, in contrast, are the phenomena described by ethnosymbolists. The distinction would make it possible to acknowledge that modern nations are the result of a process that goes in two directions. On the one hand, the *top-down* represents the role of political units and elites in developing national identities. On the other hand, the *bottom-up* captures the collective forms of identity that serve as building blocks for national identity.[29] States or elites, by themselves, do not "create" nations and national identity. But neither do communities, for the most part, spontaneously become full-blown nations or develop strong nationalist feelings without the intervention of either states or ideological elites. Nations are often the result of proto-nations that have been individuated and mobilized by political units and also nationalist intellectuals.

In some sense, nations could be identified in a way that does not immediately portray the properties that are essential to the self-understanding of a given people. Political units and nationalist intellectuals are not always in touch with the meaningful features of the people they wish to portray—a state of affairs that seems to be prevalent in societies that have not undergone a process of modernization or industrialization. Or also think of the fact that states and nationalist intellectuals have often preceded the "nation."

But when do states and nationalist ideology reach the point in which they become meaningful for the proto-nations they represent? This is a complex matter, but for our purposes we simply need to see that national identities can be *internalized* by a group and hence become meaningful. So, for instance, members of cultural groups, that have internalized the national identities often engineered and managed by states and nationalists, can identify their cultural groups in terms of such national identities. But note that this is possible because the group has appropriated and internalized features, symbols, narratives, and practices that then become essential to the self-understandings of group members.

An example will help us to illustrate the point at stake. When I characterize myself as a "Mexican," I may be describing experiences and properties that are essential to my self-understanding—in this way I identify my culture from the inside. Since I am a member, in a significant manner, of the culture I am identifying, then my identification is meaningful. But the category "Mexican" would be unintelligible without a nation-state and certain nationalist principles. Thus my characterization of Mexican culture coincides with certain nationalist notions of Mexicaness. This example shows that meaningful identification, from inside the culture, has effectively merged with a type of identification that might have been historically external. The latter, however, is possible because external identification has been internalized by members of the culture. We can say then that identification from outside a culture could be meaningful when such a form of identification is internalized by the culture at stake. Drawing on Weber's illustration, we could say that peasants can identify themselves as French citizens, in a meaningful and relevant sense, when they have internalized Frenchness.

CONCLUSION

In this chapter I raised the following question: how do we characterize groups that have the function of endowing members with the type of membership that is central to members' identities? The groups that have the function at stake generally satisfy three conditions. First, there is the condition of relevant identification, which sustains that group members are identified according to properties that are essential to their self-understandings, i.e., properties that make their membership basic. The second condition is that of differentiation. Here, basic membership is necessarily connected with groups that have difference-sensitive attributes—what I called us-type groups, which contrast with them-type groups. Groups with difference-sensitive attributes possess what I called the status of discernibility. The third and last condition I discussed is that of intrinsic identification. Under this condition, groups and members are identified from what was described as the "inside" of a group and not the "outside." Two important elements discussed within this condition are group identification and national identity formation. We will see at a later point the significance of these two elements for understanding Hispanic identity making.

I have now completed my discussion of membership and groups. With this framework in mind, I will now turn to the discussion of the Hispanic group and membership. The general question guiding subsequent chapters is this: does the Hispanic group, and its corresponding membership, satisfy the conditions discussed so far?

NOTES

1. Although the discussion in this chapter is concerned with a different set of issues, I have found David Copp's discussion on the concept and individuation of societies, to be distinguished from "societal populations," helpful. See *Morality, Normativity and Society* (Oxford: Oxford University Press, 1995), 124–43. I also follow Avishai Margalit and Joseph Raz in the strategy of focusing on group characterization instead of group types—a strategy that lies behind their notion of "encompassing groups." See "National Self-determination," in *Ethics and the Public Domain: Essays in the Morality of Law and Politics*, Joseph Raz (New York: Oxford University Press, 1994), 113–17.

2. This is similar to the point I made in the previous chapter when highlighting the social dimension of identity.

3. Benedict Anderson, *Imagined Communities: Reflection on the Origin and Spread of Nationalism*, rev. ed. (New York: Verso, 2002[1983]), 6.

4. For literature that expresses the view succinctly, see Christopher W. Morris, "Peoples, Nations, and the Unity of Society," in Cultural Identity and the Nation-State, eds. Carol C. Gould and Pasquale Pasquino (New York: Rowman and Littlefield, 2001), 24; and Sami Zubaida, "Nations: Old and New. Comments on Anthony D. Smith's 'The Myth of the "Modern Nation" and the Myths of Nations,'" *Ethnic and Racial Studies*, 12, 3 (1998): 330–31.

5. An important assumption in the illustration is that there is no "generational gap." Experiences for people belonging to different generations can vary, but there would still have to be enough elements in common between people from different generations for them to recognize each other as fellow nationals.

6. Since the group is identifiable, according to my characterization, it is also stable. The point I make here is similar to the one made by Will Kymlicka when high-

lighting the identifiable character of ethnocultural groups, and countering the claim, made by Iris Marion Young and others, that certain groups, e.g., ethnocultural, do not fall under identifiable types. According to Kymlicka, ". . . ethnocultural groups do not form a fluid continuum, in which each group has infinitely flexible needs and aspirations," but rather "there are deep and relatively stable differences between various kinds of ethnocultural groups." Will Kymlicka, *Politics in the Vernacular: Nationalism, Multiculturalism and Citizenship* (New York: Oxford University Press, 2001), 59.

7. Bhikhu Parekh makes a similar point when he comments that "cultures are distinguished from each other both by the content of their beliefs and practices and the manner in which these are internally related and form a reasonably recognizable whole." *Rethinking Multiculturalism: Cultural Diversity and Political Theory* (Cambridge, MA: Harvard University Press, 2000), 149. The point might seem trivial, but it is being contested and thus it is worth arguing.

8. Thus not all properties by which members can be identified are relevant. If I am right, then the claim made by Iris Marion Young that attributes are relational and thus shift according to the context has limitations. "Together in Difference: Transforming the Logic of Group Political Conflict," in *The Rights of Minority Cultures*, ed. Will Kymlicka (New York: Oxford University Press, 1995), 157. Whereas it is true that attributes are context-sensitive, some attributes will simply be relevant and others irrelevant; so the range of context-sensitive attributes in my account is more limited than what Young allows. This difference is due to varying conceptualizations of groups, a topic to which I will return in the next section.

9. Young believes the following: "Different groups always potentially share some attributes, experiences or goals. Their differences will be more or less salient depending on the groups compared and the purposes of the comparison. The characteristics that make one group specific and the borders that distinguish it from other groups are always *undecidable*." "Together in Difference," 161. While I agree with the first part of the passage, i.e., groups have overlapping attributes and group boundaries are sensitive to contexts, I do not see how the final claim follows, i.e., that group boundaries are "undecidable" (by which I assume she means indistinguishable or indiscernible). My claim is that, in fact, groups are distinguishable from other groups—and only groups that have this quality are capable of endowing members with basic memberships.

10. Differentiation and discernibility are of course a matter of degree. What degree of differentiation is then necessary for distinguishing groups that might endow members with basic memberships? This question is extremely hard to answer and is likely to furnish varying answers according to the circumstances. Copp, for instance, addresses a similar problem when trying to identity a specific "society." Comparing three group levels—a town, somewhere in France, a nation, France, and a continent, Europe—he posits that, according to some criteria that differentiate the three groups, the town is not a society with regard to the nation, but the nation is indeed a society with regard to the continent. Although this might indeed be true in this particular example, I doubt that relations of this kind can be extrapolated to all towns and nations. See *Morality*, 136.

11. Harold Isaacs and Lucian W. Pye, *Idols of the Tribe: Group Identity and Political Change* (Cambridge, MA: Harvard University Press, 1997 [1975]), 40.

12. Michael Walzer, *Thick and Thin: Moral Argument at Home and Abroad* (South Bend: University of Notre Dame Press, 1994), 83. For a similar view, see also Avishai Margalit, *The Ethics of Memory* (Cambridge, MA: Harvard University Press, 2002).

13. I defined group primordialism in the previous chapter when discussing membership. My notion of basic membership is intended to be a non-primordialist one with regard to groups.

14. For an account along these lines, see Russell Hardin, *One for All: The Logic of Group Conflict* (Princeton: Princeton University Press, 1995).

15. How these particular groups may come into being is widely addressed in the literature of nations and nationalism. Group configuration follows different routes and is caused by a variety of factors, e.g., spontaneous bonds of solidarity, influence of elites, political individuation, conflict, deliberate exclusion. For a discussion on different models of group configuration and boundary shifting, see Donald L. Horowitz, *Ethnic Groups in Conflict* (Berkeley and Los Angeles: University of California Press, 2000), 64–70. In mentioning multiple group configurations in a previous footnote, I also referred the reader to Anthony D. Smith, *National Identity* (Reno: University of Nevada Press, 1991), 23–26.

16. Jean-Paul Sartre, *Anti-Semite and Jew: An Exploration of the Etiology of Hate* (New York: Schocken Books, 1965), 82.

17. So while Young puts forward an account in which difference does not entail otherness, in my view difference of a certain kind does entail otherness. See "Together in Difference," 156–66.

18. Incidentally, one might add that groups are different from each other due not only to social markers, but also norms of exclusion. For a discussion on exclusionary group norms, see Hardin, *One for All*, 72–106.

19. I thus agree with Parekh when he says the following: "Since cultures are created against the background of the shared features of human existence, it is impossible for them not to share at least some beliefs and practices in common. This does not mean, as is sometimes argued, that they form a continuum and cannot be distinguished or individuated." Couture, Nielsen, and Seymour, *Rethinking Multiculturalism*, 149.

20. "How European Can We/Will We Be?," in *Citizens: Towards a Citizenship Culture*, ed. Bernard Crick (Oxford: Blackwell, 2001), 57.

21. Clifford Geertz, *The Interpretation of Cultures* (New York: Basic Books, 1973).

22. Eugen Joseph Weber, *Peasants into Frenchmen: The Modernization of Rural France, 1870–1914* (Stanford: Stanford University Press, 1976).

23. This seems to be the predominant approach. For authors in this camp, see Benedict Anderson, *Imagined Communities*; John Breuilly, *Nationalism and the State*, rev. ed. (Chicago: Chicago University Press, 1994[1982]); Ernest Gellner, *Nations and Nationalism* (Ithaca: Cornell University Press, 1983); Eric Hobsbawm, *Nations and Nationalism since 1780: Programme, Myth, Reality* (Cambridge: Cambridge University Press, 2002[1990]); Eric Hobsbawm, *The Age of Capital: 1848–1875* (Vintage Books: New York, 1996[1975]), 82–97; Eric Hobsbawm, *The Age of Revolution: 1789–1848* (Vintage Books: New York 1996[1962]), 132–45; Liah Greenfeld, *Nationalism: Five Roads to Modernity* (Cambridge, MA: Harvard University Press, 1992); Elie Kedourie, *Nationalism* (New York: Frederick A. Praeger Publisher, 1961).

24. John Hutchinson remarks the following: "It is implausible [. . .] to conceive of modernizing nationalists as outside their society mobilizing it from above. It implies that invoked ethnic memories have an independent force with which they have to negotiate. What modernists have failed to explore is the relationship of nationalism to other belief systems and the complex symbolic mediations by which nationalists are able to canalize the past for their purposes." "Nations and Culture," in *Understanding Nationalism*, eds. Montserrat Guibernau & John Hutchinson (Malden, MA: Polity Press, 2001), 77.

25. The most prominent author within this approach is Anthony D. Smith. See "The Origins of Nations," *Ethnic and Racial Studies* 12, 3 (1989): 341–67; "State-Making and Nation-Building," in *States in History*, ed. John Hall (Oxford: Basil Blackwell, 1986); *The Ethnic Origins of Nations* (New York: Basil Blackwell, 1987). Likewise, Smith offers a useful discussion on the topics and issues at stake in the current literature: *Nationalism: Theory, Ideology, and History* (Malden, MA: Polity Press, 2001). There is also a useful review on the different types of approaches and authors who have studied the origins of nations in "Introduction: Questioning the Ethnic/Civic Dichotomy," in *Rethinking Nationalism*, Canadian Journal of Philosophy, Supplementary Volume 22, eds. Jocelyne Couture, Kai Nielsen and Michel Seymour (Calgary: University of Calgary Press, 1996), 10–23.

26. It is important to point out that the notion of ethnicity is a problematic one. Smith believes, for example, that ethnic groups may be characterized in a more or less clear way. See "The Origins of Nations," 345. Others believe that the notion of ethnicity confuses more than it clarifies things, especially in the study of nations and nationalism. For this view, See Walker Connor, "A Nation Is a Nation, Is a State, is an Ethnic Group, Is a . . .," in *Ethnonationalism: The Quest for Understanding* (Princeton: Princeton University Press, 1994), 100–103. And yet others, like Jorge J. E. Gracia, believe that ethnicity may be characterized in terms of clusters of properties (a position that seeks to avoid the pitfalls of other misleading characterizations, but does not do away with the notion completely). See "The Nature of Ethnicity with Special Reference to Hispanic/Latino Identity," *Public Affairs Quarterly* 13, 1 (1999): 25–42.

27. In fact, nations have to be analyzed in terms of "political, technical, administrative, economic and other conditions and requirements." Hobsbawm, *Nations and Nationalism*, 10.

28. For this notion, see Hobsbawm, *Nations and Nationalism*, 46.

29. Hobsbawm expresses this point in *Nations and Nationalism*, 10–11.

III

HISPANIC IDENTITY

7

Nationality and Hispanics

As we saw previously, the American federal government officially recognizes certain groups by means of the Standards for the Classification of Federal Data on Race and Ethnicity. One of the reasons for such recognition is a governmental attempt to identify, classify and gather data on diverse population groups that have historically "experienced discrimination and differential treatment because of their race or ethnicity."[1] But the purpose behind the classification and recognition of racial and ethnic groups is not only to identify groups that have experienced discrimination. These groups are also recognized by governmental agencies, policy-makers and society in general because membership in racial or ethnic groups is often thought to be central to members' identities. As I argued in chapter 3, this is the presumption of relevant membership.

"Hispanic" is one of the groups recognized by the federal government, policy-makers and society. A Hispanic in American society is someone who has a particular cultural or national origin. According to the official definition of the federal standards, a Hispanic or Latino is a "person of Mexican, Puerto Rican, Cuban, Central or South American or other Spanish culture or origin regardless of race."[2] In focusing on this group, the question that arises is whether membership in the Hispanic group is indeed central to members' identities. Another way of formulating the question is this: Is Hispanic membership basic? In order to shed light on the basicness of Hispanic membership, I will compare this membership with another membership, i.e., nationality. I will argue that national membership is basic for most members of the Hispanic group; but, in contrast, Hispanic membership is not basic for most members of the Hispanic group. In the following chapter, I will discuss the implications of this finding for the claim that Hispanic membership is central to members' identities.

THE NATIONALITY OF HISPANICS

When we think of Hispanic membership, what type of membership is it? The question is whether Hispanic membership can be thought of as basic. The first step for examining the basic membership of Hispanics is to take a closer look at the *nationality* of Hispanics. After all, Hispanics are characterized in terms of national groups, i.e., Mexican, Puerto Rican, Cuban, Colombian—or any other Latin-American nation—culture or origin.

I will begin by highlighting the fact that people included in the category of "Hispanic" generally have different national memberships.[3] By national membership, in this specific context, I have two variables in mind: (a) feelings of loyalty toward a nation, i.e., national identity, or (b) citizenship, i.e., the formal acknowledgment of a state that someone is a member of such a state.[4] Taking into account the national identities and citizenships of Hispanics we find at least four different groups. Part of what I will show is that although citizenship and feelings of loyalty toward a nation often coincide, they do not always do so. Nonetheless, the larger point I wish to discuss is twofold: all Hispanics have a national membership and such membership corresponds with a wide variety of nationalities.

The first group of Hispanics is composed of American citizens who identify themselves with the American nation. These citizens might be either born in the United States or naturalized. We can think here of second-generation Mexican or Cuban Americans or someone who was born in Latin America, but then becomes a U.S. citizen and pledges allegiance to the American nation. A second group is composed of American citizens who identify themselves with their nation of origin in Latin America. In this second group, people are nominal members of the American nation since—despite their American citizenship—their feelings of loyalty are primarily oriented toward a Latin-American nation. As an example, let us think of a Cuban exile who immigrates to the United States and becomes a naturalized American citizen; and yet his or her national allegiance remains in the former birthplace and homeland. According to the 2002 National Survey of Latinos conducted by the Pew Hispanic Center and the Kaiser Family Foundation, "Hispanics who are American citizens are still more likely to identify themselves primarily by country of origin (44%) than to identify primarily as an 'American' (33%)...."[5] It is reasonable to expect that at least some of those who identify themselves by country of origin do indeed have feelings of loyalty toward their nations.

One could contend at this point that someone from Colombia, who then becomes an American citizen, might have mixed allegiances. She could have, say, both a Colombian and an American national identity. This might indeed be true. Suppose, however, that there were a highly conflictive situation, e.g., a war, between the United States and Colombia. In a conflictive situation someone with a mixed identity is likely to be partial to either one side or the other. Considerations such as a sense of justice might determine the choice of partiality. But a crucial element in taking sides will be the person's national identity. Conflict might force the person to choose between competing identities, and identify primarily with one of the groups while renouncing, temporarily or nominally at least, the other. Despite a mixed identity, one of her identities becomes *dominant* due to a situation that no longer makes the compatibility of identities sustainable.[6] Thus, given that one of her identities is being threatened—the one that might become dominant in the conflictive context—she will probably feel compelled to be partial and defend her dominant identity.[7] I will return to this point below since it is important for understanding the basicness of Hispanic membership. It is important to incidentally point out that there are significant incentives for group partiality in cases of conflict. This is one of the reasons why conflict is so revealing in analyses of group membership and thus figures prominently in my understanding of the contrast between members and nonmembers. Given a situation of conflict, group member will benefit from strict partiality.

Let us continue with the third group of Hispanics: those who are not American citizens and do not identify themselves with the American nation. We could think, for instance, of a migrant worker from Mexico who crosses the border purely for the purpose of obtaining a particular job. Accordingly, there is no interest in the American nation as such; but rather the interest is oriented toward an economic opportunity that as a matter of contingency happens to be found in American territory. The worker presumably continues to identify herself with her nation of origin, i.e., Mexico, and has no interest in American citizenship.

The fourth and last group consists of those who are not American citizens, but identify themselves with the American nation. In this category, we might think of someone who was born in Panama and has the citizenship of her birthplace, but then comes to the United States as a child. The parents of the child are not American citizens and thus the child, who was not born on American soil, is not an American citizen either. Since the person in mind grows up in American society, it is possible that she feels identified with the American nation. As she becomes an adult, it would be quite natural to have feelings of loyalty and an identity related to the United States, despite not being an American citizen.

In the four groups I have outlined, two points must be highlighted. First, all Hispanics have a national membership. Here we must remember that the Hispanic category is defined and understood in terms of nationality, a very important point and one that we will return to in the next chapter. A Hispanic is a "person of Mexican, Puerto Rican, Cuban, Central or South American or other Spanish culture or origin regardless of race."[8] It is worth pointing out that the nations mentioned in the definition are from Latin America, but there is also an implied nation, i.e., the United States of America. The category "Hispanic" does not attempt to define Mexicans in Mexico, or Colombians in Europe. The category attempts to define Mexicans, Colombians, Venezuelans, Cubans, etc., who are now in American territory. As pointed out, a Hispanic might be an American citizen or not, but must now be residing, whether legally or not, in the United States. As a matter of attribution, Hispanics are an American phenomenon.[9] A Venezuelan who might have been seen in Venezuela as a German due to having fair skin and a German-sounding last name, or as a "Moreno" due also to skin complexion, becomes a Hispanic once she enters the U.S.[10]

The second point is that Hispanics have a variety of national memberships. I mentioned earlier that when speaking of national membership I loosely used the term with two variables in mind: (a) national identity, and (b) citizenship. In accordance with the four groups I described, it is fair to say that Hispanics have both a variety of national identities and citizenships. Throughout the discussion, I have assumed that Hispanics have a single citizenship and a single national identity, regardless of whether both variables coincide or not. But consider that some people might in fact have multiple citizenships and more than one national identity. It would not be hard to imagine someone who was born from a Colombian mother and an American father, and thus has two citizenships and also possibly two different national identities. I think, however, that we also find limitations in the range of possible citizenships and identities. The range of citizenships will most likely be limited to perhaps three—imagine someone who is born on U.S. soil from a Salvadorian mother and a Mexican father, and thus acquires all three citizenships. Similarly, the range of identities will also be limited. Despite multiple influences, a person with a mixed identity is most likely to identify herself more strongly with a set group of traits than others. And even if these traits are distributed among several particular groups, the range of groups, and thus the options for strong identification will be limited. At any rate, although interesting, cases of multiple citizenships and mixed identities are not prevalent and thus may be put aside without undermining my general argument. We must also bear in mind that even in those strange cases of multiplicity, the options are limited and, as suggested earlier, one membership might become dominant over competing memberships in, say, a situation of conflict.

Another complication that might arise when looking at Hispanics is that, as we saw, national identity does not always overlap with a corresponding citizenship. Such a distinction and potential complication is an important one, but since it is not crucial for my argument, I will ignore it in much of the discussion. I will speak of national membership focusing primarily on national identity, namely, feelings of loyalty toward a nation. Hispanics have different national membership—by which I mean that they have different national identities. Some Hispanics have feelings of loyalty toward Mexico, others toward Cuba or Venezuela, and yet others toward the United States of America. The latter observation is in line with the way different Hispanics identify themselves: "Foreign-born Latinos (the first generation) have a powerful preference for identification by their country of origin. Indeed, that is usually not only the country of their birth but also where some spent their childhood years." Also, "over half (57%) of Latinos with U.S.-born parents (the third generation and beyond) identify themselves first and foremost as an American."[11]

NATIONALITY AND BASIC MEMBERSHIP

How significant are the national identities of most Hispanics? I wish to suggest, first, that the national identities of Hispanics actually matter to a significantly large extent. And, second, the reason why the national identities of Hispanics matter to such a large extent is because their national identities are a type of basic membership. I will begin with some illustrations.

Imagine a Hispanic family in which the mother, Claudia, is not an American citizen and does not feel identified with the American nation. Despite the fact that she has lived in the United States for many years and is a U.S. permanent resident, she retains strong feelings toward her native country Mexico, and particularly toward her native town, Tijuana. Her daughter, Maria, was born and raised in the United States and is a U.S. citizen. Maria has a vague memory of a visit to Mexico as a child, but Mexico does not represent much to her because she was born and raised in America, and feels identified with the American nation.[12] Now suppose a war broke out between the United States and Mexico. The war is characterized—as all wars normally are—by particularly bitter sentiments against the other side. Stories that Claudia, from Mexico, heard in her childhood come to her memory: stories, imaginary or real, about the heroic resistance against an establishment largely sponsored by the *gringos*. Life on the border for her, like many others, kept alive the largely historical bittersweet feelings that many Mexicans on the border feel toward the rich and sometimes "kind neighbor" who is also the "suspicious enemy."[13] Now that the war breaks out, all these memories come to mind and Claudia finds it impossible to avoid strongly bitter feelings against Americans. Her daughter, however, is in a different position since she is a member of the American nation. Maria would naturally tend to side with the United States. Her patriotism is aroused by what she sees as an essentially just war against Mexico. In a situation like this, mother and daughter would perhaps find themselves divided by national loyalties. Even if not completely alienated from each other, the affinity of mother and daughter would at least be seriously tested. The situation I am describing now is not wholly inconceivable. It has, in fact, occurred before throughout history. Think, for example, of the families that were divided over loyalties to the Empire or the Colonies in the context of the American Revolution. Likewise, families in Latin America were divided in the nineteenth century over support to the cause of the Realists, Spaniards, or the cause of Independence led by the Creoles, natives of the colonies. Illustrations of this sort show the power of regional sentiments and loyalties, which are often sufficiently manifest in nationalities.

Consider now an important soccer game between Mexico and Costa Rica, or Colombia and Argentina, games that will determine the classification to the World Cup. It is likely that these games will draw a high number of nationals that will support their team, and in many instances show antagonism, even if in a "friendly" way, toward the opposite team. Why are these national sporting events so important? What do they reveal about the supporters that fervently cheer for their national teams? A victory of the national team is a source of collective pride and a defeat is a source of collective humiliation. National teams are generally positive representations of "wide selves." And as David Copp puts it: "when we have wide selves, the accomplishments and failures of certain other people, groups, or entities are important to us emotionally, for their accomplishments and failures can ground emotions of esteem."[14] In the context of sport teams, we find that if they triumph, we all triumph; if they lose, we all lose. These sorts of feelings are true of sports teams in general, but tend to be particularly true of *national* teams. David Copp, in discussing the consolidation of nationhood between 1915 and 1950, highlights the role of sports in national feelings. He comments that national sports became for national members ". . . an expression of national struggle, and sportsmen representing their nation or state, primary expressions of their imagined communities." Similarly,

> what has made sport so uniquely effective a medium for inculcating national feelings (. . .) is the ease with which even the least political or public individuals can identify with the nation as symbolized by young persons excelling at what practically every man wants, or at one time in life has wanted, to be good at. The imagined community of millions seems more real as a team of eleven named people. The individual, even the one who only cheers, becomes a symbol of his nation himself.[15]

The feelings expressed in the latter paragraph can be witnessed in—to use examples only limited to Latin America—the classificatory rounds for the Soccer World Cup; say, for example, a game between Uruguay and Argentina. Other events, such as the Pan-American Games, the South American Games, the Cup of Liberators and the Caribbean Series, may also be the occasion for nationalist feelings to emerge in the benign context of sports.

According to Alejandro Portes and Rubén Rumbaut, "patriotism [in Latin America] is often sharpened by periodic revivals of conflict with a neighboring Latin nation. Thus, Colombians and Venezuelans, Ecuadorians and Peruvians, Chileans and Argentines have traditionally reaffirmed their sense of national pride in actual or symbolic confrontations with each other."[16] The sporting events I have in mind could be seen as symbolic confrontations between Latin-American nations.

Given the confrontation between nations, whether actual or symbolic, the question that arises is this: what is so special about nations? The question demands a complex answer, but we know indeed that there is something about nations in Latin America that arouses deep passions and feelings of loyalty. Someone growing up in Venezuela, or any nation in Latin America or North America, most likely has a national identity. Having a national identity means that one has feelings of loyalty toward one's nation and these feelings often matter to a significantly large extent. But why do these feelings matter to a significantly large extent?

Nations give people a sense of commonality.[17] In a way, national configurations represent communities bound together by a dynamic that was discussed earlier: a strong sense of *we* that separates people from *them*. More specifically, when I speak of "we" and "they" here, I am alluding to the condition of differentiation described in the previous chapter. I wish to highlight the point that membership among Latin Americans and Americans in this national "we" is generally basic.[18]

Suppose we asked a Venezuelan, an American, or a Peruvian to characterize herself according to those traits that are essential to her own self-understanding. Among those traits, she could most likely count her language, her birthplace, the people to whom she is related, certain tastes, habits, beliefs, etc. It is likely that many of the essential traits she uses to characterize herself are the traits that make her a member of a national group. Let us recall that these were precisely the two characteristics of basic membership discussed in chapter 2: (a) certain traits are essential to someone's self-understanding; and (b) those traits make the person a member of a particular group. Let me now refine the point about nationality as a type of basic membership. Take, for example, the language of the person just mentioned. Suppose an essential trait of her self-understanding is the language she speaks, e.g., Spanish. If she did not speak the language she currently does, she would not be the person she is. But consider that it is not only Spanish; it is rather the kind of Spanish that makes her sound like a Venezuelan, a Mexican, an Argentinean, a Puerto Rican or a Peruvian; thus making her a member in one of those national groups.

Think also of another possible essential trait: her sense of "home." We can picture asking her: "where is home for you?" It is quite possible to imagine her, and a good number of people from Latin America and the United States of America, answering this question in national terms. Home is Chile, San Salvador, Cuba, etc.[19] We can imagine people answering this question in more specific regional terms—this is particularly true of Americans. Home is Boston, Texas, Chihuahua, Maracaibo, or Buenos Aires. But even in these instances, we must bear in mind that these regions are part of an overarching national community defined by political boundaries. Without this sense of homeland, the person in our example would perhaps not be who she currently is. Thus, a birthplace and sense of homeland, which makes her a member of a national group, is essential to her self-understanding.

What I have said about the specific person in our example will tend to be true for many people in Latin-American nations. Latin-American nationals tend to identify themselves with their nation of origin.[20] The point I wish to make, at any rate, is that many of the essential traits people from Latin America (and also the United States) will use to characterize themselves are precisely those traits that often make them members of their respective nations. If this is correct, it is possible to say that national membership is generally a type of basic membership for Latin-American nationals.

To see the collective strength of national identities among Latin-American nationals, due to national basic memberships, let us compare nations with an us-type group such as "Latin America." One could say, for instance, that Latin Americans—according to José Vasconcelos, a "cosmic race"[21]—have a strong sense of solidarity as a group. We could, in fact, think of Latin America as a large and overarching community. Ernesto "Che" Guevara speaks, for example, about "we" who are in constant confrontation with "them." The "we" Guevara has in mind is at times quite broad: it consists of those people who have been born not only in Latin America, but more widely in poor countries. In a famous speech delivered on February 26, 1965, at the Afro-Asian Solidarity Conference in Algiers, he speaks about the Latin American, Asian, and African peoples as a "family" with a common aspiration that unites every one of them. One of his opening sentences is: "*Our* common aspiration, the defeat of imperialism, unites us in *our* march toward the future; *our* common history of struggle against the same enemy has united *us* along that road" (my italics).[22] The sort of we-versus-them rhetoric, as evinced in Guevara himself, has certainly served to mobilize Latin American (and so called "third world") countries against imperialist powers, which happen to be "foreign."[23]

Note, however, that the sense of "us" among those born in poor or Latin American countries has often been superseded by a stronger sense of "us," e.g., national groups. Guevara himself ended some of his speeches with a slogan that became one of the trademarks of the Cuban Revolution: *Patria o Muerte!* (roughly translated as "country or death!"). "Patria" (*patrie* in French or *das Heimatland* in German) conveys the idea of a "homeland" or "birth soil" to which one is inalienably bound by virtue of being born in such soil. This "patria" is a national community. The observation illustrates the strength of national memberships among Latin Americans.[24]

Consider some historical examples in support of my previous point. Let us think, for instance, of the War of the Pacific between Bolivia and Chile (1879–1884) after which Bolivia became a landlocked country; or the Chaco War between Paraguay and Bolivia (1932–1935) with the latter seeking to gain access to the Atlantic Ocean. Also, think of the peculiar conflict known as the Soccer War between El Salvador and Honduras (1969) in which armed confrontations broke out after a series of preliminary soccer games for the World Cup.[25] Examining the history of war and conflict between Latin-American *nations*, one can see the power of nationality, which is often stronger than the Latin American "we." Throughout Latin-American history, projects of national unification have failed and the power of nations has proved to be rigid. In 1826, Simón Bolivar "convened the Congress of Panama to foster the uniting of Spanish America into one political-economic entity." The project of unity failed. Similarly in Central America several countries were united in the Central American Federation, an attempt that also failed. Not until after World War II did Latin-American countries, paying attention to the creation of the European Common Market in 1957, start speaking about economic integration.[26] Even here, economic integration—if it happens—is a distance away from political and cultural integration.

But let us also remember that bellicose confrontations are not the only kind of events showing the differences that separate Latin-American nationals. We need to bear in mind here our earlier comment about symbolic confrontations reflected in sporting events. At any rate, a Colombian is not to be confused with a Venezuelan, an Argentinean with a Chilean, or a Mexican with a Salvadorian. All these nations represent geopolitical units of their own that are often guided by fierce nationalism in their policy-making,[27] and have a set of symbols and rituals that give expression to an exclusive national "us."[28] Let us bear in mind at this point that nationality remains strong even when Latin-American immigrants become Hispanics in the U.S, a point that I will continue to elaborate in subsequent discussions.[29] Contrasting national and Hispanic memberships, this is how Portes and Rumbaut describe the situation of Hispanics in the U.S.:

> Colombian immigrants certainly know that they are Colombian and Mexicans that they are Mexican; what they probably do not know when they arrive in the United States is that they belong to a larger ethnic category called Hispanics. Colombians, Mexicans, Cubans, and other immigrant groups from Latin America are generally aware that they share common linguistic and cultural roots, but this fact seldom suffices to produce a strong overarching solidarity. National experiences are too divergent and national loyalties too deeply embedded to yield to this supranational logic.[30]

By way of conclusion here, let me make a clarification. I am not suggesting that nationality is the only type of basic membership among Latin Americans.[31] In line with what I have suggested when discussing membership, we can think of transnational or subnational basic memberships, e.g., membership in a religious community. I am rather suggesting that national membership is generally basic because many of the essential traits Latin Americans (and Americans) use to characterize themselves are precisely the traits that make them members of a national group, which has a corresponding state. The distinction is important because it allows us to see that national membership is basic, but it is not the only type of basic membership.

I began the current section with illustrations showing the intensity of national feelings. Illustrations of this sort raise questions about the significance of nationality. Why is nationality so significant among Latin Americans and Americans? I suggested that nations are communities with a strong sense of "we" and membership in this national "we" is generally basic. Once we see that national membership is generally basic, we can also begin to see what is so significant about nations and why they draw intense feelings of loyalty.

HISPANICITY AND BASIC MEMBERSHIP

We set out to inquire about the status of Hispanic membership. Can Hispanic membership be thought of as basic? We have seen that Hispanics do, as a matter of fact, have different national identities. Furthermore, I have suggested that the national memberships of people included in the category of "Hispanic"—whether American or Latin American—are generally basic. But even if we acknowledge that nationalities among Hispanics are a type of basic membership, the question that must be raised is whether Hispanic membership can also be thought of as basic. For reasons that I will explain in the next chapter, I think that the answer is negative. But for the sake of discussion, let us grant for now that the answer to the possibility of Hispanic basic membership seems to be, at least in part, affirmative.

Think of someone born in the United States under the name of Maria Alonzo in a family of Salvadorian immigrants. Such a person will most likely possess traits—many of them perhaps nonvoluntarily acquired—that are essential to her own self-understanding. Some of the traits that are essential to Maria Alonzo's self-understanding—her parent's homeland and history—will perhaps make her think of herself as a Hispanic. But we must also remember that Maria Alonzo has a nationality, which is presumably a type of basic membership. Maria Alonzo was born in the United States and thus has an American national identity. We could imagine that this national identity is highly significant for her because her membership in this national "we," like the membership of other Americans, is generally basic.[32] Maria Alonzo has a Hispanic and a national membership, both of which seem to be basic. Comparing these two memberships will help us to understand the status of Hispanic membership. As I will have occasion to point out later, this comparison is not only illuminating but also necessary, given that Hispanicity is defined by nationality —or more precisely, national origins.

I wish to suggest that Hispanic membership might have some degree of basicness for some of the people included in the category of "Hispanic," but the degree of national basicness among Hispanics is pervasive and higher than Hispanic membership. My suggestion entails three claims. First, national membership is basic for all Hispanics—or at least a vast majority of them. I will call this the criterion of *pervasive basic membership*. A second claim is that Hispanic membership is basic for some, but not all Hispanics. Let me mention here again that speaking about the basicness of Hispanic membership is an overstatement, for reasons that will be explained in the next chapter. But I grant, for the time being, the possibility of basic Hispanic membership for the sake of argument. Call this the criterion of *partial basic membership*. Third, even when Hispanic membership has a certain degree of basicness, e.g., as with Maria Alonzo, national membership has a higher degree of basicness. I understand by "robust membership" a membership that has a higher degree of basicness than other memberships. If membership X has a higher degree of basicness than membership Y in situation S, then X is robust with regard to Y. According to the third claim then we have the criterion of *robust membership*. The first two criteria are about the scope of basic membership among members of the category, whereas the third criterion is about the qualitative degree of a kind of membership in relation with other comparable memberships. I will now turn to a discussion of the three criteria.

I have already pointed out that all (or almost all) Hispanics have a nationality, by which I primarily understand "national identity" or "feelings of loyalty towards a nation." It is hard to imagine a Hispanic without a nationality, i.e., someone who has a Hispanic identity, but not a national identity. Here we must remember that Hispanics have an American or a Latin-American nationality since Hispanics are second-generation Americans or originally from Latin American nations. As we saw in the four groups discussed above, some Hispanics have an American national identity, whereas others have national identities from Latin American nations —regardless of whether national identity coincides with citizenship or not. The point now is that despite differences in national identities, all (or almost all) Hispanics do in fact have national identities. I also argued above that national identities are very powerful for people from Latin America (and America) because nationality is a type of basic membership among them. If I am right so far, we can then see that all (or almost all) Hispanics have national identities, and these national identities derive from a type of basic membership in a national community. The corollary is that national membership among Hispanics is pervasive, i.e., national membership is basic for all (or almost all) Hispanics. In sum, the criterion of pervasive basic membership among Hispanics is met by the attribute of nationality.

Let us now assume for a moment that Hispanic membership is also basic. The question then is whether Hispanic membership is basic for all (or almost all) Hispanics. I have granted that Hispanic membership might be basic for some Hispanics, e.g., Maria Alonzo. But are all other Hispanics in the same position? Consider one of the groups we discussed above, i.e., those who are not American citizens and do not identify themselves with the American nation. I used the example of a Mexican migrant worker from Mexico who crosses the border purely for the purpose of obtaining a particular job. Such a migrant has no interest in the American nation as such, but rather a particular economic opportunity that happens to be found in American territory. Once the migrant crosses the American border he will become a Hispanic. The migrant presumably has a Mexican identity, but how significant is his "Hispanic" membership? One could imagine that probably not very significant. In fact, one could easily imagine his Hispanic membership not being basic. Suppose we asked the migrant to characterize himself according to those traits that are essential to his own self-understanding. He mentions, for instance, language and homeland, which make him a member of the Mexican nation. One could point out that the Spanish language and Mexican origin also make him a member of the Hispanic group. It does not mean, however, that his Hispanic membership is then basic. The migrant's essential traits make him view himself primarily as a Mexican and not necessarily as a Hispanic.[33] Whereas his Mexican membership contains traits that are essential to his own self-understanding, his Hispanic membership does not. My point is that the migrant's membership in the Mexican nation is basic, but his membership in the Hispanic group is not.

Let us recall a point that was made in chapter two with regard to the characteristics of basic membership. The two components of basic membership are (a) certain traits are essential to my own self-understanding and (b) these traits make me a member of a particular group. Keeping these two components together is important because, if isolated from each other, we will have two misleading pictures. First, one might simply think of traits that are essential to someone's self-understanding, but these traits usually derive from and are associated with a particular group. Second, one might think that being a member in a particular group might be essential to a member's self-understanding. But this is not always the case because membership does not always entail the sorts of traits that are essential to someone's self-understanding. The upshot is that membership is basic if and only if group traits are essential to a member's self-understanding.

Now let us think again of the Mexican migrant who becomes a Hispanic in the U.S. by virtue of the fact that he speaks Spanish and has a Mexican homeland. But note that these traits, which are essential to his own self-understanding, make him a member of a particular group, the Mexican nation. This particular group is an us-type group because, among other reasons, membership in the group is basic and the group is identified from the inside—two of the conditions discussed in chapter six with regard to relevant groups. When it comes to Hispanic membership, however, it cannot be said that the traits that are essential to the migrant's self-understanding make his membership in the Hispanic group similar to national membership. He may indeed be, in some sense, a member in the Hispanic group, but this group *per se* is not characterized exclusively or primarily by the Spanish language and Mexican homeland (the traits that are essential to the migrant's self-understanding).[34] Now recall that membership is basic if and only if group traits are essential to a member's self-understanding. Whereas this condition can be applied to the particular group, Mexican, it cannot be applied to the Hispanic group. So despite the fact that the migrant is, in some sense, a member of the Hispanic group, this membership is nonbasic.

Another brief example will also make the point of the nonbasicness of Hispanic membership. One might think of someone who has a Cuban relative three generations back, e.g., her grandfather. But other than a relative the person has no ties with Cuba. She considers herself an American and many of the features that are essential to her own self-understanding are the ones that make her a member in the American nation, and thus her American membership is basic. She might additionally consider herself a Hispanic, but her Hispanic membership is not basic because none of the traits that are essential to her own self-understanding are also the sorts of traits that make her a member in the Hispanic group. The person I have in mind might have a Hispanic membership, but such a membership will not be basic for her. One could go even further. Since Hispanicity does not have much relevance for her identity, she might also choose not to consider herself a Hispanic. We could perhaps imagine someone choosing not to view herself as a Hispanic because the essential traits of her own self-understanding make her an American, but not necessarily a Hispanic. She might choose to think of herself as a Hispanic American, but she might also choose to think of herself as an American *simpliciter*. If my observations are correct, Hispanic membership as a type of basic membership seems to have a partial extension. Hispanic membership is basic for some, but not all Hispanics.

Incidentally, I suspect that many Hispanics will see their Hispanic membership as a matter of choice. Thus they might choose to pick out some traits that will be considered "Hispanic," but they may also choose not to pick out those traits. As we saw earlier, Mary Waters describes a kind of identity that is voluntary and thus selective. So, for instance, "you can choose those aspects of being Irish that appeal to you and discard those that do not."[35] Hispanics might choose some traits of Hispanicity that they find appealing and also discard the unappealing traits. Once choice is introduced, i.e., you choose and discard traits, then questions about basicness emerge. Are voluntary traits essential to someone's self-understanding? If I can discard certain traits at will, are they really essential to my own self-understanding? I will ignore the questions having to do with choice in the present context and simply assume that, whether a matter of choice or not, Hispanic membership is basic for some but not all group members. Even if that is the case, the crucial point is that Hispanic membership as a type of basic membership has a partial extension. My conclusion then is that whereas, as we saw before, nationality meets the criterion of pervasive basic membership, Hispanic membership does not meet this criterion. Hispanic membership meets, at best, the criterion of partial basic membership.

In our previous examples, I have implicitly compared national and Hispanic memberships. We must now make this comparison explicit and turn to the degrees of basicness between national and Hispanic membership. I will now discuss the third criterion mentioned above, robust membership. I mentioned before the way in which Portes and Rumbaut describe Hispanics and their national memberships. Among Latin-American nationals and Hispanics, national experiences "are too divergent and national loyalties too deeply embedded to yield to this supranational logic [i.e., Hispanic identity]."[36] The idea described here is that the national membership of Hispanics is robust, i.e., national membership has a higher degree of basicness than Hispanic membership. I suggested above that Latin-American nations are communities with a strong sense of "we" and membership in this national "we" is generally basic, which is one of the reasons why nations draw intense feelings of loyalty. I now wish to develop this notion further and argue that national membership when compared with Hispanic membership is robust.

Let us begin with an observation about robust membership and conflict. Robust membership does not exclude other basic memberships. As suggested, one might be a Hispanic and an American, and both memberships might be basic. But robust membership does often exclude other memberships that might have a similar degree of basicness in a given situation or context. What I mean is that under a set of circumstances robust membership can often be exclusive, precluding other memberships with a similar degree of basicness. Robust membership is one of the reasons why in a situation of conflict we are likely to see people taking sides and defending those groups with traits that are most essential to their own self-understandings—Serbs and Croats, Hutus and Tutsis, Catholics and Protestants, Mexicans and Americans. As mentioned in chapter 6 and in our previous discussion, it is certainly true that people usually have different layers of membership in different (and sometimes conflicting) us-type groups. It does seem to be the case, however, that in certain instances one of the basic memberships in an us-type group could have the potential for overriding other basic memberships. One can particularly see one membership prevailing over others in situations of conflict.

If the observation is right, then it is possible to anticipate that in the case of a confrontation between the nationalities of Hispanics, Hispanic membership will subside and national membership will prevail. The reason why national membership prevails over Hispanic membership is because national membership is much stronger than Hispanic membership. If membership X has a higher degree of basicness than membership Y in situation S, then X is robust with regard to Y. In situation S, e.g., conflict, national membership will show a higher degree of basicness than Hispanic membership, as seen by actions of partiality toward the nation, and hence the former membership is robust with regard to the latter. The question that arises is whether there can be a situation S in which Hispanic membership overrides national membership. Given the traits about the groups themselves, which will be discussed in the next chapter, I think the answer is negative at this point in time. As the qualities of the groups might change in the future, the answer at that point may be a different one. An analogy between the Latin American and Hispanic groups in relation to national groups will support my claim that national membership is robust with regard to a supranational category such as "Hispanic."[37] One of the points I made in our earlier discussion is that national membership is robust with regard to Latin American membership. Being a Hispanic is akin with being a Latin American in that it is a category that encompasses different national memberships. If it is true that national membership is robust with regard to Latin American membership, one could say a fortiori that national membership is robust with regard to Hispanic membership. The point follows because both categories, Latin American and Hispanic, are defined by virtue of nationality. We might encounter a different situation if we compared two categories, one of which was defined by nationality and the other was not—e.g., a religious category. But the Hispanic category is deeply intertwined with nationality and nationality remains strong. My claim then is that the criterion of robust membership is met by national membership and not Hispanic membership.

CONCLUSION

I set out to inquire whether membership in the Hispanic group is central to members' identities. In order to understand the identity of Hispanics, I raised the question of whether Hispanic membership is basic. I attempted to answer this question by exploring national membership and comparing national membership with Hispanic membership. I suggested that national membership is basic for all (or almost all) Hispanics, but Hispanic membership is basic for only some Hispanics. Additionally, national membership is more robust than Hispanic membership.

Three points follow from my line of thought. First, if national membership is a type of basic membership for most Hispanics, national membership is likely to be highly significant for them. Thus for most Hispanics, national membership is at the center of their identity. Second, granting that Hispanic membership is actually basic for some Hispanics, Hispanic membership could be said to be highly significant for them. Hispanic membership would then seem to be central to the identity of some Hispanics. But here we must also remember that national membership is generally robust with regard to Hispanic membership. Hence, my third point, if national membership has a higher degree of basicness than Hispanic membership, national membership is likely to be more significant to more people than Hispanic membership; and also more significant as a type of membership. Given that nationality is more significant, it has a greater claim to being at the center of someone's identity. Even in cases in which Hispanic membership might indeed seem to be central to someone's identity, the situation for most Hispanics is that national membership is at the center of their identities.

NOTES

1. See "Revisions to the Standards for the Classification of Federal Data on Race and Ethnicity," in *Federal Register*, vol. 62, no. 210 (Thursday, October 30, 1997, Notices, 58782).

2. As we saw in chapter two, the definition was officially issued by the Office of Management and Budget on May 12, 1977, in the "Race and Ethnic Standards for Federal Statistics and Administrative Reporting," otherwise known as "Statistical Directive No. 15." As I pointed out in chapter 2, according to the latest revision, the definition remains the same, but the category is now "Hispanic" or "Latino," and "Spanish Origin" could also be used. See "Revisions," 58789.

3. I am aware of the terminological difficulties here. Nations do not always overlap with states, and thus state membership does not necessarily mean national membership. Walker Connor provides an illuminating discussion on the different groups that are often mistaken for nations and different kinds of states in "Who are the Mexican Americans? A Note on Comparability," in *Mexican-Americans in Comparative Perspective*, ed. Walker Connor (Washington, D.C.: The Urban Institute Press, 1985). See also "A Nation Is a Nation, Is a State, Is an Ethnic Group, Is a . . ." in *Nationalism: The Quest for Understanding* (Princeton: Princeton University Press, 1994), 90–100; and Max Weber's discussion on nationhood in *From Max Weber: Essays in Sociology* (New York: Oxford University Press, 1946), 172. Nonetheless, given the strong political dimension of nationalities, citizenships often imply a national identity—or as in the case of Canada, a set of identities; and thus I use the term "national membership" with two variables in mind. For the kind of terminological ambiguity that gives rise to these variables, see Robert Ware, "Nations and Social Complexity," in *Rethinking Nationalism*, Canadian Journal of Philosophy, Supplementary Volume 22, eds. Jocelyne Couture, Kai Nielsen and Michel Seymour (Calgary: University of Calgary Press, 1996), 134–36. Beyond the terminological difficulty, one of my points will be that there might be discrepancies between the national identity one possesses, in fact, and the national identity that one's citizenship represents.

4. The two variables distinguish types of memberships. Similar distinctions, for instance, would include separating formal and substantive citizenships. "The former refers to a formal link between an individual and the state . . ." And "the latter refers to the bundle of civil, political, social, and also cultural rights enjoyed by an individual, traditionally by virtue of her or his belonging to the national community." Marco Martiniello, "Citizenship in the European Union," in *From*

Migrants to Citizens: Membership in a Changing World, eds. T. Alexander Aleinikoff and Douglas Klusmeyer (Washington D.C.: Carnegie Endowment for International Peace, 2000), 345.

5. Mollyann Brodie, Annie Steffenson, Jaime Valdez, Rebecca Levin, and Roberto Suro, *2002 National Survey of Latinos*. Report prepared by the Pew Hispanic Center and the Kaiser Family Foundation, December 2002, 29.

6. This interesting point is one of the premises underlying Russell Hardin's analysis of group membership and conflict. See *One for All: The Logic of Group Conflict* (Princeton: Princeton University Press, 1995), particularly 142–82.

7. Donald L. Horowitz observes that in situations of conflict boundary lines between groups are sometimes shaped and hardened. See *Ethnic Groups in Conflict* (Berkeley and Los Angeles: University of California Press, 2000), 74. Assuming that boundaries are hardened, a member of two groups, that become antagonistic toward each other, might have to identify with one of the groups and thus exclude or minimize the other. If we add to this picture that states often place strong demands of allegiance among their subjects, sometimes making memberships exclusive, it is not hard to see how these demands might be heightened in times of conflict, thus requiring in fact that dual citizens express a strong and definite allegiance to one of the states involved. Consider for instance, the renunciation element for naturalized U.S. citizens when they take the Oath of Allegiance. See T. Alexander Aleinikoff, "Between Principles and Politics: U.S. Citizenship Policy," in *From Migrants to Citizens*, 147–50.

8. See "Revisions," 58789.

9. This phenomenon has consequences that may be viewed as both positive, social benefits derived from a disadvantaged status, and negative, racial stigmatization. Martha E. Gimenez, "U.S. Ethnic Politics: Implications for Latin Americans," *Latin American Perspectives*, 19, 4 (1992): 13–14.

10. Social ascriptions change from one context to the other. So, for instance, someone who might be classified under a category in Mexico, say, Indian, becomes a Hispanic or Mexican-American in the U.S.—although of course, given the ethnic and racial differentiation in the federal standards such a person might choose to identify herself as both Hispanic/Latina and American-Indian. See Connor, "Who Are the Mexican-Americans?" 24–25. Similarly, someone who might have never thought of herself in racial terms is compelled to do so once she encounters the classificatory scheme in the U.S. See Linda Martin Alcoff, "Is Latina/o Identity a Racial Identity?" in *Hispanics/Latinos in the United States: Ethnicity, Race, and Rights*, eds. Jorge J. E. Gracia and Pablo De Greiff (New York: Routledge, 2000), 24.

11. *2002 National Survey*, 28.

12. The level of continuity between generations is often disrupted or diminished by migration. The children of immigrants often find themselves in a world—with values, problems and identities—that is very different from the parent's world. Roberto Suro, for instance, opens his narrative on Latinos in the U.S. with the story of Imelda, the teenage daughter of immigrants from a village in Central Mexico who becomes a welfare mother. Using the story as an illustration of striking contrasts between the life experiences and worldviews of immigrants and their children, he comments that "Imelda's parents had traveled to Texas on

a wave of expectations that carried them from the diminishing life of peasant farmers on a dusty *rancho* to quiet contentment as low-wage workers in an American city. These two industrious immigrants had produced a teenage welfare mother, who in turn was to have an American baby. In the United States, Imelda had learned the language and the ways. In the end, what she learned best was how to be poor in an American inner city" (original emphasis). *Strangers Among Us: Latino Lives in a Changing America* (New York: Vintage Books, 1999), 4.

13. Due to the long border they share, along with cultural, political and economic differences, the history between the U.S. and Mexico is a complicated one. The relationship has been characterized by failed expectations, although agreements have also been put in place in order to satisfy common interests. Historically, each country has perceived the other one as a threat. In the case of Mexico, the perceived threat was partly the case because "every Mexican child knew that the United States had 'taken' half of Mexico's territory during the 19th century while, during the 20th century, outright military intervention had been replaced by less tangible forms of intervention or interference." Susan Kaufman Purcell, "The Changing Nature of U.S.-Mexican Relations," *Journal of Inter-American Studies and World Affairs* 39, 1 (1997): 138.

14. David Copp, "Social Unity and the Identity of Persons," *The Journal of Political Philosophy* 10, 4 (2002): 383.

15. David Copp, *Nations and Nationalism since 1780: Programme, Myth, Reality* (Cambridge: Cambridge University Press, 2002[1990]), 143.

16. Alejandro Portes and Rubén Rumbaut, *Immigrant America: A Portrait*, sec. ed. (Berkeley and Los Angeles: University of California Press, 1996), 135.

17. These commonalities are often expressed in and reinforced by symbols and ceremonies. John Breully's observation with regard to the use of symbols in nationalist movements is helpful. "Nationalist movements, like all mass movements, make use of symbols and ceremonies. These give nationalist ideas a definite shape and force, both by projecting certain images and by enabling people to come together in ways which seem directly to express the solidarity of the nation." *Nationalism and the State*, sec. ed. (Chicago: University of Chicago Press, 1994), 64.

18. This is not a universal statement, i.e., that national membership, under all circumstances, will always be basic. My claim applies to the specific context of the Americas. Benedict Anderson argues that modern nations originate in Latin America. The view, which has not gone unchallenged, helps to understand historically why national feelings in Latin America are quite strong. Along with cultural forces, the key for understanding Latin-American nations has to do with the fact that since colonial times they had been "administrative units." These historical units roughly correspond with the modern geo-political units. *Imagined Communities: Reflection on the Origin and Spread of Nationalism*, rev. ed. (New York: Verso, 2002[1983]), 50–52.

19. According to the *2002 National Survey*, "foreign-born Latinos' attachment to their country of origin emerges from their choice of the nation they consider their real homeland, in Spanish 'patria,'" 34.

20. Note that I speak in terms of tendency and proportion. My claim is that national membership for most Latin Americans is basic. But the degree of basicness, although quite strong for many people, will also be weak for some people. This

happens to be true among some indigenous groups that have not internalized the national features of the states in which they happen to be members. I mentioned previously that the state is not always in touch with the collective identities of all its members. Similarly Connor reminds us that Indian consciousness is quite high in Mexico and might even shatter the image of Mexican national identity. "Who are the Mexican Americans?" 15. This is seen, for instance, in the 1994 Zapatista rebellion in Chiapas. Although, I think the point is exaggerated, national identities are much more pervasive and powerful than Connor seems to think, the reminder is well taken. For the role of ethnic identity in the Chiapas revolution, see José Alejos García, "Ethnic Identity and the Zapatista Rebellion in Chiapas," in *National Identities and Sociopolitical Changes in Latin America*, eds. Mercedes F. Durán-Cogan and Antonio Goméz-Moriana (New York: Routledge, 2001), 160–63.

21. See José Vasconcelos, "The Cosmic Race," in *Latin American Philosophy for the 21st Century: The Human Condition, Values and the Search for Identity*, eds. Jorge J. E. Gracia and Elizabeth Millán-Zaibert (New York: Prometheus Books, 2004), 269–78.

22. Ernesto "Che" Guevera, "Our Common Aspiration: The Death of Imperialism and the Birth of a Moral World," in *Venceremos: The Speeches and Writings of Ernesto Che Guevara*, ed. John Gerassi (London: Panther Books, 1969), 524. Guevara is an icon often displayed, but seldom read. In my view, his writings are worthwhile reading, for they give us valuable insights into the "us-type" mentality.

23. Hugo Chavez, current president in Venezuela, is a recent example of how effective a political weapon the we-versus-them rhetoric could be. Given that the rhetoric has been quite effective when used along the lines of social class, one might speculate that, despite claims to the contrary, class affiliations could indeed trump national affiliations. See Horowitz, *Ethnic Groups*, 89–92.

24. This is not to say that conditions could change; so that a pan-Latin-American identity gains strength. But this has not been the case historically and does not seem to be the case in the foreseeable future. Alcoff makes the following remark with regard to a "U.S. pan-Latina/o identity," which originates in Latin America with integrationist visions voiced by Bolivar, Marti, and Guevara: "It is important to note that populations 'on the ground' have not often resonated with these grand visions . . ." "Is Latina/o Identity a Racial Identity?," 27.

25. See my example above regarding the manifestation of national feelings in sporting events.

26. Harry E. Vanden and Gary Prevost, *Politics of Latin America: The Power Game* (New York: Oxford University Press, 2002), 168.

27. See Thomas E. Skidmore and Peter H. Smith, *Modern Latin America*, sixth edition (New York: Oxford University Press, 2005), 414.

28. Part of the reason why this "we" is so resilient has to do with the political individuation of nations. As I have noted, group boundaries and configurations might change. But given the institutional and relatively stable characteristic of states, groups individuated by political boundaries tend to be self-perpetuating.

29. So a survey brief on the *2002 National Survey of Latinos* compares populations in different states and comments that "country of origin, or the birthplace of Latinos and their ancestors, is one of the biggest differentiators between the Latino populations in California, Texas, New York, New Jersey and Florida." *Latinos in*

California, Texas, New York, Florida and New Jersey: Survey Brief, Pew Hispanic Center and The Henry J. Kaiser Family Foundation, March 2004, 1.

30. Portes and Rumbaut, *Immigrant America*, 135.

31. The claim I have made is that nationality for Latin Americans represents what Robert McKim calls "strong identification." Although this is the case, I agree with McKim's reminder: "even when one identifies strongly with one's nation, clearly this is almost always only one of several competing sources of identity. Other obvious sources of identity include, for example, one's association with groups as various as one's family, friends, neighbors, coreligionists, and those who share one's economic interests." "National Identity and Respect among Nations," in *The Morality of Nationalism*, eds. Robert McKim and Jeff McMahan (New York: Oxford University Press, 1997), 260–61.

32. What it means to be an American will, of course, have different points of emphasis for different people. Some will focus on the linguistic and geographic criteria, whereas others will focus on the belief that America is a land of immigrants, and might even conclude that it ought to be intentionally a multicultural nation. In a way, varying normative versions of America are not only different, but also potentially conflicting. But despite points of emphasis, there is an identifiable American geopolitical entity that has a set of distinguishing values and attributes. For various normative statements on the traits of American nationhood, see *Postethnic America: Beyond Multiculturalism* (New York: Basic Books, 1995); Michael Walzer, *What it Means to Be an American: Essays on the American Experience* (New York: Marsilio, 1996); and Arthur M. Schlesinger, Jr. *The Disuniting of America: Reflections on a Multicultural Society*, rev. ed. (New York: W. W. Norton & Company, 1998).

33. In this case, the attribution of Hispanic properties might still be in the ascriptive stage, so that properties have not been internalized by the migrant.

34. This point will be developed in more detail in the next chapter.

35. Mary Waters, *Ethnic Options: Choosing Identities in America* (Berkeley and Los Angeles: University of California Press, 1990), 115.

36. Portes and Rumbaut, *Immigrant America* 135.

37. This analogy is helpful, but also has certain limitations. It is true that both the Latin-American and the Hispanic category represent attempts to unify at the supranational level national distinctions. And as Alcoff points out, the process in Latin America precedes "pan-Latina/o identity" in the U.S. "Is Latina/o Identity a Racial Identity?" 27. But whereas supranational identity has been an ideological project led by Bolivar, Marti, etc., the ideological component in the U.S. is not as strong. Hispanic identity, an American phenomenon, emerges not primarily on the basis of ideological calls for unity, but rather as the by-product of government policies toward Latin-American immigrants. In a sense, then, what I will call Hispanic identity making in chapter 9 is an unintentional phenomenon. See Geoffrey Fox for a discussion on the limitations of the analogy that adduces different reasons from the ones I have mentioned. *Hispanic Nation: Culture, Politics and the Construction of Identity* (Tucson: The University of Arizona Press, 1996), 9–11.

8

Hispanic Identification and Common Identity

I have looked at Hispanic membership in comparison with national membership. In this chapter, I wish to examine the Hispanic group and query whether the group as such satisfies the conditions of groups that have the function of endowing members with basic memberships. I will concentrate on the first two conditions formulated in chapter six—the conditions of relevant identification and differentiation—and leave the third condition, intrinsic identification, for the next chapter. The general question to be addressed now is this: Does the Hispanic group satisfy the conditions of relevant groups?

RELEVANT IDENTIFICATION

We know that according to the first condition outlined in chapter 6, relevant identification, groups are identified according to properties that tend to make membership in a group basic. Is the Hispanic group identified according to properties that make Hispanic membership basic? The answer to this question, I will argue, is negative. Recall that I granted for the sake of argument in the previous chapter that Hispanic membership might indeed have a certain degree of basicness, but I now move a step beyond and discuss the reasons why I do not think that Hispanic membership could in fact be basic. Let us look at two components in the question being raised: (a) is the Hispanic group identifiable, and (b) is it possible to single out the relevant properties of Hispanic membership? I will address these two questions in turn and make two points.

First, there is a difficulty lying in the fact that Hispanics are not a clearly identifiable group. Second, the reason why Hispanics are not clearly identifiable is because Hispanic membership is an epiphenomenon of national membership—a type of membership that is currently robust with regard to Hispanic membership.

I will now begin with the point on whether Hispanics are identifiable. Let us here recall that the sorts of groups we are concerned with are identifiable. A group is identifiable when given a process of interaction, group members can discriminate members from nonmembers by recognizing certain social markers in fellow members. The question that now arises is this: are members of the Hispanic group able to recognize each other as fellow members (and discriminate those members from nonmembers)? In order to address this question, let me begin with another one: what are the criteria according to which Hispanics are classified? According to the U.S. Census Bureau, for instance, the criteria for classifying Hispanics are either *birth* or *heritage*. So, for example, "... people of Mexican origin [i.e., a Hispanic] may be either born in Mexico or of Mexican *heritage* [my emphasis]."[1] So, in other words, "Hispanic" may refer to at least three possibilities. First, a Hispanic is someone who is born in Mexico (or more generally, Latin America) and migrates to the U.S. Second, a Hispanic is someone who is born in the U.S. from Mexican, or Latin-American, parents, and thus presumably has a Mexican (or Latin American) heritage.[2] Lastly, since there are no constraints upon the idea of "Mexican heritage" one could perhaps include a third possibility: people who believe they have enough affinity with Mexican or Latin-American "heritage" and are thus entitled to be classified as Hispanics.

The first criterion for classification posits that a Hispanic is someone who was born in a certain place. But note that it is not just any place; it is rather a *nation*. One clearly sees in this criterion that some Hispanics are first-generation immigrants who were born in Latin America, whereas other Hispanics consist of the second generation or those born and reared in the U.S.[3] Note again the significance and pervasiveness of nations: a first group of Hispanics comprises people born in Latin-American nations, whereas the second one consists of American nationals.[4] For the first group, those born in Latin America, the criterion of birth would be enough to make them classify as Hispanics.[5] But for the second group, those born in the U.S., the criterion of birth is not enough for counting as Hispanic, since many non-Hispanics are born in the U.S. Now let us look more closely at the group of those that classify as Hispanics under the birth criterion. A Hispanic is someone who was born in Mexico, Honduras, Venezuela, etc. But here we must bear in mind that all those national places are different from each other, both culturally and politically.[6] The predictable result, as I have already suggested, is that we are attempting to subsume a set of different national identities under an overarching category. So the Hispanic category consists of Mexican-Venezuelan-Honduran-Chilean-Argentinean-Colombian-Bolivian-Ecuadorian-Peruvian-Uruguayan-Paraguayan identities—and we have not finished mentioning all the possibilities. We must here remember, however, that Hispanics may be classified under a second criterion, namely, heritage—which includes those born in the U.S. This, I think, makes the situation more complicated. Under this criterion, those born in Latin-American countries and the U.S. are supposed to have a common heritage that makes them identifiable. Here we must bear in mind that, as already mentioned, all the national places at stake are different from each other. Thus, we are attempting to subsume under a single category a set of different national identities, or rather, "heritages."[7]

Let me now return to the original question about whether the Hispanic group is identifiable. I said above that (based on the condition of relevant identification formulated in chapter 6) a group is identifiable when, given a process of interaction, group members can discriminate members from nonmembers by recognizing certain social markers in fellow members. The question that arises is this: could one say that the Hispanic group is identifiable according to a set of social markers that makes recognition among fellow members of the group possible? Given the differences in identities among members of the Hispanic group, I doubt that the answer to the question is affirmative. The answer to this question would be affirmative if either national identities were weaker than what they currently are, or Hispanic identity was stronger than what it is. But given the current state of affairs, members of the Hispanic group would probably not recognize each other as fellow members in a relevant sense—meaning that the group is not identifiable in the sense that interests us. I have not yet said everything I intend to cover about the criteria for Hispanic classification, Hispanic common identity and the process of Hispanic identification. I will return to these topics below.

I will now turn to the reason why the Hispanic group is not relevantly identifiable. Let me begin my argument by emphasizing the fact that, as we have seen, national memberships tend to be different from each other and also, under some circumstances, exclusive. So a Mexican is not an Argentinean or a Chilean. Similarly, a Colombian is not a Venezuelan or a Salvadorian. Now, let us note that categorizing different and exclusive memberships is not the problem as such. After all, we do this when we speak of Mexicans, Venezuelans and Bolivians as Latin Americans, or, say, Roman Catholics. In these instances, we could even acknowledge that there are cases in which a Bolivian and a Paraguayan are united by their Catholic membership in a way that takes precedence over their national differences. In such a situation, it could be the case that their religious membership competes with or is even more basic than their national memberships.

Nonetheless, the problem with the notion and phenomenon of Hispanicity begins when differentiated and exclusive national memberships are categorized as a single group in which membership is supposed to have a certain degree of basicness. We must remember that the importance of being a Hispanic presumably lies in that Hispanicity is very important to someone's identity. For if Hispanic membership is simply nominal (without a high degree of significance for someone's identity), then it would be irrelevant (from the government's perspective) whether someone classifies as a Hispanic or not. Given the presumed value of membership in the Hispanic category and the way the category is defined, the following dilemma arises. Either membership in the single Hispanic category is robust with regard to the nationally differentiated and often exclusive memberships comprised by the category, or the exclusive national memberships are more robust than membership in the single category. I argued in the previous chapter that the latter is the case, i.e., national memberships are robust with regard to Hispanic membership.

Let me now pause for a moment and, before moving on, summarize some of the elements that have come up to this point. In my discussion so far, we see that the following is the case: (a) Hispanics are classified by virtue of national memberships, (b) Hispanic membership is presumably basic, and (c) national memberships are more basic than Hispanic membership. Note that Hispanics are classified by virtue of memberships that are more basic than Hispanic membership itself. The problem here lies in the attempt to subsume under a single categorial membership a set of national memberships that is robust with regard to the categorial membership.[8] What this attempt shows is that the apparent basicness of Hispanic membership is an *epiphenomenon* of national membership.[9] National membership is basic. Hispanic membership might have the appearance of basic membership, but the apparent basicness of Hispanic membership really derives from national memberships.

For the sake of clarity, let me explain the argument in more detail and also more formally. I will begin by thinking of a person P, whose Hispanic membership is presumably basic. Let us remember that if P has a basic membership, she has a set of traits that are essential to her self-understanding and make her a member of a particular group. In this hypothetical case, the particular group would be the Hispanic group. Suppose we tried to identify the traits that are essential to P's self-understanding and that also make her a member in the Hispanic group. P, for instance, has two traits that are essential to her self-understanding: she speaks Spanish and she was born in Ecuador. But now consider two points. First, Hispanic membership is characterized by Latin-American national traits. A Hispanic, for instance, is someone who speaks Spanish, was born in Colombia (or from Colombian parents) or has a Mexican heritage. Thinking of P, the reason why she is considered to be a Hispanic is because she speaks Spanish and was born in Ecuador. Put in more formal terms, we can say, for instance, that for every P, if she is a Hispanic the traits by virtue of which she is identified as such are national traits. Incidentally, we can also say that Hispanic membership is a function of national membership, where the value of the former variable is related to and contingent upon the latter.

The second point moves us to a crucial step in the argument. Let us recall that national membership is robust with regard to Hispanic membership. What this means is that nationality has a higher degree of basicness than Hispanicity. More precisely, there are more traits that are essential to P and make her a member in a national group than traits that are essential to P and make her a member in the Hispanic group. The latter statement assumes, of course, that there are certain traits that could be essential to P's self-understanding and make her a member in the Hispanic group. I make this concession for the sake of argument, but we will see that such a concession is not entirely true. According to this second point, let us say that the degree of basicness for national membership is always higher than the degree of basicness for Hispanic membership.

Given the two points I have just mentioned, consider that it would be counterintuitive to say that Hispanicity is basic. Given that Hispanicity is defined by virtue and is a function of nationality, and nationality has a higher degree of basicness than Hispanicity, it does not follow that Hispanicity is basic. It rather follows that nationality is basic and the apparent basicness of Hispanicity derives from the basicness of nationality. Put briefly, Hispanicity is an epiphenomenon of nationality.

The argument is confirmed in practice. Think of P again. The traits that are essential to P's self-understanding are traits that probably make her a member in a national group, e.g., Ecuador. Thus her Ecuadorian membership is basic. We might think that the two traits that are essential to P's self-understanding also make her a Hispanic (in a way that makes her Hispanic membership basic). But the seemingly Hispanic traits (language and birthplace) are really traits of a particular national group, i.e., Ecuador. We can then see that the Hispanic traits are epiphenomena of Ecuadorian traits. When we attempt to identify the traits that are presumably essential to P and make her a member in the Hispanic group, we are really identifying national traits. If I am right, it would then make sense to say that P's Ecuadorian membership is basic, but the claim that her Hispanic membership is basic would beg the question and point toward national membership.[10]

It is important to clarify what I am saying. I am not saying that P could not be considered a Hispanic. For purposes of census classification or media targeting, to mention just two examples, she is certainly seen as a Hispanic. She could also even view and think of herself this way. But the fundamental question is whether her Hispanic membership is basic, and thus given the value of identity—or any other criteria—merits official classification and the sort of recognition that is currently granted by the federal government. My point now is that given the robustness of national membership, and the way Hispanicity is defined, Hispanic membership is nonbasic. I will return to considerations on the merits for official classification and recognition in the final chapter. But if Hispanic is nonbasic, the immediate question that comes to mind is whether Hispanic membership could indeed become basic. I will deal with this possible transformation in the next chapter. Let me just mention here that Hispanic membership could indeed become a type of basic membership. But I think that two conditions would need to be the case. First, Hispanicity would have to become an identity in itself and not simply a category or identity defined by virtue of other national memberships. A second condition is closely related to the first one. The nationalities that are currently included in the Hispanic category will need to lose their strength and cease to have the high degree of basicness that they currently have. As we will see in the next chapter, this trend follows what have been historically common cases of national identity making.

Let me briefly deal here with a possible objection that might be raised. I said earlier that in our hypothetical case P has two traits that are essential to her self-understanding and make her a member of the Ecuadorian nation. But imagine that P has now migrated to the U.S., has become an American citizen and has renounced Ecuadorian citizenship. In fact, she no longer considers herself Ecuadorian. So, it would be more precise to say that the traits that are essential to P's self-understanding formerly made her a member of the Ecuadorian nation. Would it not follow that P's Hispanic membership in the U.S. in then basic? Two observations are in place. First, bear in mind that basic membership entails (a) traits that are essential to someone's self-understanding and (b) make her a member in a particular group. P renouncing a particular group does not automatically make her a member in another particular group—assuming that the Hispanic group was a particular one. Note that P has voluntarily renounced a group to presumably become a member, out of her own choice, in another group. But we have now introduced the element of voluntary membership. As I suggested previously, voluntary traits do not necessarily preclude the traits that are essential to someone's self-understanding, but nonvoluntary traits have a higher propensity to be essential, given the fact that they cannot be changed and are thus stable. Note that even if we do not introduce new voluntary traits that become essential to P's self-understanding, she has explicitly renounced her membership in a particular group, i.e., the Ecuadorian nation. The case is then that since traits that are essential for P's self-understanding are not necessarily dependent upon P's membership in a group, she might retain those traits without being associated with the group any longer. Thus, given the explicit renunciation from the particular group, her membership ceases to be basic.

Second, let me point out here that, as I said before, the Hispanic group is not a particular group because members of the group do not recognize each other as fellow members. The reader might have thought of this point already, but I have avoided making the claim explicit because it would make my argument circular. I would be saying that Hispanic membership is nonbasic because the Hispanic group is not particular and the reason why the Hispanic group is not particular (and hence properly identifiable) is because membership is nonbasic. My claim that the Hispanic group is not properly identifiable because Hispanic membership is nonbasic is made on different grounds—i.e., Hispanicity is an epiphenomenon of nationality. But the fact of the matter is that Hispanics cannot be considered a particular (and properly identifiable) group because the group does not have a common identity, a topic to which I return in the next section. The essential point now is that since the Hispanic group is not a particular group with a common identity, and thus the sort of group in which membership might be basic, P's membership in the Hispanic group is not likely to be basic.

At this point, we can then finally return to the question guiding our current discussion: What is the reason why Hispanics are not identified in the sense that interests us? If my argument is correct, we can see the reason why the Hispanic group is not properly identifiable. According to the condition of relevant identification, groups are identified according to properties that tend to make membership in a group basic. But if we look for these properties among Hispanics, we will find that these kinds of properties are the ones that tend to make Hispanics members of their respective nations. Properties of basic membership are primarily national, and only epiphenomenally Hispanic. Thus when we attempt to identify the properties of basic membership among Hispanics, we are really turning to national properties. The end result is that nations satisfy the condition of relevant identification across the board. Hispanicity, in contrast, borrows from national traits, but does not generally satisfy the condition of relevant identification.

DIFFERENTIATION AND COMMON IDENTITY

I will now turn to the condition of differentiation. According to this condition, basic membership is necessarily connected with the difference-sensitive attributes of groups. In chapter 6, I argued that there is a necessary connection between group differences and the properties that are essential for the self-understandings of group members. The way I put it was this: groups in which basic membership is possible tend to be those groups that can be distinguished by way of exclusion—G and not G. These groups have what I called the status of discernibility. Much of what was said in the previous section can be applied here as well. We could virtually paraphrase the previous argument and see why the Hispanic group does not satisfy the condition of differentiation. I will not, however, proceed this way. What I will do here is raise the question of whether the Hispanic group possesses the status of discernibility and suggest that the group does not have the status. The discussion in this section will draw from previous arguments and return to some earlier points. But the present discussion will also add additional elements to my previous arguments by engaging two theoreticians of Hispanic identity, namely, Jorge Gracia and Angelo Corlett. My aim is not to engage these authors exhaustively. Instead, I address their views in the context of a broader discussion that aims to shed light on the point of discernibility and the condition of differentiation.

Let us recall that groups have the status of discernibility when two circumstances are the case. The first one is that group members have traits in common. And, second, these common traits are such that they make the group distinguishable from other groups. Another way of formulating these circumstances is by saying that groups have a "common identity" that is unique to such a group. Focusing now on this notion of common identity, the question is: Do Hispanics have a common identity in the sense that matters? Gracia and Corlett have argued that this is certainly the case. By examining some of their arguments, I will contend that the Hispanic group does not have a common identity in the sense that matters.

Jorge Gracia adopts a historical family view according to which the category of "Hispanic" reflects a "common identity" and thus the category is useful for the self-understanding and empowerment of Hispanics.[11] He claims, for instance, that "to adopt a name and define one's identity is. . . . an act of empowerment because it limits the power of others to name and identify us."[12] Elsewhere, he says that "the category 'Hispanic' is useful to describe and understand ourselves. It also serves to describe much of what we produce and do, for this product and these actions are precisely the results of who we are. "[13] To grasp the way Gracia believes we should use the category of "Hispanic," a way that allows us to acknowledge the unity and yet diversity of the group, we must look at his conception of ethnic names. In Gracia's view, ethnic labels can be misleading because of their ambiguity and yet we should be able to retain those labels because they play a crucial role in the groups they name. Accordingly, a satisfactory conception of ethnicity must account for the unity and also diversity of ethnic groups. The parameters of ethnic explanation should be: "first, the unity of ethnic groups and their difference from other groups; second, the diversity found within ethnic groups themselves."[14] Part of the confusion about ethnic groups and the reason why ethnic labels run the risk of becoming too broad and thus useless, is that we use the wrong criteria for ethnic identification. Gracia examines five criteria for the identification of ethnic groups—political, linguistic, cultural, racial and genetic—and contends that the criteria must be abandoned because they do not provide necessary or sufficient conditions for ethnic identification. Gracia's purpose then is to propose a criterion of ethnic identification that does not necessarily entail political units, language, culture, race or genetic relations; so that we can still identify ethnic groups but not have to link them to traits such as race, language, etc.

According to Gracia, we can successfully identify ethnic groups, acknowledging their unity and yet diversity, by implementing a *historical* criterion: "What ties the membership of an ethnic group together, and separates them from others, is history and the particular events of that history; a unique web of changing historical events supplies their unity."[15] The historical understanding of ethnic groups allows for a cluster of properties that makes ethnic groups unique without requiring that every single member of the group possesses the same exact properties. A cluster of properties distinguishes ethnic groups by virtue of relationships that vary at times, but yet make the group distinguishable. Gracia explains the point this way: a group of members ABCD is identifiable due to the relationship (aRb) between A and B; (bRc) between B and C; and (cRd) between C and D. Now is A necessarily related to D or C? Maybe or maybe not, but those specific relationships are not crucial. What matters is that there is a cluster of historically relational properties within the set ABCD; and such a historically relational cluster of properties is enough for making the group identifiable.[16]

Gracia's argument can now be illustrated with respect to the ethnic understanding of Hispanics. We assume that Hispanics constitute an ethnic group, but then wonder about the criterion by which we can determine whether they are an identifiable ethnic group or not. Can we distinguish Hispanics by virtue of their nationalities? The answer is obviously negative because some are Chilean, whereas others are Mexicans, Paraguayans, etc. How about language? The answer is once again negative because some Hispanics speak Spanish, but not all do. The same goes for culture, race, and genetic relationships among Hispanics. It would then seem highly unlikely that we would be able to identify Hispanics as an ethnic group, unless we turn to Gracia's historical criterion for ethnic identification. Gracia points out that:

> the concept of Hispanic should be understood historically, that is, as a concept that involves historical relations. Hispanics are the group of people comprised by the inhabitants of the countries of the Iberian peninsula after 1492 and what were to become the colonies of those countries after the encounter between Iberia and America took place, and by descendants of these people who live in other countries (e.g., the United States) but preserve some link to those people.[17]

So Hispanics may have different races and come from various linguistic groups, cultural backgrounds and national communities. But if someone is historically related to some segment of the group stemming from a specific region, i.e., the continent known as Latin America, after a particular date, i.e., 1492, he or she belongs to the ethnic group known by the term of "Hispanic." In short, Hispanics are an identifiable ethnic group because of a historical criterion.

I will now raise two objections to Gracia's account on the ethnic identification of Hispanics. My first objection is directly related to Gracia's notion of historical relations as the criterion for ethnic identification. The second objection goes against Gracia's claim that Hispanics have a common identity and such an identity is a source for the self-understanding and empowerment of Hispanics. In Gracia's account, Hispanics are an identifiable and distinguishable ethnic group because they possess a cluster of properties. Were we to raise the question about the origins of the cluster of properties that distinguish Hispanics, Gracia's account will point toward historical relations. But let us now raise another question: Where do the historical relations that form the basis for the cluster of properties of ethnic groups come from? When raising the question about the origin of historical relations, I am assuming three elements: (a) history consists of narratives about certain events; (b) those narratives are shaped by those who tell the narratives; and (c) a way in which narratives are shaped by those who tell them is by means of categories.[18]

The bottom line with regard to the last element is that we cannot think of historical relations or narratives without using categories and those categories shape the content of the story. A quick example will illustrate the point. Fifty years ago the 1492 event between Columbus and indigenous people in the now "Latin-American continent" would have been classified under the category of "discovery." Given a change in social sensibility and the need to use a different designation, the same event now goes under the category of "encounter."[19] So my specific question now is this: What is the origin of the categories used in telling the historical narrative that describes and characterizes Hispanics? In other words, who defines the categories that shape the narrative of Hispanic identity? The question I have posed requires a complex and multifaceted answer that would need to take into account shifting social sensibilities. I would like to focus, however, on an important generator for the categories used in the historical narrative of Hispanic identity: the state. We could naturally turn to Latin American states, except that the phenomenon of Hispanic identity is primarily an American phenomenon and thus we must turn to the American state.

The Proclamation of George W. Bush inaugurating the 2001 National Hispanic Heritage Month gives us an interesting example of what I have in mind. Quoting different examples and pointing out how Hispanics "have played an integral role in our country's exceptional story of success,"[20] the Proclamation classifies Hispanics under the category of "contributors to the American experience." We can now think of a contrasting example. People of Mexican origin would have hardly been classified under the just mentioned category by the American state, approximately a hundred years ago, in the context of the Mexican-American war. We could use illustrations of several shifting categories, but I want to now address the category of "Hispanic" itself. The definition of Hispanic was put forth in 1977 by the American government and has been kept to this day in the Standards for the Classification of Federal Data on Race and Ethnicity. A "Hispanic" is a "person of Mexican, Puerto Rican, Cuban, Central or South American or other Spanish culture or origin regardless of race."[21] Let us note several elements in this definition. First, a Hispanic is a person with a particular origin. Not any kind of origin would do, since the person under description originates from one of the national frameworks delimited in the category. There is now a very important second element strongly implied in the category. As we have had occasion to note, a Hispanic is a person of a national origin who is presumably now a member of the American nation or resides in American territory.[22] Without this qualification, the category would not make sense—since the category is not trying to capture Mexicans who are now living in Mexico, but rather Mexicans who now live in the U.S.—and presumably have interests in the U.S. There is a transferal or addition of membership: a person was, in the past tense, a member of the Mexican nation, and is now, present tense, a member of the American nation—although the person might indeed retain her previous membership and add a new one.

Now let us compare the Mexican who is a member of the Mexican nation and the person of Mexican origin who is currently a member of the

American nation, and raise the following question: What do they have in common? Or let us pose the question this way: Is there enough affinity between the two people (the Mexican in Mexico and the American of Mexican origin) to subsume them under the same category? According to Gracia, the two people in our comparison are connected with one another by means of historical relationships and thus they both can be justifiably subsumed under the category of "Hispanic." Several interesting points could be brought up in our example and in a reply to Gracia, but let me focus on the starting point of the Hispanic category. The category as it is being used in the current context, and indeed as it is used by Gracia, originates with the American government. Were it not for Statistical Directive No. 15 released in 1977 by the Office of Management and Budget, the term "Hispanic" would probably not have the same relevance it has now in our vocabulary and understanding of American society. The category originally arises due to an effort of the American state to identify a segment of the American population who happen to have a particular background. The attempt to identify people by means of the category "Hispanic," has had as a result an increasing awareness in American society about the existence of "Hispanics." In the next chapter, we will come back to identification.

The upshot of the present discussion is that the identification of Hispanics as an ethnic group cannot only be understood in terms of historical relations. The identification of Hispanics has to be understood within the context of the needs and policies of the American state. If the latter claim is true, there is a political dimension in the understanding of Hispanics as an ethnic group. The result, in fact, is that Gracia can speak of historical relations as the criterion for ethnic identification only because there is a previous political criterion that makes identification possible.[23] So the very criterion for ethnic identification that Gracia has rejected, the political unit, is the one that makes it possible for us to speak of Hispanics as an identifiable ethnic group. In conclusion, the understanding of Hispanics as an ethnic group is not only historical; the understanding is also to a very large extent political.[24] My observation does not necessarily undermine the thrust of Gracia's view, but I think that the observation does force him to rethink his justification for the criteria of ethnic identification.

Let me now move on to a second objection, which I believe is more crucial. In Gracia's view, Hispanics have a common identity and this form of identity is a source for the self-understanding and empowerment of Hispanics. The claim has two components: (a) Hispanics have a common identity and (b) this identity is a source of self-understanding and empowerment. In looking at (a), we must ask ourselves: What do we mean when we say that Hispanics have a "common identity"? There is a sense in which we might identify Hispanics as people who have a Latin-American origin, which is, as we have seen, the way the category is defined by the American state. But if "origin" is the principle of identification, why not do the same with other groups like the Irish, Germans, French, Finnish, or for that matter the English who traveled to American soil from Boston, England? We could propose, for example, that "the set of people in the now American nation who can trace their origins to the group of people who arrived in Boston in or after 1630 form a distinct and identifiable group." The latter is certainly possible: one could gather the group of people who trace their genealogical background to one of the members of the Boston group. The group would indeed be identifiable in accordance with a principle of "origin." Compare then two groups that are identified on the basis of the principle of "origin:" "Hispanics" and "descendants of the Boston group." We must wonder whether we are talking about identification with respect to each group in the same sense. Or more precisely: are the implications for identifying Hispanics the same as the implications for identifying descendants of the Boston group? The answer to these questions is negative due to the following presupposition: there is a degree of significance in the identification of Hispanics that is absent in the identification of the Boston group descendants. In other words, there is presumably something extremely relevant about being a Hispanic, so relevant that it requires official classification and recognition by the American state. Such relevance and need for classification and recognition does not apply to other types of groups that could conceivably be identified in some sense—as, for example, the descendants of the Boston group.

My comparison raises the following point: What do we mean by "common identity"? The question is not so much whether Hispanics have a common identity. Clearly, in some sense they do, just as many other groups do. The question is rather whether Hispanics have a common identity in the sense that matters. I believe the questions that need to be asked are these: Is the common identity of Hispanics such that it reflects how meaningful it is to be a Hispanic? Are the elements that unite Hispanics robust enough to give them meaning and direction? Are the properties that seem to make Hispanics identifiable in some sense such that they endow Hispanics with basic membership?[25] As I have explained, I believe that the answers to these questions tend to be negative due to the property of nationality among Hispanics. As I suggested earlier the notion that Hispanics have a relevantly distinctive cluster of properties is falsified because of the one property that pulls them apart, namely, nationality. Identifying Hispanics, in the relevant sense, is not generally possible because of two reasons. First, there is the fragmentation caused by national identities. And second, there is the fact that properties of basic membership are primarily national, and only epiphenomenally Hispanic.

Thus it is difficult to identify Hispanics in the relevant sense as a distinct group of people that are unified by and have a common identity due to a cluster of properties.

If I am right so far, we can see not only why the thesis on the common identity of Hispanics in the pertinent context is put into question, but also why the second half of Gracia's claim, i.e., (b) Hispanic identity is a source of self-understanding and empowerment, is doubtful. For given the robustness of national identities, people subsumed under the category of "Hispanic" tend to find the primary source of self-understanding and empowerment in their nationalities, and not their Hispanicity. The bottom line, once more, is that the significance and robustness of nationality tends to overshadow the thinness of Hispanicity.

I have raised two objections against Gracia's view on the ethnic identification of Hispanics. First, I pointed out that Gracia's notion of historical relations as the criterion for ethnic identification cannot be understood independently from the political criterion. As a matter of fact, the category "Hispanic" stems from and is defined by the administrative apparatus of the American state. The second point was related to Gracia's claim that Hispanics have a common identity and such an identity is a source for the self-understanding and empowerment of Hispanics.

Angelo Corlett presents us with another attempt to depict Hispanics as a group with a "common identity."[26] The general concern for Corlett has to do with ethnic classification for the purposes of civil rights policies. Given Corlett's concern, it helps to distinguish between two different issues at stake. First, Corlett claims that ethnic classification serves the interests of justice. Certain groups of people in the United States have been discriminated against based on the racial or ethnic group to which they belong. Identifying groups that have suffered discrimination is then extremely important. Such is, as we have seen before, part of the rationale behind the Standards for the Classification of Federal Data on Race and Ethnicity. The government attempts to identify and gather data on populations that have historically "experienced discrimination and differential treatment because of their race or ethnicity."[27] The requirements of justice entail distinguishing and classifying those individuals for the purposes of retribution. According to Corlett, we distinguish those individuals by means of a necessary and sufficient condition for ethnic classification: genealogical ties.[28] I will not have much to say in this chapter about the issue of ethnic or Hispanic classification for the purposes of justice and retribution. Although I will anticipate some points here, I will leave most of the discussion about this topic, classification and civil rights, for the final chapter.

My main interest now is in the second issue underlying Corlett's account: the presumed claim that ethnic identity, and particularly Hispanic identity, is essential for defining personhood. If one wants to argue, for example, that Hispanics have certain civil rights, and a violation of those civil rights is a wrongdoing, one ought to be able to identify and classify Hispanics. The latter observation is true because considerations of justice "are based on assumptions that certain names have referents," and so the name "Hispanic" refers to members of the Hispanic group who are genealogically related to one another. When we identify Hispanics we assume that they have properties in common or a "common identity," for "if there are no properties that are shared in common by all Latinos and if we cannot know what they are, then this poses a fundamental difficulty for the understanding of who we are."[29]

Now, why is the presumed fact that Hispanics have a common identity for the sake of justice so important? Here I return to my previous example about the members of the group that can trace their ancestors to a traveler of the Boston group. Let us compare "Hispanics" with a group whose common identity consists in being the genealogical "descendants of the Boston group," and ask ourselves whether the common identity of Hispanics is equally important in comparison with the common identity of the Boston group descendants. The answer is negative because there is a degree of significance in the common identity of Hispanics that is absent in the common identity of the Boston group descendants. The implication is that there is something extremely relevant about being a Hispanic.

Another illustration like the one I used in chapter three will help us to see the point. Suppose I am applying for a job in a field in which I have no previous professional experience. I am applying for a job as a publisher, but have no previous experience as one. Given my circumstance, I could be said to be a member of the group known as the "publishing novices," and have some properties in common with other members of the group. I am turned down for the job and have grounds to believe that the reason for my rejection lies in the fact that I am a member of the "publishing novices," and the hiring committee strongly preferred a member of the "publishing experts." Now suppose instead that I have grounds to believe that the reason why I was turned down for the job is because I am a Hispanic, African American or American Indian. Whereas the rejection for being a member of the "publishing novices" would not count as legal discrimination, the rejection for being a "Hispanic" certainly would be discriminatory.

The illustration allows us to see that the issue at stake is not simply the common properties of groups. Many groups have common properties, but this is irrelevant for public justice. There is something vicious about discriminating against Hispanics because there is something particularly relevant about being a Hispanic. Highlighting the connection between justice and identity, the issue is that the "common properties" of Hispanics are such that they say something extremely important about who Hispanics are. In short, Hispanic identity is essential for defining personhood. Corlett fleshes out the assumption this way: "the problems of Latino and ethnic identities fall under the more general problems of personal and/or group identity. That is, whatever turns out to make me a Latino, for instance, is part of what turns out to make me who and what I am more generally, for example, as a person."[30] So Latino identity is essential for defining personhood. Elsewhere, quoting Walzer, he sustains that "ethnic identity is important because it enables us to relate to and connect with others who are like ourselves in both experience and circumstance."[31] The implication in the latter statement is that since Latino identity is essential for defining personhood, the properties that Latinos have in common are extremely relevant.

In Corlett's view then: (i) Hispanic identity is essential for defining personhood, and thus (ii) the common identity of Hispanics is relevant.[32] But I believe this view to be flawed. The first claim says that Hispanic identity is extremely relevant because it expresses who I am. In this context, Hispanic membership presumably classifies as what I have characterized as basic membership. But the question here is whether Hispanic membership is indeed basic. My answer to this question is no, for the national identities of Hispanics are far more significant than their Hispanic membership. In fact, as I argued earlier, the apparent basicness of Hispanic membership is an epiphenomenon of national membership. If Hispanic identity is not essential for defining personhood, then claim (ii), on the relevance of Hispanic common identity, hardly follows. The implication of Hispanic membership not being basic is that it is then not possible to speak of the common identity of Hispanics in the relevant sense. The notion that Hispanics have a distinctive cluster of properties that creates a common identity in the relevant sense is false.

CONCLUSION

In this chapter I have argued that the Hispanic group does not satisfy two of the conditions of groups that endow members with basic memberships, relevant identification and differentiation. The Hispanic group does not satisfy the condition of relevant identification because the properties by which the group is identified are not those that make membership in the group basic. Members of the Hispanic group may be identified according to certain properties, but those are not properties that constitute basic membership. I argued that this is the case because the properties of basic membership among Hispanics are really national properties. Hence, I made the point that the apparent basicness of Hispanic membership is an epiphenomenon of national membership.

In turning to the second condition, differentiation, I raised the question of whether the Hispanic group has the status of discernibility. Groups that satisfy the condition of differentiation are those that have the status of discernibility, i.e., a common identity by which the group can be distinguished from other groups. Much of the discussion here focused on some of the views regarding Hispanic common identity advanced by Jorge Gracia and Angelo Corlett. I argued that Hispanics do not have the status of discernibility because they cannot be said to have a common identity that distinguishes them from other groups. Thus the conclusion is that the Hispanic group does not satisfy the condition of differentiation.

NOTES

1. Roberto Ramirez and Patricia de la Cruz, *The Hispanic Population in the United States: March 2002* (U.S. Census Bureau, June 2003), 1. The meaning of the word *heritage*, or what it means to have a certain *heritage*, is not made clear in the report. The report is alluding to the Standards for the Classification of Federal Data on Race and Ethnicity. See "Revisions to the Standards for the Classification of Federal Data on Race and Ethnicity," in *Federal Register*, vol. 62, no. 210 (Thursday, October 30, 1997, Notices, 58789).

2. A parent's nationality or heritage is irrelevant for U.S. citizenship, since the law operates under both the principle of *jus soli* and *jus sanguinis*. In principle, anyone born in the U.S. or outside the territory but from a parent who is a U.S. citizen is entitled to citizenship. Although certain restrictions apply to these principles, e.g., residency requirements for the transmission of citizenship to children born in foreign territory, they have generated little controversy, except perhaps for the question of children born in the U.S. from undocumented parents. For a discussion of citizenship acquisition, see T. Alexander Aleinikoff, "Between Principles and Politics: U.S. Citizenship Policy," in *From Migrants to Citizens: Membership in a Changing World*, eds. T. Alexander Aleinikoff and Douglas Klusmeyer (Washington D.C.: Carnegie Endowment for International Peace, 2000), 123–34.

3. The distinction between foreign-born and American-born Hispanics, or first and second generations, is crucial for surveys and reports on the general group. See, for instance, Roberto Suro and Jeffrey Passel, *The Rise of the Second Generation: Changing Patterns in Hispanic Population Growth*, Pew Hispanic Center, October 2003; *Generational Differences: Survey Brief*, Pew Hispanic Center and The Henry J. Kaiser Family Foundation, March 2004; and Roberto Suro, *Attitudes toward Immigrants and Immigration Policy: Surveys among Latinos in the U.S. and in Mexico*, Pew Hispanic Center, August 2005.

4. I made the point earlier that the Hispanic category entails in addition to Latin-American nations an implicit nation, i.e., the U.S. Hispanics are those who

either have a Latin-American nationality and reside in the U.S., whether legally or illegally, or those who are American nationals with a Latin-American background.

5. Although the point would be highly relevant in other contexts, the legal status of these Latin-American nationals in U.S. territory is of little concern for my argument here.

6. National differences have significant implications for explaining, for instance, labor-market and political participation trends for each group within the Hispanic category. These national differences also determine incorporation conditions in the U.S., and these various conditions, in turn, affect and differentiate group behavior. For a discussion on how incorporation conditions affect groups, see Alejandro Portes, "From South of the Border: Hispanic Minorities in the U.S.," in *Immigration Reconsidered: History, Sociology and Politics*, ed. Virginia Yans-McLaughlin (New York: Oxford University Press, 1990), 170–74. For another study discussing modes of incorporation and how they affect the rise of ethnic consciousness in varying groups, see Helen I. Safa, "Migration and Identity: A comparison of Puerto Rican and Cuban Migrants in the United States," in *The Hispanic Experience in the United States: Contemporary Issues and Perspectives*, eds. Edna Acosta-Belén and Barbara R. Sjostrom (New York: Praeger, 1988).

7. In addition to the national element we need to add the generational one that was pointed out above: first and second-generation Hispanics are fundamentally different. According to the survey brief *Generational Differences*, a key factor for understanding Hispanics in the nationwide *2002 National Survey of Latinos* "was how long Latinos and their families have been in the United States." The report adds that "the Hispanic population is very diverse in this regard, covering a range from recently arrived immigrants to those whose ancestors have lived in the United States for many generations," 1.

8. This problem has been a standard one in the process of identity-formation carried out by the modern state. Official designations often did not have the presumed content, and were often weaker than other memberships. In part, the success of the modern state is to have overcome this state of affairs and actually be able to subsume many memberships under one. I have already mentioned, drawing on Eugen Weber, how peasants were turned into Frenchmen. We will see other examples in the next chapter.

9. I borrow the term "epiphenomenon" here from the literature on the philosophy of mind, although the discussion and the point made proceeds on a very different terrain. In the context of the mind-body problem, the question is whether a mental event M might indeed have any causal powers. M is an epiphenomenon of some other event E, when the causal work is undertaken not by M but by the underlying event E, despite the appearance that M brings about some new event. In other words, given a causal relationship between C and C*, event M might have the appearance of causing C*, whereas C* is in fact caused by C. Borrowing terms from other bodies of literature, although having certain limitations, is also instructive. Jorge L. A. Garcia, for instance, in speaking about identities provides a "deflationary" account—a term he borrows from the philosophy of language. See "Is being Hispanic an Identity? Reflections on J. J. E Gracia's Account," *Philosophy and Social Criticism*, 27, 2 (2001): 33.

10. We observe a somewhat similar phenomenon in the relationship between subnational and national groups in some post-colonial African nations. In Rwanda and Burundi, for example, self-identification may not coincide with the official category of nationality. The Rwandan state categorizes members as Rwandan nationals, disregarding ethnic identification. The official policy since 1994 is that ethnic categories do not exist. People, however, have identified themselves as either Hutu or Tutsi—a form of identification that has fatally superseded national identification. See Peter Uvin, "On Counting, Categorizing, and Violence in Burundi and Rwanda," in *Census and Identity: The Politics of Race, Ethnicity, and Language in National Censuses*, eds. David I. Kertzer and Dominique Arel (Cambridge: Cambridge University Press, 2002), 161.

11. Jorge Gracia, *Hispanic/Latino Identity: A Philosophical Perspective* (Oxford: Blackwell, 2000). And also "The Nature of Ethnicity with Special Reference to Hispanic/Latino Identity," *Public Affairs Quarterly*, 13, 1 (1999): 25–42.

12. Gracia, *Hispanic/Latino Identity*, 46.

13. Gracia, *Hispanic/Latino Identity*, 66.

14. Gracia, "The Nature of Ethnicity," 33.

15. Gracia, "The Nature of Ethnicity," 34.

16. Gracia, "The Nature of Ethnicity," 33–36; and *Hispanic/Latino Identity*, 47–55.

17. Gracia, *Hispanic/Latino Identity*, 48.

18. The elements I mention do not mean, however, that historical descriptions are "subjective" or that descriptions do not have truth-conditions. For a discussion on these matters, see Behan McCullagh, *The Truth of History* (New York: Routledge, 1998), 13–61. For interesting discussions on the role of historical narratives in group identity, see Arthur M. Schlesinger, Jr. *The Disuniting of America: Reflections on a Multicultural Society*, rev. ed. (New York: W. W. Norton & Company, 1998), 51–77. See also Robert Fullinwider, "Patriotic History," in *Public Education in a Multicultural Society: Policy, Theory, Critique*, ed. Robert Fullinwider (Cambridge: Cambridge University Press, 1998).

19. The attribution of racial categories, for example, also provides a good example of different social sensibilities. On this point, see a helpful discussion by Lawrence Blum, *I'm Not a Racist, But . . .: The Moral Quandary of Race* (Ithaca: Cornell University Press, 2001), 98–108. For a historical study of shifting categories, comparing the U.S. and Brazilian censuses, see Melissa Nobles, *Shades of Citizenship: Race and the Census in Modern Politics* (Stanford: Stanford University Press, 2000).

20. George W. Bush. "Proclamation 7471 of September 28, 2001," in *Federal Register*, vol. 66, no. 191, Tuesday, October 2, 2001, Presidential Documents, 50097.

21. "Race and Ethnic Standards for Federal Statistics and Administrative Reporting;" otherwise known as Statistical Directive No. 15, Office of Management and Budget, May 12, 1977. As mentioned in previous discussions, the definition remains the same, but the category is now "Hispanic" or "Latino," and "Spanish Origin" could also be used. See "Revisions," 58789.

22. The proposition of membership, of course, depends on how one counts membership. If one means citizenship, only a limited set of members, excluding legal residents, in the Hispanic group will in fact be members of the American

nation. Illegal immigrants are residents but not members of the American state, although they might indeed be cultural members. For official U.S. membership policies, see Aleinikoff, "Between Principles and Politics."

23. The point I make here is similar to the one made by Kwame Anthony Appiah when he says that "sharing a common group history cannot be a *criterion* for being members of the same group, for we need something by which to identify the group in order to identify *its* history; and that something cannot, on pain of circularity, be the history of the group" (original emphasis). *The Ethics of Identity* (Princeton: Princeton University Press, 2005), 136–37.

24. This point is connected with an earlier discussion in chapter 2 on the political dimension of categorization and classification.

25. Without the sense of membership and common identity that matters, the case for Hispanics as plausible holders of group rights or subjects of legal protection is undermined. I will return to this point in the final chapter. If the Hispanic designation is "helplessly vague," then "the ascription of rights to such a fuzzy group is bound to yield erratic, inconsistent, and at times morally erratic results." Leonardo Zaibert and Elizabeth Millan-Zaibert, "Universalism, Particularism, and Group Rights," in *Hispanics/Latinos in the United States: Ethnicity, Race, and Rights*, eds. Jorge J. E. Gracia and Pablo De Greiff (New York: Routledge, 2000), 173–74.

26. Angelo Corlett, *Race, Racism and Reparations* (Ithaca: Cornell University Press, 2003).

27. "Revisions," 58782.

28. Corlett, *Race, Racism and Reparations*, 129.

29. Corlett, *Race, Racism and Reparations*, 41.

30. Corlett, *Race, Racism and Reparations*, 46.

31. Corlett, *Race, Racism and Reparations*, 128.

32. I also take these two propositions to mean that the common identity of Hispanics constitutes reasons for action—such as, for instance, showing group solidarity. See Appiah's discussion on black identity. *The Ethics of Identity*, 184–86.

9

✣

Hispanic Identity Making

In the previous chapter, I argued that the Hispanic group does not satisfy two of the conditions, relevant identification and differentiation, of groups that have the function of endowing members with relevant memberships. There is yet a third condition, intrinsic identification, according to which groups are identified from the inside. I have saved the discussion on the condition of intrinsic identification until now because this condition might be the key for understanding the potential future of the Hispanic group.

It is reasonable to say that Hispanics do not currently satisfy the condition of intrinsic identification. Given that the group cannot be identified in the relevant sense and does not have the type of difference-sensitive attributes that matter, one can expect that the question of intrinsic identification is at bottom an irrelevant one. The reason for the latter claim is that the condition of intrinsic identification builds on the other two conditions. If the two first conditions are not satisfied, then a fortiori the third one will not be satisfied either. If a group cannot be identified according to properties that make membership in such a group basic, and the group does not have the type of difference-sensitive attributes necessarily connected with basic membership, it is worthless to raise the question of whether the group can be identified from the inside. Accordingly, Hispanics cannot be said to satisfy the condition of intrinsic identification.

Nonetheless, discussing this condition is very important because, as I mentioned, such a discussion could provide one of the keys for understanding what the direction of Hispanic identity might be. The discussion might help us see how Hispanicity could become a "tipping phenomenon."

In the context of this discussion, I wish to advance the following hypothesis: a process of identification and identity making could push the Hispanic group along a line in which the group approximates the sort of entity that satisfies the conditions of relevant groups. Thus, the Hispanic group could, in effect, come closer to becoming the sort of group that endows members with basic memberships. Put differently, my conjecture is that the attempt to identify Hispanics from the outside prescribes a set of beliefs, principles and customs that may be internalized by the Hispanic group. In this process of internalization, the group could acquire the kinds of properties that endow members with basic memberships. Succinctly, Hispanic identification could foster and strengthen Hispanic identity.

In formulating my hypothesis, I will make two points. First, there is a parallel between national identity making and Hispanic identity making. Second, the American state is one of the most significant agents in the process of Hispanic identity making. Throughout the discussion of these two points, we will see that the notion of "heritage" in historical cases of national identity formation is a crucial one. I will end this chapter with a discussion addressing the view that Hispanics have a disuniting effect on American society.

HISPANIC IDENTIFICATION

A certain group of people are ostensibly identified as "Hispanics." But how is Hispanicity identified? My suggestion is that there are some very important parallels between the process by which national identities have been shaped and the way in which Hispanic identity is also being shaped. Incidentally, part of the reason why the phenomenon of Hispanic identity is so interesting is because it represents a laboratory for exploring nationalism. John Hutchinson remarks that "the European Union offers scholars of nationalism a fascinating experiment in progress."[1] The same is true about Hispanic identity.

Like national identity, Hispanic identity is the result of a process that generally has at least two core elements: first, an identity making agent, which in the case of modern nations is often a political unit; and second, basic forms of collective identity, e.g., language, myths, rituals, religion, social practices, etc.[2] The political unit represents a *top-down* direction in the emergence of Hispanic identity.[3] As we have seen in earlier discussions, there is a significant public policy dimension in the identification of Hispanics. The notion of "Hispanic" makes an appearance due to the need of the American government to identify and standardize the data on a particular population for policy purposes. As we know, the origin of the category is found in documents such as the Office of Management and

Budget Statistical Directive No. 15, released in 1977, and the Standards for the Classification of Federal Data on Race and Ethnicity, which is a revision of the standards in Directive 15. The category originally arises due to an effort of the American state to identify a segment of the American population that happens to have a particular national background or origin.[4]

But official categories, by themselves, would not be sufficient for the emergence of Hispanic identity. Thus we must turn to the other direction of the process, i.e., *bottom-up*. Certain linguistic and cultural traits would have to come together to form the basis on which Hispanic identity is built. These are the "building blocks" of identity. Without these collective forms of membership, which are sometimes generated and often shaped by political individuation, it would be impossible to have Hispanic identity as such. Thus, there are presumably certain features, e.g., language, customs, shared histories and events—and particularly for Hispanics, national origin—that would serve as the building blocks for Hispanic identity. A careful look at this process of identity formation will reveal that from the top-down direction, there is apparently a somewhat clear and distinguishable Hispanic identity. After all, it would seem that having a coherent category depends on the existence of an identifiable population. But the situation from the bottom-up direction is different. As I have insisted, Hispanics are not identifiable in the relevant sense because their identities are anchored in the robustness of nationality. If we look at the bottom-up direction of identity formation, we will realize that Hispanicity attempts to capture a set of different national identities. I have suggested that those national identities, and not Hispanicity, are the source of meaning and direction among members of the group known as "Hispanic." Thus until members of the Hispanic category see their national identities fading and, at the same time, develop a common identity as a group, top-down identification will simply put into a single category a set of disparate groups without a relevant set of common properties.

The important point in the dynamic of top-down identification, however, is that a process of identification is underway. The fact is that such a process of identification has not completely penetrated the bottom-up, and thus Hispanics are not relevantly identifiable, but top-down identification might very well lay its roots at the bottom. This situation would represent a typical case of peasants turned into Frenchmen. To restate the point in a slightly different manner, Hispanicity is currently identified from the *outside* by the American state and its governmental agencies. Nonetheless, could this form of identification be assimilated and internalized by a group of people and thus become relevant and meaningful to them? Such could certainly be the case. If this were the case, Hispanicity could then come closer to representing a primary source of meaning and direction, and being the sort of group in which membership is basic.

THE NATIONALIST IMPULSE

To imagine how the top and the bottom, or the outside and the inside, might merge, let us look at some nationalist statements that have had profound historical consequences. First, I will look at a nationalist statement that represents the romantic notion of nationhood. In his *Addresses to the German Nation*,[5] Johann Gottlieb Fichte, the seventeenth century German philosopher, argues that in order to preserve and promote the existence of the German nation a new system of education must be created. The argument that Fichte develops is based on the premise that nations are communities bound together by a certain purpose and, more importantly, a certain mission. This is, in Fichte's view, certainly true of the German nation, which is his main concern. The concern of the *Addresses* is that at some point in history the German nation saw its unity and integrity threatened and destroyed. But, according to Fichte, the German nation possesses certain features which make it original and unique, and such features are retrievable. Given the assumption of common and retrievable national features, it follows that it is necessary and possible to create a new order of things, i.e., a new system of education, to restore and further enhance the development of the German nation.[6]

In what follows, let us take a closer look at the assumption that nations have common and retrievable features. The key point for understanding this premise is that national communities have a certain *purpose* and, more importantly, a *mission*. This first point puts forth the idea that nations are communities of a certain kind. To comprehend the sense in which nations have a given purpose, we must examine what is the makeup of a nation. National communities are first of all composed of self-interested individuals —a trait not unlike that of classical liberalism, but with a particular twist. Such individuals are linked to each other in order to fulfill their particular goals and satisfy their own well-being. The satisfaction of every individual's well-being fosters the well-being of the whole. But at the same time the well-being of the whole is necessary for individuals to be able to enjoy their personal well-being. Hence nations are primarily organisms that guarantee the individual well being of each of its members. For individuals to be able to pursue their welfare they must belong to an organism that ensures the fulfillment of such a pursuit. The interests of individuals then generate a common interest.[7] Such a common interest is to create and preserve an atmosphere in which individuals may flourish and thus the purpose of a nation is to guarantee the well-being of its members.

But many organizations exist with the primary purpose of protecting the interests of their members. A labor union, for example, is a group whose objective is to safeguard the well-being of its members in the labor force and also to protect their interests. A labor union, however, is not a nation in Fichte's sense. What is it that distinguishes a group like a labor union from a nation since the purpose of both types of communities is to promote the well-being of their members? At this point, Fichte would say that a nation is not only a group with a given purpose, but also a group with a historical mission. It is here where certain cosmic considerations come into the picture.[8] A nation is a group whose origin is of a special kind and whose endurance is also eternal, i.e., nations are transcendental communities. Nations are transcendental in the sense that they came into existence long before their current members were born, and will also continue to exist long after current members are gone. The reason why there exist such transcendental communities is because individuals, in their self-interest, are not only concerned with their material well-being. According to Fichte "the natural impulse of man (. . .) is to find heaven on this earth, and to endow his daily work on earth with permanence and eternity."[9] Since individuals strive to endow their daily work with "permanence" and "eternity," it follows that the individual's well-being encompasses the need for transcendence.[10]

The way to satisfy this need for transcendence is to belong to a transcendental community. Individuals then desire to belong to a community with a long-term mission. The mission of a nation is to guarantee the well-being of its members throughout the ages. For this reason, nations have been endowed with a special divine or quasi-divine origin and will likewise persist eternally or at least for a very extensive period of time. The essential point I want to highlight in Fichte's account is that nations are far more than a mere aggregation of individuals who come together in order to mutually satisfy their self-interests and solve coordination problems. National groups are supposed to have a high degree of permanence that is bound with a sense of transcendence and mission.

I want to look now at two typically nationalist statements that have also had historical consequences. The first was written by Jules Michelet in the wake of the 1789 French Revolution; the second by Giuseppe Mazzini in 1861.

The first statement goes like this:

Like children gone stray, and lost till then, they have at length found a mother; they had been so humble as to imagine themselves Bretons, Provencaux. No, children know well that you are the sons of France; she herself tells you so; the sons of that great mother, of her who is destined, in equality, to bring forth nations.[11]

The second statement is this:

[Mazzini speaking of the person who is called to write the national history of Italy]. . . . The writer will then proceed to trace the origin of our nationality from those Sabellian tribes, dwelling, as I have said, round the ancient Amiternus; who, along with the Osque, Siculians, and Umbrians, first assumed the sacred name of Italy, and initiated the fusion of the different elements spread over the Peninsula, by planting their lance—the symbol of authority—in the valley of the Tibur, in the Campagna, and beyond.[12]

The first element to be highlighted in these two passages is that several groups are merged into one large overarching entity. So people who are formerly known as "Bretons" and "Provencaux" are now the children of *France*. Similarly, people from the former "Sabellian" tribes along with the "Osque," "Siculians," and "Umbrians" are fused into a single group comprising the people of *Italy*. Note also that there is a strong rationale for such a merger of groups. For Michelet, groups are like "children gone astray." These children have finally "found a mother" with the advent of France.

The quasi-religious motive of someone who was once lost but now finds her way home has to do with *destiny*. The lost children find themselves in that "great mother" who has a certain destiny: "in equality, to bring forth nations." One is left wondering what is meant by "bring forth nations," but for our present purposes what needs to be highlighted is the fact that France is supposed to fulfill some sort of destiny. A quick glance at the way in which the French have conducted themselves in world affairs since the eighteenth century, would certainly seem to confirm the directive of "destiny"—one may, for instance, think of the so called First (1804–1814) and Second (1852–1879) French Empires.

The rationale for Mazzini is somewhat different, since he believes that writing the national history of Italy entails tracing the moment in which diverse groups "first assumed the *sacred* name of Italy" (my italics). Mazzini is not only concerned with the possibility of different groups coming together and forming a species of alliance or consortium. It is rather that those groups altogether assume a "sacred" name. The sacredness of the name presumably stems from the fact that the community represented by the name is also sacred. In the sacred character of the community, we find the rationale for the merger. Formerly different groups are fused together because of their sacred connection.

The theme of sacredness has often made nationalist feelings very potent, like we saw in Fichte. In highlighting the quasi-religious nature that are sometimes taken on by nationalism, Smith points out that the nation,

> is invested with sacred qualities that it draws from older beliefs, sentiments, and ideals about the nature of community, territory, history, and destiny. The result is a national community of faith and belonging, a sacred communion,

every bit as potent and demanding as that sought by the ancient Jewish prophets and psalmists.[13]

The latter comment does not imply that all forms of nationalism actually have (or need to have) explicit religious overtones, such as the ones we find in Zionism or the Afrikaner movement.[14] The comment rather implies that certain religious categories can often help us "explain the scope, depth, and intensity of the feelings and loyalties that nations and nationalism so often evoke."[15] Admittedly, the path toward national unity in Italy has been slower when compared with the French—we do not, for instance, find a unified "Italy" until the twentieth century. Nevertheless, the statements of two of their respective nationalist ideologues, Michelet and Mazzini, have yielded the intended result in both groups, since they are currently stable nations.

What I have considered so far is a typical cluster of themes characteristic of nationalism. First, we have the normative principle of unity: national groups ought to have a common unity. Such a common unity often stems from the fusion of several formerly different groups—which has been, historically, the case in the emergence of many nations. But the fusion of groups as such is not necessarily a nationalist theme. Many groups might, after all, mingle with each other by means of, say, intermarriage, conquest and coercion. Similarly, one may think of unity in terms of a common alliance. But mingling or creating alliances are not necessarily the result of nationalist themes. Ernest Renan, another famous nationalist ideologue, puts it this way: "Common interests bring about trade agreements. But nationality is also partly a matter of conscious feeling; it is simultaneously body and soul; a customs union is not a homeland [une patrie]."[16]

In the nationalist framework I am discussing, the fusion, alliance and unification of groups is intended to produce strong bonds of solidarity. Now, if a nation is more than a trade union or a common alliance, these feelings of solidarity must be justified in a certain way—for instance, by appealing to a common destiny, mission or a community with a sacred character. Justification might be either retrospective or prospective. It is retrospective when the fusion of groups in the past is explained. Such an explanation often requires an exercise of selective memory or what Renan calls "forgetfulness" (l'oubli): "forgetting, I would even say historical error, is essential to the creation of a nation."[17] In contrast, we have a prospective justification when there is a call for a consolidation of national or group unity—such as the one we see in current African nations and some types of ethnic nationalism.

A question that arises here is whether this conception of nationhood is the one that motivates America's national self-understanding. To grasp my point, consider, for instance, John Stuart Mill's conception of nationhood. According to Mill:

> A portion of mankind may be said to constitute a Nationality, if they are united among themselves by common sympathies, which do not exist between them and any others—which make them cooperate with each other more willingly than with other people, desire to be under the same government, and desire that it should be government by themselves or a portion of themselves, exclusively.[18]

Notice how Mill speaks of common sympathies that unite a group of people and, at the same time, separate them from other groups. But these common sympathies are not necessarily a matter of having a common past or a common mission. The tone of the passage does not invoke collective transcendence or sacredness. Instead, an important element in the constitution of nations according to Mill is that people "desire to be under the same government, and desire that it should be government by themselves or a portion of themselves, exclusively." The consensualist and voluntarist element with regard to political association in this phrase is evident: people *desire* to be under the same government.[19] The assumption is that since members desire to be under the same government, they need to provide their consent. As Mill puts it in another passage, "the question of government ought to be decided by the governed."[20]

Now consider the Preamble of the U.S. Constitution:

> We the People of the United States, in Order to form a more perfect Union, establish Justice, insure domestic Tranquility, provide for the common defence, promote the general Welfare, and secure the Blessings of Liberty to ourselves and our Posterity, do ordain and establish this Constitution for the United States of America.[21]

Notice first the strong voluntarist element, the people ordain and establish the Constitution.[22] Additionally, notice the lack of a transcendental mission, a common past or the language of sacredness. The purpose of the Union is simply to establish justice and pursue certain common goals, domestic tranquility and defense, promotion of general welfare and protection of freedom. Although I will not pursue the point any further here, I simply point out that the conception of nationhood underlying America's national self-understanding, at least historically, seems to be different from the conception of nationhood set forth by the nationalist ideologues I discussed above.[23]

HISPANIC IDENTITY MAKING

An examination on the way in which the identification of Hispanics displays the nationalist themes I have discussed merits a complete study and is certainly well beyond the scope of the current chapter. What I wish to do now is simply to draw attention to some trends that illustrate how the identification of Hispanics is interwoven with some of the nationalist themes that have been discussed. The Hispanic category aims to identify a segment of the American population that happens to have a particular national background or origin. Beyond formal definitions, the category is also supposed to have some content. This content comes partly in the form of a "heritage" which is built to some extent on the nationalist principles I mentioned before.

Suggesting that Hispanic nationalism has the strength and vehemence of Fichte's or Mazzini's nationalism would be a terrible exaggeration. Strictly speaking, Hispanic nationalism, for the most part, does not seem to expect the birth or revival of a new nation with its own state.[24] Hispanics are well entrenched in the American nation. In addition, the full-blown nationalism discussed above has been a very intentional phenomenon. In contrast, many of those contributing to the making of the Hispanic people would probably reject any intentional attempt to engender a new group with a common identity. What I call Hispanic nationalism here is the attempt to characterize an identity group, which has the, often unintentional, consequence of engendering and consolidating a distinct group with an identity of its own. Looking at some of the nationalist themes that appear in the background will help us to understand the phenomenon of Hispanic identity making.

The presidential proclamations of the Hispanic Heritage Month will illustrate how some nationalist themes appear in the background and will also help us to understand the phenomenon of Hispanic identity making. Each year, running from September 15 to October 15, the American nation celebrates the Hispanic Heritage Month, an observance that began as a week in 1968 under the Lyndon Johnson administration and was expanded to a month in 1988. The celebration, a good example of top-down identification, is inaugurated with presidential proclamations. Some of the themes that tend to appear constantly in the proclamations are: diversity in American society, the achievements of Hispanics, and the contribution made by Hispanics and other groups to the American way of life. Along with these themes, one of the most salient features of the proclamations is that Hispanics are identified as a *community* or *people*. Interestingly, these themes are not only present in the proclamations inaugurating the Hispanic Heritage Month, but also, for instance, in the proclamations for the National African American History Month and the Asian/Pacific American Heritage Month. The standard view expressed in the presidential addresses seems to go along the following lines. There is a nation that is composed of diverse cultures or peoples, all of whom make a contribution to the American way of life. Among the set of peoples that make up American society, we find one group, namely, Hispanics.[25] Thus one can speak of the Hispanic *people*, and the Hispanic *culture* and *heritage*.

The 2000 Proclamation, for instance, states that "the vibrant Hispanic influence can be seen in all aspects of American life and culture, from distinctive cuisine to colorful festivals."[26] The 2001 Proclamation speaks of how all Americans "celebrate the vibrant Hispanic American spirit that influences our Nation's art, music, food, and faiths."[27] The 2002 Proclamation states that "the Hispanic American *community* has a long and important history of commitment to our Nation's core values, and the contributions of this *community* have helped make our country great" (my italics).[28] And the 2003 Proclamation contains the following statement: "During Hispanic American Month, I join with all Americans in recognizing the many contributions of Hispanic Americans to the United States, and in celebrating Hispanic *heritage* and *culture*" (my italics).[29] In 2004, we celebrated "the heritage, culture, spirit, and contributions of Hispanic Americans."[30] The 2005 proclamation highlights the contributions to freedom from "our Nation's Hispanic community," and asks everybody "to recognize the proud history and rich culture of Hispanic Americans."[31] Finally, the 2006 proclamation, albeit somewhat more ambiguous in its reference to Hispanics than previous ones, speaks of a "rich Hispanic culture."[32]

The claim that Hispanics are a *people* or *community* with a common *heritage* is in no way unique to the government. Although the government is a critical source for generating and legitimizing the category, the government also replicates and reinforces views originating in agencies and organizations that advocate the recognition of a Hispanic identity. An instance of those views may be seen clearly in a report released by one of the oldest agencies aiming to represent Hispanics in the United States, the National Council of La Raza[33]—which describes itself as "the largest national constituency-based Hispanic organization and the leading voice in Washington D.C. for the Hispanic community."[34] In the foreword of the report—adapted from a speech delivered by Raul Yzaguirre, former president of NCLR, to the Congressional Hispanic Caucus Institute, September 24, 2003—the current state of affairs is described in the following terms: "we are closer than ever to a national Latino *community* with a *shared past*, a *common agenda* and a *united future*" (my italics). Interestingly, as the growth of Hispanic political power is celebrated, the question is posed: "power to do what?" The answer is that "we seek power to help this nation [presumably the American nation] fulfill its destiny, to live up to its ideals, and to go beyond the sometimes too narrow definition of what it means to be an American."[35] Note the relationship between the attainment of power for a community and the task of fulfilling a national destiny. Similarly, note the way in which "heritage" is described: "we believe in the *sanctity* of the heritage of language and culture and we treasure these gifts" (my italics).[36] These themes have a clear nationalist tone. Referring back to Michelet and Mazzini, we think of destiny and communities with a sacred character.

To continue with the presidential proclamations of Hispanic Heritage Month, it is indeed acknowledged that Hispanics have diverse backgrounds and origins. Thus "the Hispanic American community is a collage of distinct groups, including people with roots in Central and South America, Mexico, the Caribbean, and Spain."[37] But by the same token, as already mentioned, Hispanics are characterized as a people who have what appears to be a common history or heritage. Let me highlight the point that the notion of a heritage has been historically vital for the existence of many nations or peoples. One of the elements constituting, in Renan's view, the "spiritual principle" of nationhood is "the shared possession of a rich legacy of memories of the past." Renan also puts it this way: "A heroic past, great figures, glory (true glory, that is) this is the social capital on which we base a national idea." An essential component of the legacy or social capital of a people is that of glorious heroes, "for our ancestors have made us who we are."[38]

With the point on the significance of heritage in mind, it is interesting to note that one of the standard sections of the proclamations is a hagiography in which the accomplishments of Hispanic figures are emphasized. One of those hagiographic sections describes the legacy of Hispanics thus:

> The achievements of today's Hispanic Americans build upon a long tradition of contributions by Hispanics in many varied fields. Before Dr. Ochoa and other Hispanic Americans began to explore the frontiers of space, Hernando de Soto and Francisco Vázquez de Coronado ventured into the vast uncharted land of the New World. A thousand years before Mario Molina calculated the effects of human actions on the atmosphere, Mayan priests accurately predicted solar and lunar eclipses. And before Oscar Hijuelos described a Cuban family's emigration to the 1940's America, Miguel de Cervantes Saavedra gave us the classic adventures of Don Quixote and Sancho Panza.[39]

One of the most striking features of this list is that it combines apparently dissimilar and unrelated figures. Some of the people described on the list are indeed American nationals: Ellen Ochoa was born in California and Oscar Hijuelos was born in New York from Cuban parents. Nevertheless, Hernando de Soto, who died in Mississippi during one of his expeditions, was born in Badajoz, modern-day Spain; and Francisco Vázquez de Coronado, who died in Mexico City, was born in Salamanca, also in modern-day Spain. Mario Molina, professor at MIT, was born in Mexico City, although I ignore whether he has become a U.S. citizen or not.

As a matter of fact, some of the figures on the list would have hardly acknowledged any affinity with each other. It is hard to imagine any degree of significant affinity between Cervantes and the Mayans. It is also hard to imagine Soto or Coronado acknowledging any noteworthy degree of affinity with the Mayans or, more broadly, natives from the New World. Similarly, Mexicans and Americans do not often think of themselves as people who belong to the same group in any pertinent sense. What I am trying to illustrate is that some of the figures mentioned on the list, if confronted with each other, would probably not have many significant characteristics in common, or recognize each other as fellow members of a relevant group. Nevertheless, having significant features in common or recognizing each other as fellow members is not essential for being included in a group of national heroes or becoming part of a nation's heritage. Think of the American heritage. A puritan settler would probably not have had much affinity with a Pequot, or have acknowledged a Pequot as a fellow member in a relevant group, e.g., a coreligionist. The situation would have been similar between a Virginian citizen and a slave from West Africa in the eighteenth century. Likewise, a Roman Catholic in colonial Maryland would not have seen someone from Congregational and Unitarian New England as a fellow member in a relevant group. We could even think not only about lack of recognition as fellow members, but also conflict across groups—the Pequot War or, most notably, the American Civil War.

But what we need to see is that all the characters mentioned so far would, in some way or another, be thought of as part of the *American* "history" or "heritage." In connection with all the disparities and even conflict among these characters, the point about "forgetfulness" made by Renan is well taken. Formerly disjointed groups and figures are now a source of American national identity. There is then an important implication in combining dissimilar and unrelated figures. Whether Cervantes and Ochoa, or the Mayans and Hijuelos, have significant degrees of affinity—or whether they all in fact equally belong to a relevant group—is not the essential point. The point at stake is that we see in the combination of these characters the crafting of a heritage. These characters ostensibly inform the lives of a community that has a "common heritage" and a "shared past."

The crafting and consolidation of such a heritage is an important element of Hispanic identity making. As I said, Renan would have put it this way: in order to apply the spiritual principle of nationhood one needs shared memories. Having a shared past is essential for identifying Hispanics as a community or a people. Identifying Hispanics as a *people* could eventually have the following result: a series of fragmented (and sometimes conflicting) identities, e.g., Mexicans, Cubans, Puerto Ricans, may become a community of solidarity, with a given heritage, subsumed under the single category of "Hispanic." As I have suggested, the American government by means of policies and celebrations is playing an important role in identifying, shaping and reinforcing the presumable heritage of a community or people designated as "Hispanic."

Although it may seem exaggerated to believe that the emergence of Hispanic identity could command the sort of loyalty that nation-states command, a possible tension may arise as Hispanic identity grows stronger. Caught between national and ethnic loyalties Hispanics might have a somewhat similar task to the one of Irish Americans at the end of the nineteenth and beginning of the twentieth centuries. In discussing the interesting phenomenon of Irish nationalism on American soil, Kerby Miller describes the situation of Irish-American nationalist elites during the first part of the twentieth century in the following way:

> Except for some extreme Irish-American nationalists, most nationalist leaders made tortuous efforts to reconcile Irish and American patriotism and to reassure the American middle class, as well as hesitant middle-class immigrants and Catholic clergy, that Irish-American nationalism was fully compatible with aspirations to respectability and assimilation.[40]

We already see a similar situation in the tension that arises between Hispanic nationalism and the view that such nationalism, and the identities developed on American soil, might undermine American unity. Samuel Huntington, for example, believes the following about Mexican immigration: "along with immigration from other Latin American countries, it is advancing Hispanization throughout America and social, linguistic, and economic practices appropriate for Anglo-Hispanic society."[41] Huntington sees this trend as a threat to the "American dream created by Anglo-Protestant society."[42] Hispanic nationalists like Raul Yzaguirre would perhaps reply that Hispanic nationalism is not only compatible with, but actually helps to "expand the *American* agenda" (my italics).[43]

IMMIGRATION AND AMERICAN IDENTITY

The growing influence of Hispanics is presumably shaping the future of American society. As mentioned, Huntington sees this trend as a threat against American national unity and American values. In a book on national identity that received a great deal of attention, *Who are We?: The Challenges to America's National Identity*, Huntington makes three claims.[44] First, Anglo-Protestant values are the core of American culture. Second, this culture is currently being eroded. And third, one of the reasons for this cultural erosion is the influence of Hispanics. It is the third claim that interests us.

According to Huntington, the reason why Latin-American immigrants, and particularly Mexicans, pose a threat to American unity and values is because of certain immigration trends. Mass immigration and lack of assimilation are not the only causes for the erosion of American identity—Huntington speaks, for instance, of the denationalization of elites—but what he calls "Hispanization" certainly plays a prominent role. People from Latin America are immigrating to the U.S. in massive numbers and are not integrating fast or efficiently enough into American mainstream culture.[45] Massive immigration might eventually cause a bifurcated American culture. Huntington believes the following:

> The high continuation of high levels of Mexican and Hispanic immigration plus the low rates of assimilation of these [Latin American] immigrants into American society and culture could eventually change America into a country of two languages, two cultures, and two peoples. This will not only transform America. It will also have deep consequences for Hispanics, who will be in America but not of it.[46]

Now consider that, as pointed out previously, people from Latin America currently have a set of fragmented national identities. As mentioned earlier, the variety of identities stems from the fact that "Hispanics see themselves more as having separate and distinct cultures based on the country of origin rather than sharing a single culture as Hispanics or Latinos."[47] Given the variety of national origins and identities, it may then be difficult to speak of "Hispanic identity" in any relevant or robust sense. Immigrants from Latin America generally see themselves not as Hispanics, but rather as Puerto Ricans, Mexicans, Argentineans, Salvadorians, etc. This point is very significant because it shows that there is currently no common or coherent Hispanic identity and culture. It may then be true that Latin-American immigrants are not integrating themselves into the American mainstream fast and efficiently enough—let us grant this point for the sake of argument. But notice that neither is there a Hispanic identity or culture. As a consequence, if Latin-American immigrants do not become part of American mainstream culture fast enough, the result will not be a parallel Hispanic culture. The result might be a set of parallel subnational cultures and identities: Mexican American, Cuban American,

Venezuelan American, Peruvian American, Brazilian American, Spanish American, etc. Huntington does distinguish between different immigrant groups, e.g., Mexicans, Cubans, etc. And, in fact, it is particularly Mexicans and Mexican Americans who are the object of his observations. In my view, however, he skews the analysis and goes wrong when he conflates different national groups from Latin America and assumes that they might have a common identity. In other words, he wrongly assumes, at times, that diverse groups have a common Hispanic identity and that this Hispanic group is the protagonist of a phenomenon he labels "Hispanization."

But now we must also consider another angle having to do with the identity making phenomenon that was discussed above. As already pointed out, members of the Hispanic group may currently have a set of fragmented national identities, but they are also a people in the making. Several agents are tapping into and shaping the emerging feelings of commonality that exist in a group still largely consisting of Latin-American immigrants. I pointed out above that among the agents of Hispanic identity making we may count, among other agents, the American state and its governmental agencies. Although unaware of the causal effect, the government is indeed a crucial agent in the engineering of Hispanic identity, and is thus helping to transform Latin-American immigrants into "Hispanics." If my perspective is right, Huntington's view of the situation is, at best, incomplete.[48] The Hispanic influence on American society—and consequently what he and others perceive as a threat to American unity and values—is more complex than what he assumes. Latin-American immigration and the presumed lack of integration into a core national culture are not the only factors contributing toward the formation of Hispanic identity. The embryonic emergence of Hispanics, and their identity, results from a process of identity making in which one of the most significant agents is the American state. If these observations are on target, the issue of Hispanic identity in American society takes on a new meaning. The question is not only how Latin-American immigration as such, or any other kind of immigration, would transform national identity, which is one of the premises Huntington is working with. The question is rather one of public philosophy in which a model of nationhood, the value of membership and national integration guide policies toward immigrant groups.[49]

CONCLUSION

In this chapter I spoke about what Hispanics could become, namely, a people with an identity. I began by observing that Hispanics do not satisfy the third condition of relevant groups, intrinsic identification. But looking at this condition might help us to understand Hispanic identity as a tipping phenomenon. In analyzing the condition of intrinsic identification, I have advanced a particular hypothesis. A process of identification and identity making may move the Hispanic group along the continuum of groups that satisfy the conditions we discussed in chapter 6. I elaborated on this hypothesis by making two points. First, we must see Hispanic identity making in the context of national identity formation. I suggested that there might be a parallel between both processes. Second, one of the most important agents (among other agents) in the identity making process of the Hispanic group is the American state. The last point has important implications for a recent discussion by Samuel Huntington on immigration and American national identity. Here, I suggested that the formation of Hispanic identity must be understood not only as an immigrant phenomenon, but also a phenomenon that is caused by the American state.

NOTES

1. John Hutchinson, "Nations and Culture," in *Understanding Nationalism*, eds. Montserrat Guibernau & John Hutchinson (Malden, MA: Polity Press, 2001), 93.

2. This is what Eric Hobsbawm calls a "proto-nation." *Nations and Nationalism since 1780: Programme, Myth, Reality* (Cambridge: Cambridge University Press, 2002[1990]), 46. See my discussion in chapter 6.

3. The political unit is not the only crucial component of the top-down dimension. One could also include lobbying organizations, intellectuals, religious organizations, the school system and particularly the media and marketing campaigns. See, for instance, Arlene Dávila, *Latinos, Inc.: The Marketing and Making of a People* (Berkley: University of California Press, 2001).

4. For a discussion on official categories and identity making, see David I. Kertzer and Dominique Arel, "Censuses, Identity Formation, and the Struggle for Political Power," in *Census and Identity: The Politics of Race, Ethnicity, and Language in National Censuses*, eds. David I. Kertzer and Dominique Arel (Cambridge: Cambridge University Press, 2002).

5. Johann Gottlieb Fichte, *Addresses to the German Nation* (New York: Harper Torchbooks, 1968).

6. I deal with a historical statement here, but for a discussion of Germany's contemporary self-image and ethnocultural model of nationhood in connection with immigration policies, see Christian Joppke, *Immigration and the Nation-State: The United States, Germany and Great Britain* (New York: Oxford University Press, 1999), 62–99.

7. It is not clear whether Fichte believes that individuals are prior to a community, or rather the community is prior to individuals. At different points he seems to make the two claims.

8. At this point Fichte's "self-interested individuals" cease to have any similarities with classical liberalism or contractualist theories.

9. *Addresses*, 113.

10. Charles Taylor aims at fulfilling the "explanatory gap" in Gellner's theory by adducing a similar point: nations are not simply the product of historical events, but part of their force is derived from the fact that they satisfy certain psychological needs and impulses. According to Taylor, nationalism satisfies a human need for dignity and recognition. "Nationalism and Modernity," in *The State of the Nation*, ed. John A. Hall (Cambridge: Cambridge University Press, 1998), 209–16.

11. Giuseppe Mazzini, "On the Unity of the Fatherland," in *Nationalism: its Meaning and History*, ed. Hans Kohn (New York: Van Nostrand Reinhold Company, 1965), 98.

12. Mazzini, "On the Unity of Italy," in *Nationalism: its Meaning and History*, 119.

13. Anthony D. Smith, *Chosen Peoples: Sacred Sources of National Identity* (New York: Oxford University Press, 2003), 23.

14. For a different kind of explanation of national or group identification, one that draws on rational choice theory, see Russell Hardin, *One for All: The Logic of Group Conflict* (Princeton: Princeton University Press, 1995).

15. Smith, *Chosen Peoples*, 15. Why is nationalism such a potent force in mobilizing people? This is the question Smith attempts to examine. His analysis focuses on the "sacred foundations" of the nation and the "relationship to the older beliefs, symbols, and rituals of traditional religions." 4. Nationalism is often cast in religious language. Renan, for instance, rejects religion as the basis of national unity and nevertheless speaks of "this sacred thing we call a people." He speaks of nations in the following terms: "a spiritual principle, originating in the profound complexities of history; it is a spiritual family, not a group determined by the configuration of the soil." See his 1882 lecture in the Sorbonne, *Qu'est-ce Qu'une Nation?/What is a Nation?* (Toronto: Tapir Press, 1996), 44–45.

16. Sorbonne, *What is a Nation?*, 43.

17. Sorbonne, *What is a Nation?*, 19.

18. John Stuart Mill, "Considerations on Representative Government," in *On Liberty and other Essays* (New York: Oxford University Press, 1991), 427.

19. For different conceptions of political belonging and their policy consequences, see Jean Hampton, "Immigration, Identity and Justice," in *Justice in Immigration*, ed. Warren A. Schwartz (New York: Cambridge University Press, 1995), 68–77. See also Christopher W. Morris, *An Essay on the Modern State* (Cambridge: Cambridge University Press, 1998), 7–8 and 255–61.

20. "Considerations," 428.

21. For a brief historical introduction and overview of the Constitution, see Richard H. Fallon, Jr., *The Dynamic Constitution: An Introduction to American Constitutional Law* (New York: Cambridge University Press, 2004), 1–10. I take this quote from the book's appendix, 278.

22. Commenting on this consensual aspect in the genesis of the nation, Akhil Reed Amar makes the following remark: "The very process by which Americans in thirteen distinct states ordained the Constitution in the late 1780s and the early 1790s confirmed that they were not a single indissolubly united people prior to the act of ordainment. But that act, along with key words in the Preamble and

companion language later in the document, put all concerned on fair notice: After ordainment, Americans from consenting states would indeed 'form a more perfect Union' that prohibited unilateral exit. Thus the establishment of 'this Constitution' was not just the world's most democratic moment, but also, in a manner of speaking, the world's largest corporate merger." *America's Constitution: A Biography* (New York: Random House, 2005), 21.

23. Although the passage I quoted from the Constitution does not mention destiny, we must think of the Manifest Destiny doctrine in the 1840s, which did indeed posit that America has a destiny with regard to expanding the boundaries of freedom. Nonetheless, I think that the general point stands. America's notion of nationhood is different from other nations. But again we also encounter difficulties here. Typically, France and the U.S. are seen as civic nations, whereas Germany and Japan are considered ethnic nations. Consider, however, that despite similarities the U.S. and France have different models of nationhood as seen in the way the two countries integrate their immigrants and address culture in the public sphere. For a comparative discussion of France's model of nationhood, see Adrian Favell, *Philosophies of Integration: Immigration and the Idea of Citizenship in France and Britain* (New York: Palgrave, 2001). For a critical discussion of civic nationhood, see Bernard Yack, "The Myth of the Civic Nation," in *Theorizing Nationalism*, ed. Ronald Beiner (Albany: State University of New York Press, 1999), 103–18.

24. I refer here to Ernest Gellner's description of nationalism. He opens his seminal study on nationalism with these words: "nationalism is primarily a political principle, which holds that the political and the national unit should be congruent." *Nations and Nationalism* (Ithaca: Cornell University Press, 1983), 1.

25. Note that the view is similar to the one found in the Standards for the Classification of Federal Data on Race and Ethnicity. See the discussion on diversity in chapter 2.

26. "Proclamation 7338 of September 14, 2000," in *Federal Register*, vol. 65, no. 182 (Tuesday, September 19, 2000, Presidential Documents, 56457).

27. "Proclamation 7471 of September 28, 2001," in *Federal Register*, vol. 66, no. 191 (Tuesday, October 2, 2001, Presidential Documents, 50097).

28. "Proclamation 7591 of September 13, 2002," in *Federal Register*, vol. 67, no. 182, (Thursday, September 19, 2002, Presidential Documents, 58955).

29. "Proclamation 7706 of September 17, 2003," in *Federal Register*, vol. 68, no. 184 (Tuesday, September 23, 2003, 55253).

30. "Proclamation 7816 of September 17, 2004," in *Federal Register*, vol. 69, no. 182 (Tuesday, September 21, 2004, 56661).

31. "Proclamation 7931 of September 16, 2005," in *Federal Register*, vol. 70, no. 182 (Wednesday, September 21, 2005, 55505).

32. *National Hispanic Heritage Month, 2006: A Proclamation by the President of the United States of America* <http://www.whitehouse.gov/news/releases/2006/09/20060914-7.html> (November 24, 2006).

33. See *State of Hispanic America: Latino Perspectives on the American Agenda*, National Council of La Raza, February 2004.

34. *State of Hispanic America*, presentation.

35. *State of Hispanic America*, iii.

36. *State of Hispanic America*, iv.
37. "Proclamation 7338," 56457.
38. *What is a Nation?*, 43.
39. "Proclamation 7220 of September 14, 1999," in *Federal Register*, vol. 64, no. 180 (Friday, September 17, 1999, Presidential Documents, 50417).
40. Kerby Miller, "Class, Culture, and Immigrant Group Identity in the United States: The Case of Irish-American Ethnicity," in *Immigration Reconsidered: History, Sociology and Politics*, ed. Virginia Yans-McLaughlin (New York: Oxford University Press, 1990), 117.
41. Samuel Huntington, *Who are We?: The Challenges to America's National Identity* (New York: Simon & Schuster, 2004), 221. Huntington's views on Hispanics are also presented in "The Hispanic Challenge," *Foreign Policy* (March/April 2004), 30–45.
42. Huntington, *Who are We?*, 256.
43. *State of Hispanic America*, iv. See the exchange between Yzaguirre and Huntington in *Foreign Policy*, May/June 2004, 4 and 90.
44. For a critical response to Huntington's views, see *The Hispanic Challenge? What We Know About Latino Immigration*, eds. Philippa Strum and Andrew Selee (Washington D.C.: Woodrow Wilson International Center for Scholars, 2004).
45. See Huntington, *Who are We?*, 221–56.
46. Huntington, *Who are We?*, 256.
47. Mollyann Brodie, Annie Steffenson, Jaime Valdez, Rebecca Levin, and Roberto Suro, *2002 National Survey of Latinos*. Report prepared by the Pew Hispanic Center and the Kaiser Family Foundation, December 2002, 33.
48. For a discussion on the incompleteness of Huntington's perspective with regard to immigration as the mechanism contributing to cultural erosion, from an economic perspective, see Christopher J. Coyne and Peter J. Boettke, *Institutions Immigration and Identity*, Global Prosperity Initiative Working Paper 61, Mercatus Center, George Mason University, 2005.
49. For a comparative discussion between models of nationhood in France and Great Britain and how they affect policies toward immigrants, see Favell, *Philosophies of Integration*.

10

✢

Are All Minorities Equally "Minorities"?

In 1915, Horace Kallen argued that democratic principles required a "federal republic" view of American society. The substance of such a republic would be "a democracy of nationalities, cooperating voluntarily and autonomously through common institutions in the enterprise of self-realization through the perfection of men according to their kinds."[1] Despite the year in which Kallen's writings were published, his views—an early version of what some people now see as "multiculturalism"—capture a contemporary thesis. Following Kallen, let us call this thesis "cultural pluralism." According to cultural pluralism, the composition of American society entails a set of ethnic or cultural minorities whose membership in their cultural groups is central to their identities.

Several assumptions underlie the thesis of cultural pluralism. The first one is that membership in cultural groups is important for individual well-being, and so if cultures are not publicly recognized, the well-being of group members will be hampered.[2] Second, borrowing from Horace Kallen's metaphor, society is like an orchestra of diverse racial and ethnic voices and they should all receive an equal hearing.[3] Several cultural groups comprise society, and justice requires that all groups should be equally recognized, which is indeed the thrust of one version of multiculturalism. Combining these two assumptions, we have a picture of equal relevance across all cultural minorities.[4] In this picture, cultural membership is important for personal well-being and so all groups should be equally recognized in order to guarantee the well-being of the members of all cultural groups. In the words of Charles Taylor: "Just as all members have equal civil rights, and equal voting rights, regardless of race or culture, so all should enjoy the presumption that their traditional culture has value."[5] Given this presumption, all groups are genuine recipients of public recognition. Cultural groups may be different from each other, but what they all have in common is that their member's well-being is tied to the group and thus all groups are equally relevant.[6]

In this chapter, I wish to challenge the picture of equal relevance across groups. The picture is that in the American plurality of cultural voices, all voices are equally significant because they all give group members meaning and direction. I will suggest that memberships in different groups have varying degrees of significance. A comparative approach between two minority groups in American society, African Americans and Hispanics, will show that when looking at the status of cultural identities among different groups, one finds varying degrees of significance. I will then question the simple view that all cultural minorities are more or less the same, i.e., groups that provide members with a meaningful identity. If my claim is true, it undermines the notion that all cultural groups are equally relevant. Thus it becomes harder to see how different groups can be grouped in a common alliance of "minorities." The claim also shows that for two of the groups included in the Standards for the Classification of Federal Data on Race and Ethnicity, the points of departure are different in terms of raisings questions about who should be included.

IS AFRICAN-AMERICAN MEMBERSHIP BASIC?

A good starting point for our inquiry is to examine whether membership in the African-American group is basic. I will suggest that African-American membership has indeed a measure of basicness for members of the group.[7] Let me begin by quickly refreshing the notion of basic membership. Membership is basic when certain traits are essential to someone's self-understanding and also make her a member in a group. What is the trait (or set of traits) that is both essential to the self-understanding of African Americans and makes them a member of a particular group? The immediate answer that comes to mind is *race*. But we must be more precise about the meaning of race and the way in which it is pertinent for relevant membership. So let me now discuss race and its meaning for group members.[8]

Looking at the way in which African Americans are identified will help us to understand the meaning of race. My question here then is: what is the criterion by which members of the African-American group are identified? The answer seems to be painfully obvious. African Americans are identified on the basis of *race*. Note, however, that race as the basis of relevant identification is bound to run into a difficulty. One could wonder whether race per se is the kind of property that is essential to the self-understanding of group members. One may wonder, for that matter, whether any biological or physical trait could in itself be essential for the self-understanding of group members. The answer seems to be negative. Consider that not all members of all cultural groups are physically identical. Group members may have some physical traits in common, but not *all* physical traits in common. For example, not everybody within a single group has the same hair color, mouth size, height, weight, etc. If a group then is to be distinctively identified on the basis of physical traits that are essential to members' self-understanding, the matter that needs examination is: why those specific traits?

In the case of African Americans, we know that they are presumably identified on the basis of a physical trait related with skin color. But we also need to know why they are identified on the basis of this particular physical trait and not a different one. Claiming that African Americans are identifiable on the basis of race per se is not enough; we also need to know why race is the basis of relevant identification. The question we are then looking for is not simply what the criterion is for identifying members of the African-American group. The criterion seems to be very simply "race." We are looking instead for the answer to two interrelated questions. First, why is a particular physical feature the criterion by which African Americans are currently identified? Second, why is the criterion by which African Americans are identified essential to the self-understanding of group members? In order to address these questions, we must turn to certain *beliefs* and *social conceptions* associated with race. These beliefs and social conceptions derive from a historical process of racial formation.

Michael Omi and Howard Winant argue that racial formation has been a prominent characteristic of political and social life in the United States of America.[9] The American social structure has a racial dimension that has become crucial for comprehending human relationships and conflicts. In this social structure, "we utilize race to provide clues about who a person is."[10] Omi and Winant at times speak about "race" in general, but it is clear that their discussion specifically revolves around African Americans. The upshot of the discussion is that the racial understanding of African Americans is a salient characteristic of American social life. According to the authors, "race" is a concept that allows us to understand the conflicts and interests that arise due to different types of human bodies. It is not, however, physical features or human bodies as such that motivate conflicts and interests; the latter arise from social and historical meanings associated with human bodies. While bodily traits are understood according to social and historical meanings, one should not assume that the concept of race is extremely ambiguous and simply arbitrary. Omi and Winant concede that the concept is indeed imprecise and vague, but that does not mean it is not useful. Accordingly, "a more effective starting point is the recognition that despite its uncertainties and contradictions, the concept of race continues to play a fundamental role in structuring and representing the social world."[11] The task of the social theorist then is to examine the phenomenon of race in American society and attempt to give a causal explanation for its existence.

The causes for the racial dimension in American society are many and very complex, but one particular source for the formation and reproduction of the African-American race has to do with political institutions.[12] Omi and Winant comment, "the state from its very inception [in American history] has been concerned with the politics of race. For most of U.S. history, the state's main objective in its racial policy has been repression and exclusion. Congress's first attempt to define American citizenship, the Naturalization Law of 1790, declared that only free 'white' immigrants could qualify."[13] And the distinction and codification of races (or rather a particular race currently classifiable as "African Americans") due to governmental policies has been a continual characteristic of American political history. The self-representation of "race" among blacks has changed throughout history, but one constant feature of American society is that the conditions and rules for racial classification and identification have been replicated due to the enactment of governmental policies.

An important implication about the concept of race is that it serves not only to classify and identify African Americans, but also to define *who they are*. By defining who they are, the category of "race" becomes an important component for the self-representation of African Americans. And although Omi and Winant do not flesh out the point this way, one can draw out the following implication from their discussion: the social and historical meanings surrounding the notion of "race" have become essential to the self-understanding of African Americans. A historical process of identification and exclusionary policies has facilitated a state of affairs in which a particular group is identified according to a physical trait defined as "race." Given the exclusion of the group on the basis of this criterion, the trait has become essential to the self-understanding of group members.[14] What I mean by this is that one of the essential traits for the self-understanding of African Americans is their skin color. An African American could not presumably conceive of and characterize herself without thinking of her skin color. This state of affairs generally makes membership in the African-American group basic.[15]

RACE AND NATIONAL IDENTITY

African Americans also belong to a national group that has traits that tend to be essential to the self-understanding of its members. I will now argue that since these national traits are essential to the self-understanding of group members, including African Americans, the national membership of African Americans is also basic. I will also point out that, for African Americans, there is sometimes tension between their racial and national memberships.

In order to understand the basicness of American national membership, let us take a closer look at American national identity. In a thought experiment similar to the ones I have discussed before, imagine someone who is raised in the United States. Such a person will most likely grow up speaking a certain language, English, pledging allegiance to a national flag and other patriotic symbols, participating in a life that is organized and ruled by a set of governmental policies, adhering to the values of freedom and justice, and developing habits of mind that create a certain degree of social cohesion. Members of the American nation belong to a community that represents a whole worldview and thus they participate in a collective story. This story talks about the Pilgrims, the Founding Fathers, the saga of Independence, the Civil War, a land of freedom that attracts immigrants from the rest of the world, etc. Now, the national story also contemplates failures and contradictions. For example, one may count as failures the fate of Indians in the hands of the English-speaking settlers, the inability in the past to incorporate, effectively and immediately, and treat fairly immigrants from certain parts of the world (e.g., Ireland, China and Japan) and, in general, the inequalities of a society presumably characterized by fairness and justice.

Chief, however, among the failures told in the national story are the incidents of *slavery* and *racism* against blacks. These incidents stand as a testimony of how a group has been constantly excluded in a land of liberty and justice for all. They also stand at the center of national landmarks, i.e., the Civil War and the Civil Rights movement, which have presumably pushed the nation forward in the struggle for liberty and justice. The point that needs highlighting is that there is a *national story* that informs the identity of a whole *community*.[16] Even some of those that have been excluded are protagonists of such a national story by virtue of the fact that they have been unjustly excluded and should now be included. Inclusion in this context means that the American nation might have a diversity of backgrounds, cultures, religions and races. Nonetheless, as a matter of principle, all those groups ought to be equally recognized and have equal participation in a community that is a national unit. There is an overarching national story for a single community subsumed under a particular state.

The importance of this national community is that it represents a primary source of meaning and direction for most of its members. Membership in the American nation is central to the identity of most members, which means that the traits associated with membership in this particular group are essential to the self-understanding of group members. These members belong to a national community with a certain history and a set of practices and values that give meaning and direction, in a very vivid manner, to their lives. Now consider that African Americans are part of the American nation, which has implications for the national identity of African Americans. African Americans belong to a national community characterized by traits that are essential to the self-understanding of group members (e.g., language, history, values, etc.). Since African Americans are members in this national community, some of these national traits are presumably essential to the self-understandings of members. Thus the national membership of African Americans would seem to be basic.

At this point, however, several complications arise with regard to the status of African-American membership in the American nation. First, if we posit that basic membership entails essential traits that are essential to someone's self-understanding, and that the person is a member of a particular group, we would immediately see how the second condition of basic membership becomes problematic. African Americans might indeed have traits, essential to their self-understanding, that are associated with the American nation; but African Americans have been excluded or qualified members of the American nation. Now the picture gets more complicated if we consider how intertwined African-American history is with American history, making the first group part of the second one. Let us here remember that, as I argued earlier, membership in the African-American group has, for historical reasons, a measure of basicness. Thus African Americans possess two basic memberships: national and racial memberships. Keeping this dual membership in mind, consider the following situation: African Americans have been excluded and unassimilated members of the American nation for much of its history. As a consequence, there is tension between basic memberships that arises from the fact that African-American assimilation into the American mainstream has not been, for multiple and complex reasons, fully successful—a fact that is, according to Nathan Glazer, the driving force behind contemporary American multiculturalism.[17] The tension between national and racial memberships is perceptively pointed out by W. E. B. Du Bois. He expresses the tension this way: "one ever feels his twoness, —An American, a Negro; two souls, two thoughts, two unreconciled strivings; two warring ideals in one dark body, whose dogged strength alone keeps it from being torn asunder."[18] In conclusion, then, the national membership of African Americans, in conjunction with their racial membership, is basic. Given, however, historical circumstances of racial exclusion there has been, for African Americans, a salient tension between their American national identity and African-American membership.

HISPANICS AND AFRICAN AMERICANS

I have discussed African-American membership to this point. It is now time to compare African Americans with another group that has often been thought of as being analogous with African Americans, i.e., Hispanics. In comparing both groups, I will argue that three compelling reasons show significant differences for purposes of minority recognition in American society between African Americans and Hispanics.[19] All three reasons are closely interrelated with each other, but I will discuss them separately for the sake of clarity.

The first reason for distinguishing the groups has to do with the various basic memberships of both African Americans and Hispanics. A closer look at their basic memberships will be the point of departure for our discussion. My goal is to show several important differences that have vital implications for the relevance and public recognition of the groups. Let me begin by pointing out that the national memberships of both African Americans and Hispanics are generally basic, although complications about the membership status arise.[20] I argued in chapter 7 that the national membership of Hispanics is basic; and I also argued in the previous section of the current chapter that the national membership of African Americans is basic. In this regard, both groups are apparently similar. Note, however, that whereas there is a tension between the national and racial memberships of African Americans, which are both basic, there is no similar tension among Hispanics. I argued earlier that national membership is basic for most Hispanics, but their Hispanic membership is not generally basic—given that Hispanicity is defined in terms of nationality and the latter is trumped by the strength of national identities. Using the notion of epiphenomenon, I argued that the traits that are essential to someone's self-understanding and also seem to make such a person a member of the Hispanic group are really national traits. As a consequence, Hispanic membership is not basic and its apparent basicness is really a manifestation of the national factor. The result is that given the weakness of Hispanic membership, it is not basic and hence could not come close to competing with national basic memberships. So, unlike African Americans, there is no tension between national and Hispanic memberships.

I have spoken about the tension of two basic memberships among African Americans and also the lack of a similar tension among Hispanics. Let me turn here to the following question for a moment: Why is there no tension between basic memberships among Hispanics? Part of the answer to this question has already been mentioned: Hispanic membership is currently an epiphenomenon of national membership. But there is also more to be said. The process of identity making that I previously discussed, in chapter 9 for Hispanics and the current chapter for African Americans, will also reveal part of the answer to our question. Here we must remember that Hispanics and African Americans are to a certain extent the by-product of an identity-making process. In this process, African-American identity has developed a level of significance that is lacking with respect to Hispanic identity. In the context of the work of Omi and Winant, I suggested that the criterion of race has served to identify African Americans and has become essential to their self-understanding. A social and historical process of racial formation linked with governmental policies has brought about such a situation.

The historical and social process that has engendered and shaped the racial identity of African Americans has been absent with respect to Hispanics until recently. The latter is obvious, since (as we will see in more detail below) African Americans have been part of American national life, one way or another, for centuries, whereas Hispanics did not start making a highly visible and significant nationwide appearance until the 1960s.[21] Nonetheless, as I have also pointed out, the identity-making role of the American state with regard to Hispanics may change (and is currently changing) the significance of Hispanic membership. At this point in time, however, the fact is that there is a tension between basic memberships among African Americans that is absent among Hispanics. This is the first important difference between the two groups.

Let me now go back for a moment to the claim that both groups are similar in that national membership is basic in both groups. This is indeed true, but here the following question must be raised: When looking at the national memberships of both African Americans and Hispanics, which *national* membership is basic? An attempt to answer this question will have us turn to the other two reasons that show why both groups are significantly different for purposes of public recognition in American society.

African Americans are full members of the American polity. This should be an obvious fact, but it is often taken for granted. Understanding this fact will allow us to see a very important quality that distinguishes African Americans from many members of the Hispanic group. Assertions about the membership of African Americans in the American state must be immediately qualified because African Americans have not always had access to the social and political goods available to the rest of American society. So, as I have mentioned, African Americans have been "excluded members" or "barred citizens" of a political community, which is indeed, as we have seen, a condition that raises difficulties in analyzing African-American membership. The fact of the matter, however, is that African Americans are currently full members of the American political community. Even if this claim is contested, it is necessary to acknowledge that if African Americans are not, in fact, full members of the political community, it is clear that they *ought to be*. The fact that they have not been full members throughout American history is regarded as an evil that ought to be corrected. So either African Americans are currently, in fact, full members, or ought to have potentially full membership in the American polity.

In order to illustrate what I mean by full membership, let us look more closely at the status and implications of citizenship. The American citizenship of African Americans is normally clear and unproblematic. Given the full recognition by the Constitution in, say, the Fourteenth Amendment,[22] and that African Americans are not, for the most part, Ghanaian, Nigerian, Gambian or Malawian citizens, it follows that their American citizenship is unquestionable.[23] African Americans are not commonly recognized as subjects of particular African states, meaning that they are not entitled to the rights or liable to the duties of other citizens belonging to African states.[24] For example, African Americans are not entitled to vote in Rwanda, and are not obligated to pay taxes in Ethiopia or defend the Nigerian state. In contrast, African Americans possess rights recognized by the American state—not always recognized, but again this is part of the African-American struggle—and also have duties toward the American state, manifested, for example, in the obligation to pay taxes and defend the American territory. The fact that the citizenship of African Americans is unquestionable, showing that they are full members of the American state, should be obvious in one of the hyphenated terms that currently describes them, namely, African *Americans*.

One may observe at this time that some African Americans are immigrants. For example, Jamaicans, Haitians and black South Africans who migrate to the United States are likely to be classified as "African Americans." This might be true, but when we refer to African Americans we do not normally think of an *immigrant* group. We refer instead to a group that has been on American soil for many generations. The ancestors of African Americans were brought to the United States against their will as slaves, but the fact remains than since then several generations have gone by. Thus African Americans are a stable and well-established group in the fabric of American society and are also (or ought to be) full members of the American polity.

In describing the African-American condition, let us say, "all members of the African-American category are also members of the American state." To repeat, there might be some exceptions, e.g., black Jamaicans, but they are largely minimal and irrelevant for our discussion. Let us now turn to Hispanics. If we take the same statement and apply it to Hispanics, "all members of the Hispanic category are also members of the American state," we will immediately detect the falsity of such a statement. Surely, a more accurate statement is that "*not* all members of the Hispanic category are also members of the American state." The political membership of Hispanics, in contrast with African Americans, is problematic in that not all Hispanics are, in fact, members of the American polity.[25]

Roughly speaking, a Hispanic, from a taxonomical point of view, may be someone who (a) is born in a Latin-American country and migrates to the U.S., (b) Someone who is born in the U.S., and is thus an American citizen, from Latin-American parents or, at least, ancestry. By the same token, one may break down (a) into other two groups: (a.1) those who have the intention of returning to their original Latin-American countries, and (a.2) those who have the intention of getting permanently settled in the U.S.

We could continue refining these two groups. If (a.1), two other groups are possible: (a.1.1) those who are recognized by the American state by some type of guest worker or nonimmigrant visa, and (a.1.2) those who are not recognized by the American state, i.e., illegal immigrants. If (a.2), then two possibilities: (a.2.1) those who have already been admitted as permanent residents and (a.2.2) people aspiring to become permanent residents—some members of (a.1). One could continue refining the taxonomy, but we have enough detail for illustrating our claim that not all members of the Hispanic group are also members of the American polity. Clearly, some members of the group known as "Hispanics" are also members of the American state, whereas others are not. For instance, not all Hispanics are American citizens, or even legal residents. Among the latter group, i.e., illegal aliens, some have the *intention* of becoming members of the American state, whereas others do not. Additionally, among those intending to become members of the American state some have the *possibility* of doing so, whereas this is not true for others. In conclusion, while the political membership of African Americans is unproblematic, the political membership of Hispanics in the American state is highly problematic. It is just not possible to generally assume that Hispanics are, or ought to be necessarily, members of the American polity.

I have said that, in contrast with Hispanics, we should assume that African Americans ought to be members of the American polity. I take it that this is simply, under the current state of affairs, an uncontroversial statement. But let us now wonder: why should it be assumed that African Americans ought to be members of the American polity, whereas the same cannot be assumed with regard to Hispanics? The answer to this question will show a third significant difference between the two groups. It is necessary to look at the self-image of the American community. As I said in an earlier discussion, communities, not least, national communities, have a certain narrative. This narrative consists of a story that often includes many of the traits that are essential to the self-understanding of community members. As suggested earlier, African Americans stand at the center of the American national story. And in a certain sense the particular story of African Americans can be seen as a struggle of many generations for greater participation and full recognition in the larger national community. The point is that the history of African Americans is embedded in the history of the American nation. Now compare Hispanics and African Americans. The contrast we will notice is that while we may take it for granted that African Americans are part of the American national story and experience, the same is not true about Hispanics. I suggested that African-American history is embedded in American history, but note that Hispanic history is not—at least not to the same extent. It is perfectly possible to appreciate the American national story, encompassing its history from colonial times, without any reference to Hispanics, whereas it is virtually impossible to comprehend the national story without references to slavery, the Civil War, the Civil Rights movement, art forms such as Jazz, Blues and Rock 'n' Roll, etc. In short, it is almost inconceivable to tell an American national story that does not have any reference to those members classified under the category of black or African American.

One may reply, of course, that the American national story could contemplate events like the purchase of what is now New Mexico, the Mexican-American war, the Spanish war, etc. But two observations must be made. First, those events have not been essential for the shaping of the American national story; they are indeed important events, but they are not at the center of the story reflecting the American self-image. Second, and most importantly, those events, and generally speaking, events entailing exchanges with Latin-American countries, belong to the history of American *foreign* relations and not the *national* story. An important implication derived from the latter point is that Hispanics are originally "foreigners," i.e., people from a foreign land who migrate to the U.S. Accordingly, historically speaking, Hispanics are perceived as a subset of the category of "immigrants;" a category that implies the insertion of an outside group into American society. Thus, Hispanics have some affinity with Italians, Poles, Irish, and Koreans, all national outsiders who migrated to the U.S. It is true that "immigration" is an essential component of the American national story—America is thought of as "a nation of immigrants"—but Hispanics are only a subset of such a component. One could perfectly well understand immigration without including Hispanics—and including instead other groups such as Indonesians or French Canadians. The central point is that although immigration is essential for understanding the American self-image, the particular immigration of people from Latin-American countries—now Hispanics in the U.S.—is not. As a consequence, Hispanics are not essential to the national story and hence whether Hispanics are American nationals or not is irrelevant. In contrast, African Americans are intrinsic to the national story and are thus necessarily an element of the American national self-image. The difference between the two groups in the American self-image is an important one. This difference shows that one group is central whereas the other is peripheral to the American self-image. The difference between center and periphery also answers the question of why African Americans ought to be full members of the American policy, whereas this is not necessarily the current case with Hispanics.

DIFFERENT QUESTIONS, DIFFERENT SCENARIOS

I set out to question the simple view that all cultural minorities are more or less the same, i.e., groups that provide members with a meaningful identity. Questioning this simple view implies challenging the perception of equal relevance across groups. For all groups to be equally relevant they would have to be analogous. What is the analogy between African Americans and Hispanics—the two largest minorities in American society? It can be inferred from my previous discussion that, given the differences between both groups, not much can be said to answer this question persuasively.

Now how do the differences I have described above come up in issues of public recognition?[26] Addressing this question will allow us to see more clearly the trouble with the view that Hispanic and African-American identity are similarly relevant because they entail an equally significant degree of identity. I have claimed that African-American membership is basic, whereas Hispanic membership is not. If this claim is right, then one could suggest that two separate issues arise with respect to the public recognition, starting with but also perhaps extending beyond classification, of African-American and Hispanic identities in American society.

Since African-American membership is basic, the issue is whether African-American identity *ought* to be publicly recognized or not. One possibility here is to simply assume that either a tension may emerge between racial and national identities, or that national integration should require the public recognition of meaningful identities.[27] Another possibility is to argue that we desire a "color-blind" society and thus, in order to achieve a state of color-blind equality, we must seek to reverse or minimize the social and political mechanisms—including official classification—that have created and continue to reproduce racial consciousness.[28] The question here of course is whether, given the current significance of racial consciousness, such a reversal would be feasible without causing unacceptable degrees of social disturbance. The issue, at any rate, is this: given the basicness of African-American membership, should it be publicly recognized or not?

Since Hispanic membership is not basic, the issue of public recognition is altogether different. I pointed out in chapter 9 that, by recognizing "Hispanic identity," the American political apparatus is fostering an identity-making process. The end result of this process could be the creation of an identity and membership that may indeed come closer to becoming basic.[29] The issue is whether Hispanic identity ought to be recognized so that Hispanic membership increases any degree of basicness. Several alternatives arise with respect to the recognition of Hispanic identity. One may point out that the identity-making process is undesirable, since it will only bring further social fragmentation. According to a different alternative, the identity-making process is what the American pluralistic ideal is all about: welcoming foreigners that become hyphenated Americans. According to this last alternative, the identity-making process is harmless because, despite the fact that Hispanic membership could eventually have some degree of basicness, such an identity will not ultimately undermine American national unity. One could also acknowledge that, one way or the other, the identity-making process is irreversible—due not only to state policies, but also massive migration, interest-group organizations such as The National Council of La Raza and the League of United Latin American Citizens, and a powerful Spanish-speaking media. Given the irreversibility of the process, American society should do its best to accommodate the new internal ethnic identity.

It is important to point out here that even if one believes that the identity-making process of Hispanics is desirable or irreversible, the distinction between different members in the Hispanic group must be kept clear. The distinction, for instance, between a Hispanic who is an American citizen and a Hispanic who is an illegal immigrant is important because otherwise it will be unnecessarily difficult to address the question of Hispanic public recognition in American society. The issue of public recognition is obviously geared toward full members of American society. The issue does not have to do with the public recognition of foreigners or nonimmigrants visiting the U.S. The matter at stake is not recognizing cultures in Turkey or France, or even cultures of Turkish and French visitors to the U.S. The matter is rather related to members of the American polity, which excludes visitors and illegal aliens. Confining the question of public recognition to American nationals reinforces my point about the difference between the African-American and Hispanic situations. If we isolate *national* members, one could perhaps make a plausible case for the recognition of African Americans, whereas the case for Hispanic recognition would be far more complicated. Since, as we saw above, all African Americans are members of the American polity, the African-American community as a whole is entitled to the question of public recognition. But since, as we saw above, as well, not all members of the Hispanic category are also members of the American state, the issue of cultural recognition does not apply to all Hispanics. It would only apply to those members of the Hispanic category that are also members of the American state. The point that needs highlighting, at any rate, is that the problem of public recognition with respect to African Americans and Hispanics is crucially different. Both situations must be addressed by raising two different sets of questions and looking at separate scenarios. This state of affairs breaks the apparent analogy between both groups.[30]

CONCLUSION

In this chapter I have compared African Americans and Hispanics. The purpose of the comparison is to show that not all cultural minorities in American society are equally relevant. I began by establishing that given a historical process of racial formation, the racial membership of African Americans is basic. But the American national membership of African Americans is also basic. Hence, for African Americans, there are, at least, two basic memberships, racial and national, which due to historical circumstances of social and political exclusion, could be in tension with each other. I then compared African Americans with Hispanics and argued that there are several reasons why both groups are significantly different for purposes of relevance and public recognition in American society. At the end, my suggestion revolves around a simple point. Instead of claiming that American society consists of a plurality of voices, all of which are equally entitled to public recognition, we should take one voice at a time and ponder whether such a voice does indeed have the merits for public recognition.

NOTES

1. Horace Kallen, *Culture and Democracy in the United States: Studies in the Group Psychology of the American Peoples* (New York: Arno Press, 1970), 124. Most recently, an explicit version of this "cultural pluralism" has been proposed by Michael Walzer in *What it Means to Be an American: Essays on the American Experience* (New York, Marsilio, 1996), 23–49.

2. See Judith Lichtenberg on the "flourishing argument." "Nationalism, For and (Mainly) Against," in *The Morality of Nationalism*, eds. Robert McKim and Jeff McMahan (New York: Oxford University Press, 1997), 160–62.

3. Kallen, *Culture and Democracy in the United States*, 104 and 124–25.

4. David Miller describes this point as one of the premises in the politics of recognition: "groups should participate in the political realm *on an equal basis*, and should be encouraged to affirm their distinct identities and perspectives in the

course of doing so" (my emphasis). "Group Identities, National Identities and Democratic Politics," in *Citizenship and National Identity* (Cambridge: Polity Press, 2000), 63–64.

5. "The Politics of Recognition," in *Multiculturalism: Examining the Politics of Recognition*, ed. Amy Gutmann (New Jersey: Princeton University Press, 1994), 68.

6. Kwame Anthony Appiah comments that the potential value of multicultural education lies in creating a common loyalty and mutual understanding in a pluralist society. He claims, for example, "once I consciously grasp [. . .] the significance and value of my identity for me, I can see what the significance and value of their collective identities would be for others." "Culture, Subculture, Multiculturalism: Educational Options," in *Public Education in a Multicultural Society: Policy, Theory, Critique*, ed. Robert Fullinwider (New York: Cambridge University Press, 1998), 85. The assumption in the claim is that all acknowledged identities play a similar role in all respective groups. For an updated discussion of Appiah's views, see his *The Ethics of Identity* (Princeton: Princeton University Press, 2005).

7. Attempts have been made to show that blacks ought to be committed to principles of group solidarity without necessitating black identity. Whether there exists "black" identity or not, and what its features are, is not a topic I am concerned with. My claim is simply that given a process of racial differentiation a particular physical trait has become essential to the self-understandings of members in the group known as African Americans. See Tommie Shelby, *We Who Are Dark: The Philosophical Foundations of Black Solidarity* (Cambridge, MA: Harvard University Press, 2005).

8. Although I do not address it directly, Anthony Appiah's discussion and analysis of "race" has been very helpful. See his "Race, Culture, Identity: Misunderstood Connections," in *Color Conscious: The Political Morality of Race*, eds. K. Anthony Appiah and Amy Gutmann (Princeton: Princeton University Press, 1996), 30–43

9. Michael Omi and Howard Winant, *Racial Formation in the United States: From the 1960s to the 1990s*, sec. ed. (New York: Routledge, 1994).

10. Omi and Winant, *Racial Formation*, 59.

11. Omi and Winant, *Racial Formation*, 55.

12. I focus, following Omi and Winant, primarily on the shaping force of political institutions. But other institutions, for example religion and media, are also very important for shaping group identity. For an interesting study on the role of religion in African-American identity, see Eddie Glaude "Myth and African-American Self-identity," in *Religion and the Creation of Race and Ethnicity: An Introduction*, ed. Craig R. Prentiss (New York: New York University Press, 2003).

13. Omi and Winant, *Racial Formation*, 81. It is not exactly clear what the authors mean by the "state," but we can ignore this point without undermining the broader discussion.

14. This state of affairs gives group members reasons for actions in the form of "because I am an L, I should do X." Appiah, *The Ethics of Identity*, 184.

15. For an interesting discussion, from a social science perspective, on the elements and implications of racial identity and solidarity among African Americans,

see Paul Sniderman and Thomas Piazza, *Black Pride and Black Prejudice* (Princeton: Princeton University Press, 2002), 11–60.

16. For the role of collective histories and narratives, see Robert Fullinwider, "Patriotic History," in *Public Education in a Multicultural Society*, 205. See also Jonathan Glover, "Nations, Identity and Conflict," in *The Morality of Nationalism*, 23–25.

17. Nathan Glazer, *We Are All Multiculturalists Now* (Cambridge, MA: Harvard University Press, 1997), 78–121.

18. W. E. B. DuBois, *The Souls of Black Folk* (New York: Bantam Books, 1989[1903]), 3.

19. Even if the claim that Hispanics are a racialized or partially racialized group were true, the differences between both groups would still be evident due to the reasons I discuss next. See Linda Martin Alcoff, "Is Latina/o Identity a Racial Identity?" in *Hispanics/Latinos in the United States: Ethnicity, Race, and Rights*, eds. Jorge J.E. Gracia and Pablo De Greiff (New York: Routledge, 2000); and Lawrence Blum, *I'm Not a Racist, But . . .: The Moral Quandary of Race* (Ithaca: Cornell University Press, 2001), 149–55.

20. These complications, incidentally, apply not only to African Americans in the U.S. Other members in Latin–American nations have also had a second-class status. Indigenous groups in places like Mexico, Peru and Bolivia come to mind.

21. "Hispanos" and Mexican Americans have a long historical tradition in the Southwest of the U.S.

22. The Fourteenth Amendment, enacted in 1868 after the Civil War, dictates "all persons born or naturalized in the United States, and subject to the jurisdiction thereof, are citizens of the United States and of the State wherein they reside." It also adds what have become known as the Due Process and Equal Protection clauses. "No State shall make or enforce any laws which shall abridge the privileges or immunities of citizens of the United States; nor shall any State deprive any person of life, liberty, or property, without due process of law; nor deny any person within its jurisdiction the equal protection of the law." For an introduction to these clauses see Richard H. Fallon, Jr. *The Dynamic Constitution: An Introduction to American Constitutional Law* (New York: Cambridge University Press, 2004), 91–137. I quote the Constitution from his book.

23. Given the 1997 revision of the federal standards, the African-American category may include black people with other nationalities, e.g., Jamaicans. Nonetheless, as I will point out below, this development is a recent one and the fact remains that, unlike other groups in the federal standards, African Americans are not, for the most part, an immigrant group—a state of affairs that could indeed change in the future. See the discussion on African Americans in chapter 3; see also "Recommendations from the Interagency Committee for the Review of the Racial and Ethnic Standards to the Office of Management and Budget Concerning Changes to the Standards for the Classification of Federal Data on Race and Ethnicity," in *Federal Register*, vol. 62, no. 131 (Thursday, Wednesday, July 9, 1997, 36929).

24. Let me reinforce the point that this expectation is one of the most prominent characteristics of modern states. In characterizing modern states, Chistopher W. Morris puts the point this way: "Members of a state are the subjects of its laws and

have a general obligation to obey by virtue of their membership." Chistopher W. Morris, *An Essay on the Modern State* (New York: Cambridge University Press, 2002), 46.

25. As I have pointed out before, we must distinguish several senses of membership here. Who is a member? One will have different sets depending on the criteria, e.g., citizenship or legal residence. I speak here of political membership, by which I mean citizenship—the type of membership that entitles people to all the rights accorded by the American state, e.g., the right to vote. For distinctions on memberships and their different rights, I have relied on T. Alexander Aleinikoff, "Between Principles and Politics: U.S. Citizenship Policy," in *From Migrants to Citizens: Membership in a Changing World*, eds. T. Alexander Aleinikoff and Douglas Klusmeyer (Washington D.C.: Carnegie Endowment for International Peace, 2000).

26. I raise this question under the assumption that recognition would intentionally proceed on the grounds of identity. Since I have argued that the presumption of relevant membership is implicit in official classifications, it is not clear that the U.S. would want to recognize groups based simply on the motive of identity. As I have pointed out previously, when I speak of recognition I generally refer to any type of governmental action that highlights and acknowledges particular groups and members in a public way, which does not necessarily require an explicit stance on the significance of identity. I will return to the grounds for classification and recognition in the next chapter.

27. Based on principles of justice, and not necessarily identity-recognition as such, Will Kymlicka comments that ethnoconscious policies are necessary for the sake of integration. So even if the final goal is a color–blind society, "a degree of short-term separateness and colourconsciousness is needed to achieve the long-term goal of an integrated and color-blind society." Will Kymlicka, *Politics in the Vernacular: Nationalism, Multiculturalism and Citizenship* (New York: Oxford University Press, 2001), 184. Justice Sandra Day O'Connor has expressed a similar view in *Grutter v. Bollinger* 539 U.S. 306, 343 (2003).

28. Fears of creating and perpetuating this kind of consciousness is exactly what has prevented the French government from using official ethnoracial classifications in censuses and public documents, although this measure has generated a great deal of controversy. For an overview of the arguments for and against this kind of classification in France, see Alain Blum, "Resistance to Identity Categorization in France," in *Census and Identity: The Politics of Race, Ethnicity, and Language in National Censuses*, eds. David I. Kertzer and Dominique Arel (Cambridge: Cambridge University Press, 2002), 130–42.

29. Inasmuch as policies of identity-recognition can be regarded in some sense part of "multiculturalism" the question would also be whether a self-perpetuating identity that is generated by the very act of public recognition is desirable. Brian Barry comments "multiculturalism actually creates the reality which is then, in a circular process of self-reinforcement, appealed to as a justification for a further extension of multiculturalist policies." Brian Barry, *Culture and Equality: An Egalitarian Critique of Multiculturalism* (Cambridge, MA: Harvard University Press, 2002), 315.

30. Beyond all the differences I have described, the larger problem that needs to be addressed is that of "two nations" separated along racial lines—black-white—that have a long history and are deeply entrenched in American society. According to Nathan Glazer: "The two nations for our America are the black and the white, and increasingly, as Hispanics and Asians become less different from whites from the point of view of residence, income, occupation, and political attitudes, the two nations become the black and the others." Glazer, *We Are All Multiculturalists Now*, 149.

11

✢

Government, Classification and the Recognition of Hispanics

DO HISPANICS NEED RECOGNITION?

I began my query with the question of why the federal government would want to classify and recognize racial and ethnic groups. Two reasons can be adduced to answer this question. First, the government aims to produce accurate demographic profiles. I argued that this objective is guided by what I called the principle of diversity, i.e., the notion that the general population from which data is collected consists of subgroups and that such a state of affairs is a good. Second, the federal government collects data for purposes of civil rights monitoring and enforcement. I argued, however, that these two reasons provide an incomplete governmental justification for the task of ethnoracial categorization and datacollection. For a full justification, we need to turn to what I called the presumption of relevant membership, i.e., membership in a particular group is central to members' identities. My claim was that this presumption is necessary for understanding the government's interest in collecting ethnoracial data. I suggested that this presumption creates a connection between identity politics and classification in which, in fact, the government aims to recognize citizen's identities.

Focusing on the presumption of relevant membership, I then raised the question of whether membership in the Hispanic group is indeed relevant to group members' identities. My answer has been negative. I have made two claims. Hispanic membership is non-basic, which means that the traits that are essential to the self-understanding of group members do not generally make people members of the Hispanic group—but rather members of national groups. A second and closely related claim was that the Hispanic group does not satisfy the conditions of groups in which membership is basic; such conditions are satisfied by national groups instead. My view then is that, in terms of basic membership, Hispanicity is an epiphenomenon of nationality. Although I also suggested in chapter 9 that Hispanic identity making could transform and increase the significance of membership in the group.

Let us now return to the question of why the government would want to classify and recognize certain groups and query whether the Hispanic group merits this sort of governmental recognition. Inclusion of the Hispanic category in the Standards for the Classification of Federal Data on Race and Ethnicity can proceed on three grounds:

(a) Interest in demographic profile guided by the principle of diversity
(b) Civil rights monitoring and enforcement toward the Hispanic group
(c) Identity recognition of ethnoracial group members

To approach the question at hand we need a point of clarification. Querying whether Hispanics, or any group, ought to be included in the federal standards presupposes another question. Are all the three grounds mentioned above a legitimate function of governments? With the exception of civil rights monitoring and enforcement, under some circumstances, I do not think that it is immediately obvious whether a legitimate governmental function is to classify people on the grounds of producing diverse demographic profiles or to recognize identity groups. I will not, however, argue the point here—although I will raise the point again and offer some insights at the end of the chapter. Let us assume, for the sake of argument, that all three grounds are legitimate. The federal standards themselves explicitly assume that the first two grounds, demographic profiles and civil rights considerations, are legitimate functions. Indeed, as we have seen, the very formulation of the federal standards for ethnoracial classification is based on these two grounds. With regard to the third element, identity recognition, the standards assume implicitly that this may indeed be a legitimate governmental function, but neither the function nor the assumption that it may be legitimate is made explicit in the document. As we have seen, the standards operate on the presumption of relevant membership, but the presumption is not stated explicitly.

Granting then that the three grounds for classification stated above are related to legitimate functions, are there good reasons for including the Hispanic category in the federal standards? Let us look first at the interest in demographic profiles guided by the principle of diversity. In chapter 2, I suggested that the principle of diversity entails two points. First, the task of classification and data gathering assumes differential qualities of population subgroups. Second, this condition of differentiation is a good. Nonetheless, how do we know which form of group diversity is a good? Many kinds of diversities may be a good, but the answer to the previous question is manifestly grounded on the ethnoracial criterion. But now another set of questions arise: of all the possible criteria for group differentiation and diversity, why the ethnoracial criterion? Given that the federal standards put forward the ethnoracial criterion, how do we know that ethnoracial diversity is a good?

As I pointed out in chapter 2, the criterion for determining the differential group qualities that should count is based on a political decision. And this decision on group classification is, in turn, dependent on previous beliefs and criteria that determine who does and should count. The answer then to the question of why ethn-racial diversity is a good cannot be answered without looking at the beliefs about ethnoracial groups that motivate the decision to classify members that belong to these types of groups. These beliefs, I have argued, emerge in the presumption of relevant membership. It would then seem that in order to look at the first possible grounds for including the Hispanic category in the federal standards, we would have to turn to the third element, i.e., identity recognition. So whether the demographic profile of diverse population groups of a certain kind justifies the presence of Hispanics in the federal standards depends on identity considerations.

We also know that diversity of a certain kind is not the only reason for the task of ethnoracial classification. I suggested that a second, and in many ways more important, reason has to do with civil rights. But here we would need a significant distinction. I argued in chapter 3 that the extension consisting of Hispanic group members who have suffered discrimination is not equal with the extension of the group at large. The discrepancy between group extensions characterizes other groups in the federal standards as well, e.g., Asians and American Indians. In the specific case of Hispanics, we may indeed find subsets of the Hispanic group that, under some circumstances, have suffered systematic discrimination, e.g., Mexican Americans in the Southwest. This subset, however, should not be confused with the whole Hispanic set. The claim that some members or subsets of the Hispanic group have suffered, and continue to suffer, discrimination, is true. Nonetheless, the claim that all members or subsets of the Hispanic group have suffered, and continue to suffer, discrimination is not clearly true. The implication then is that in looking to apply civil rights justifications, we need to distinguish several groups.

Let us make a distinction between the restricted and broad extension of the Hispanic category. The restricted extension includes members of a class who have been subjected to systematic discrimination by virtue of class membership. Notice here two conditions of discrimination: (a) class membership and (b) systematic discrimination against the group. The second condition is very significant because when we speak of class discrimination and protection, we often refer to the systematic character of such discrimination. By systematic discrimination I mean a recurrent and predictable act against a class whereby if someone is a member of the class it is possible to anticipate that the person is liable to discrimination. Given the systematic character of this discrimination it is not necessary that every single member of the class be discriminated against, but rather that the group as such be the object of recurrent discrimination. It would be unnecessary to assume, for instance, that every single member of the African-American group was discriminated against with regard to voting in the 1940s and 1950s in order to argue for the necessity of the 1965 Voting Rights Act. Perhaps not every single African American was discriminated against in this regard, but nonetheless the nature and degree of voting discrimination against the class was such that it was necessary to enact legislation to protect the black vote. Similarly then, when I speak of the restricted sense of Hispanics I assume that class members, whichever way defined, are subjected to enough discrimination, in a systematic way, so that we can effectively speak of discrimination against the class—or more precisely, its members.[1]

The broad extension, in contrast, includes members of a class who have not been necessarily subjected to systematic discrimination by virtue of class membership. The claim simply acknowledges the point made throughout the book that members of the Hispanic group represent, in fact, many different kinds of subgroups. Some of these subgroups have evidently been subjected to systematic discrimination, e.g., Mexican Americans in the Southwest, but the situation is not as clear with regard to other subgroups, e.g., Spaniards, Cubans or newly arrived immigrants with different nationalities. Consider also that Hispanics show some notable differences among themselves with regard to, for example, education.[2] Whereas some subgroups are in need of targeting and intervention strategies, not all Hispanic subgroups are in the same condition. Part of the targeting effort would include collecting data that helps to assess and create intervention strategies for different groups in multiple circumstances.[3] It turns out, however, that the category in the federal standards does not make these distinctions. Hispanics are simply classified as a comprehensive group. So if we look at the second ground for inclusion of the Hispanic category in the Standards for the Classification of Federal Data on Race and Ethnicity—i.e., civil rights monitoring and enforcement —we are not really sure which group or set of groups we are referring to.[4]

Let us posit that we could apply the civil rights criterion to the Hispanic group regardless of identity considerations. In this case, only members of the group who have been discriminated against systematically—

regardless of whether group membership has been central to their identity or not—would be included.[5] In contrast, we may consider classification in the group on the basis of identity without applying the civil rights criterion. In this second case, members would be included in the group because their membership is central to their identity, regardless of whether they are members of a class that has been discriminated against systematically. We have yet another possibility. Members may be included because membership is central to their identities and they are members of a class that has been subjected to systematic discrimination. As I said, however, the federal standards do not contemplate these distinctions and all members of the Hispanic group are categorized comprehensively. It is then the case that examining whether the Hispanic category ought to be included in the Standards for the Classification of Federal Data on Race and Ethnicity on the grounds of the civil rights criterion will not take us very far. With regard to groups, or subgroups, that have experienced differential treatment the category would seem to be justified. But with regard to groups, or subgroups, that have not experienced differential treatment in a systematic form, the category would have to be justified on other grounds.

Here we come to the third grounds for classification, relevant membership or identity recognition. As can be inferred from what I have argued throughout the book, we face a complicated picture. If the condition entails that membership in the Hispanic group is central to members' identities, then clearly what is assumed about Hispanic membership is not the case. As I have argued Hispanic membership is not basic because national membership trumps the significance of Hispanicity. Put differently, part of the problem is that the Hispanic class is not clear enough because it consists of other national subsets with defined characteristics in which membership tends to be basic. It seems then that on grounds of the presumption of relevant membership, *simpliciter*, the Hispanic category, as it is currently defined, does not have a strong enough case for inclusion in the federal standards.

I raised the question of whether there is a good justification for including the Hispanic category, under its current form, in the federal standards. Based on the three possible grounds on which the category may be justified, which are only grounds under the current state of affairs, there does not seem to be a promising case. But as I suggested in chapter 9 this state of affairs might change, if we assume that identity recognition as such is indeed a legitimate reason for group classification and recognition. The government seems to operate with regard to the Hispanic group under at least two assumptions. First, membership in ethnoracial groups is very significant, which includes of course the Hispanic group. And second, it is necessary to identify these groups—either because membership is significant or due to differential treatment. But if the government identifies groups, by means of group classification and the celebration of public holidays, it may actually bring about group individuation and strengthening as a consequence. This process is what I called identity-making. Identifying Hispanics as a relevant group might actually strengthen the value of Hispanic membership. The significance of membership in the Hispanic group could indeed change if Hispanics develop a solid identity as part of a process that results, partially at least, from government identification. Identity making, however, is hardly the current and explicit goal of the federal standards or any governmental action toward Hispanics. Identity making, as it occurs now, is at best an unintentional by-product that results in part from actions such as classification and group recognition in public holidays—a novel Hispanic identity is not the immediate and manifest goal of the American state. All these considerations bring up questions about public philosophy, to which I will return below.

A MODIFIED CATEGORY

What are we to make then of the Hispanic category as it is used for public and official purposes? If the category does not capture more or less accurately a set of people, consisting of different subsets, who have been, and are, discriminated against systematically, or do not have relevant memberships that would seem to merit classification on the grounds of diversity or identity recognition, why classify Hispanics? In grappling with this question, at least two possibilities arise. First, it may be necessary to eliminate the category from the federal standards and look for different nonstandardized forms of identification, which are necessary in order to fulfill a governmental purpose. And second, the government could modify the standardized category—so that it limits the universe of people to be included under, say, the civil rights criterion, increasing accuracy. What seems to be clear is that the category needs to undergo changes, perhaps even elimination from the federal standards.

In looking at whether the current standardized category should be eliminated or the ways in which the category should be modified, let me suggest that we would have to adopt the constitutional legal framework for racial classification. Admittedly, the federal standards do not bring up situations in which there is preferential treatment per se that may be subject to constitutional challenge. In other words, given that the federal standards, by virtue of formulating mere criteria for classification, do not violate any statute as such, they are not liable to the charge of creating discrimination or contravening, for instance, the Equal Protection Clause, that grants equal protection of the laws to all citizens, as found in the Fourteenth Amendment of the U.S. Constitution. The matter at stake then is not, strictly speaking, a legal one.

The federal standards, nonetheless, constitute the point of reference for categorization and classification in programs that grant preferential treatment on the basis of diversity or the civil rights criterion. The standards represent the group and membership differentiation scheme upon which policies and programs toward groups, or members of these groups, are enacted or assessed. The case is then that the federal standards play a crucial role in classification-based initiatives, providing the skeleton for making the types of distinctions that may be subject to legal action. Based on this consideration, my suggestion is that the federal standards should then be seen through and assessed by the constitutional legal framework for racial classification.

Here we must bear in mind that the federal standards are the result of a governmental interest and mandate, which consists of classifying people and collecting data for particular purposes and that the task requires accurate classification and data. In this context, one of the discussions before the modification of the standards in 1997 considered whether self-identification, as a method of data collection, which would make it possible for individuals to identify with more than one race, could indeed compromise the accuracy of the task. The discussion of whether identifying with more than one race best serves or complicates the effort for collecting accurate data is instructive because it brings up and highlights precisely what is at stake in the governmental assignment for classification. Part of the discussion on the possible implications for modifying the standards went like this:

> Reliable and consistent information is important for enforcing Federal laws. In recent U.S. Supreme Court decisions involving education, employment and voting rights, the Court has interpreted the Fourteenth Amendment to the United States Constitution to require that governmental decision-making based on racial classifications be subjected to 'strict scrutiny' to determine whether it is 'narrowly tailored' to meet 'compelling State interests.' Changes in Directive No. 15 could affect the ability of agencies to carry out the court's mandate. If, for instance, allowing individuals to identify with more than one race would make it more difficult to identify the members and characteristics of a particular racial or ethnic group (such as American Indians and Alaska Natives, or Asians and Pacific Islanders), then determining whether a 'compelling State interest' exists with regard to such persons—and whether the government's action is narrowly enough tailored to meet that interest—could become correspondingly more difficult.[6]

In this quote, we see the elements that constitute the constitutional legal framework for racial classification: strict scrutiny, narrow tailoring and compelling governmental interest.[7]

Let me briefly explain each one of the elements and then apply them to the Hispanic category.[8] The point of departure is that racial classifications are immediately *suspect* and thus subject to *strict scrutiny* by the courts.[9] Generally speaking, any type of legislation will typically make a set of distinctions whereby people will be classified someway or another. So, for instance, suppose there is a statute according to which the higher the income, the higher the tax contribution one would have to make to the government. If I have a higher salary than someone else, then I will have to yield a higher percentage of my salary to the government. Similarly, consider that colleges often have a higher volume of applications than student slots, which means that they have to make decisions on who will be admitted and who will not. The criteria for admission generally has to do with factors such as grades, standardized test scores, achievements of a certain kind, etc. Situations like these entail some sort of classification—wealthy and less wealthy citizens to whom a certain tax regulation will apply, and eligible vs. noneligible students for admissions. This point is similar to the one I made in the first few chapters on the kinds of differential attributes that make census classifications possible and the situations in which some memberships are thought to be more valuable than others due to certain distinguishing properties. All these instances of classification, however, are for the most part benign, since they do not constitute a violation of the law.[10] Many kinds of classification occur without having any legal consequences due to violating statutes that prescribe equality.

Some kinds of classification, however, are different—they could potentially violate the law due to, say, applying the law unequally among citizens.[11] So, for instance, a school could classify citizens according to race and thus discriminate against them due to the denial of access to educational resources that should be open to all citizens.[12] Similarly, a college could discriminate against its applicants by granting special privileges to a certain group on the basis of race, and thus impose a burden on the complete set of applicants. Racial classifications could generally have the negative effect of discriminating against racial groups or placing an undue burden on one of the other groups involved.[13] In the language of the Supreme Court, racial classifications are by their very nature immediately *suspect* and thus subject to *strict scrutiny*.[14] Whenever racial distinctions are made with regard to a program or policy, the burden of proof and justification lies on the side of classification.[15] Why is it necessary to classify?

Although racial distinctions are suspect, they are also sometimes necessary in order to achieve certain goals. Thus certain goals, or *compelling in-*

terests, can trump the presumption of nonclassification. If the government has an interest that is strong or compelling enough to necessitate racial classification, then this sort of classification is within lawful limits. One might believe, like Justice Antonin Scalia, that "government can never have a 'compelling interest' in discriminating on the basis of race in order to 'make up' for past racial discrimination in the opposite direction."[16] The implication of this kind of view seems to be that official racial classifications are generally questionable in instances that involve racial distinctions. But, for the most part, the Court has considered that factors such as the remedy for specifically identified discrimination and diversity represent compelling interests.[17] These interests can only be compelling, however, when policies and guidelines are *narrowly tailored* to satisfy those specific interests and goals.[18]

The elements I want to take from the discussion so far and apply now to the Hispanic category are these: (a) the burden of proof and justification lies on racial classification; from this it follows that (b) the presumption is, or ought to be, that groups should not be classified on the basis of race; and finally (c) only a compelling interest with a program that is narrowly tailored to meet those interests can trump the presumption of nonclassification.[19] So if we ask why the government should classify on the basis of race, we need a good explanation by way of a compelling interest that is met by a program that is sufficiently narrowly tailored.

Let us begin then by placing the Hispanic category under strict scrutiny, on the assumption that this kind of classification should not generally be the case. If that is our point of departure, we can only overturn the presumption of nonclassification by finding a compelling governmental interest that would justify Hispanic classification. Some of these potentially compelling interests coincide roughly with the grounds discussed above for the Hispanic category in the federal standards. We have two possibilities: reparation for past discrimination—which would seem to coincide with the civil rights criterion—and diversity enhancement—which coincides with the goal of achieving diversity in demographic profiles.[20] Let us assume that the two interests are indeed compelling.[21]

If we now take the interest in remedying past discrimination, we are likely to run into some of the difficulties I explained above. I made a distinction between two sets with different extensions under the Hispanic category. Thus people within the category, some of whom have suffered discrimination and some of whom have not, actually encompass two different sets. I also mentioned that the federal standards do not make this distinction, since Hispanics are simply classified as a comprehensive group. If I am right, it would then seem that, to use the vocabulary of the Supreme Court, the Hispanic category or classification does not provide a sound basis for a program or policy that is sufficiently narrowly tailored in order to achieve its goal, i.e., identify a population that has been discriminated against in a systematic form and monitor policies toward this population.[22] The problem, as I have suggested, is that the Hispanic category tries to capture too much.

This state of affairs is also further complicated by the problem that the federal standards rightly identify in the passage quoted above. If self-identification is the preferred method of data collection, and individuals are allowed to identify with more than one race—which under the current standards is indeed the case, it may become increasingly harder to satisfy statutory needs. The kind of action that is tailored narrowly enough entails accurate data. But given that individuals use self-identification and may identify with more than one race, it is very hard to check the accuracy or reliability of the data. It is also very hard to determine whether the categories or the data collected do indeed satisfy the test of narrow tailoring. Here, part of the difficulty is that the federal standards are required to collect purportedly objective data with a method that is by definition subjective—since identification is based primarily on the individual's judgment.[23]

Let us turn now to the second possibility for a compelling interest, diversity. As I have mentioned diversity of a certain kind is considered a good, which is shown in the goal of identifying diversity in demographics. This is also the case for the Courts with regard to, for instance, education. But here we must also ask: assuming that diversity is indeed a compelling interest and thus overturns the presumption of nonclassification, what is the type of diversity we want to represent or achieve? The rationale for diversity aims at enhancing the variety of points of views in a particular body—e.g., a student body—and exposing people to different outlooks. A highly relevant question here is: By what criterion do we distinguish groups that will indeed contribute a variety of viewpoints or experiences to a particular body? Consider that groups with different outlooks, preferences and opinions may be distinguished by a wide range of factors. People with different religious backgrounds will tend to have different perspectives on moral issues such as abortion, and different views about the origin of the world. Similarly the set of people who like to read history, in contrast with the set of people who prefer to watch sports, will probably have a different perspective and level of appreciation for, say, the colonial period or a football game. Both groups could certainly learn from one another. Many sets could be distinguished by a wide variety of factors and thus difference alone will not be a satisfactory criterion for positing that different groups create diversity and should be classified accordingly.

What then is the criterion of differentiation according to which we make relevant distinctions and attribute a certain value to a particular group and its members? It seems to me that a possibly satisfactory criterion could be that people are members of groups that are highly valuable for them due to the fact that the traits, which are essential to their self-understanding, make them members of these groups. Another way of putting the point is that people have memberships that are what I described as basic or central to their identities. A strong criterion of this sort, which posits some type of differential qualities, would seem to be the kind of norm that separates relevant diversity-contributing groups from nonrelevant ones.[24]

Assuming that I am right so far, we then begin to run into difficulties. If my argument that Hispanic membership is not central to the identity of group members, whereas national membership is indeed central to their identities, is true, then we are using the wrong criterion to differentiate relevant diversity-contributing groups and members. But suppose further that we do indeed use the Hispanic category. In addition to using the wrong criterion for distinguishing relevant groups, we would be using a government-mandated category. Using the Hispanic category for identifying diversity-contributing group members would simply identify members according to a politically attributed category, Hispanic. The government would then seem to be interested in the kind of diversity it has already created, and mandated, by using the Hispanic category and engaging in identity making. Nonetheless, promoting diversity and engineering diversity are two different interests.[25] The question then would be whether engineering group diversity, regardless of what membership in these groups represents for actual group members is indeed a compelling governmental interest.

I do not have a straightforward or clear answer for what should happen with the definition of the Hispanic category in the federal standards or how the government should enact its policies toward that segment of the population known as "Hispanic." Nonetheless, what seems to emerge is that changes are necessary in order to have a sounder policy.

For the sake of clarification, I need to emphasize that the case presented in this book does not entail that all forms of Hispanic classification, under all circumstances, ought to be eliminated. It is necessary to recall here a distinction made in chapter 1 between weak and strong recognitions by way of classification. Weak recognition is the governmental action of classifying a certain class in order to monitor or enact certain policies. Strong recognition is the act of classifying a certain class of citizens on the grounds that membership is a good. The current classificatory scheme of the federal government is based on strong recognition. I have argued, however, that the Hispanic category, as based on this type of recognition, is untenable.

Nonetheless, I do not wish to deny that some categories might be necessary for purposes of what I call weak recognition. Referring, for instance, to the data in table 3.1, found in chapter 3, one notices that almost half of the people with a Mexican background and who speak Spanish at home have not finished high school. Such an educational deficit could potentially constitute a crisis and would need policy intervention strategies. Such intervention strategies require some type of classification for monitoring purposes. Notice now several points. Intervention strategies have nothing to do with identity recognition. Policies of this sort are simply aimed to correct or monitor a certain kind of deficit. The current ethnoracial federal standards, however, go beyond intervention strategies and make assumptions about identity recognition. Second, the act of classification does not say anything about what the right intervention strategies ought to be. They may range between claims that immigration ought to be regulated more strictly with an eye toward reduction—since immigration may increase a certain population, which has low levels of education—to full-blown affirmative action programs. We have heard both arguments in recent times. My immediate point is that classification per se does not necessarily lead to policies of a certain kind. Third, highlighting the example of a Mexican educational deficit, I suggest that the current Hispanic category cannot be of much help, since it does not aim at the population that may need targeting. The distinctions and points I have mentioned are significant, for I make a case toward modifying the current standardized classification system, but I do not wish to suggest that all types of classifications ought to be abolished across the board.

A MATTER OF PUBLIC PHILOSOPHY

Important as the changes I have referred to above are, I think that an even more significant and wider point arises. I have tried to establish that the Hispanic category does not live up to its identity self-image, a self-image thoroughly assumed by governmental classifications. But in querying the nature and justification of the category, along with the meaning of membership for members of the category, we have run into questions about public philosophy. It turns out then that examining what it means to be a Hispanic and why the government attempts to classify members of the group, has led us to encounter questions about the rationales for governmental action.

I mentioned earlier that the government operates with regard to ethnoracial group classification under several assumptions, of which I highlighted two: membership in some ethnoracial groups is very significant, and it is necessary to identify these groups because membership is significant or civil rights enforcement is necessary. As I pointed out, the first assumption is not true of the Hispanic group, but by virtue of identifying groups, the assumption may become true. The assumption on the significance of identity may turn out to be a kind of self-fulfilling prophecy as a consequence of identity making. Processes of this sort are sometimes inevitable. Historical contingencies bring about not only unforeseen consequences, but also sometimes undesirable ones. In the same vein, if we see a constant theme in studies on the emergence of nations and ethnic groups, it is that these groups and the identities of group members are often the result of a process that was only partially engineered and controlled by even the most skilled, intentional and forward-looking nationalist elites and agents. In short, group configurations and identities respond to factors beyond anyone's control. And yet the Hispanic phenomenon provides an interesting case in progress of identity formation, and also gives us the occasion to understand how the government acts toward racial and ethnic groups along with the possible consequences of this sort of action. I want to close with the discussion of three normative questions that arise in the context of our query. All of the questions have to do, in some form or another, with the proper function and purview of governments and its relationship to groups and identities.

First, when should groups be the proper object of official classification and recognition? Another way of formulating the question is by raising the point of grounds and criteria, as I have done throughout the book. I have argued that the classification scheme of the federal standards is based or justified upon certain grounds. Assuming then that all these grounds are legitimate triggers for classification, once a particular group satisfies the relevant criteria—e.g., an ethnoracial group in which membership is central to members' identities and that contributes to diversity and has suffered discrimination—the group should presumably be the proper object of official classification.

But as previous discussions have already suggested, here we really have two separate components and questions. The first component has to do with the grounds upon which the government justifies group classification. I have made this component explicit by analyzing the rationale for group inclusion in the federal standards, and highlighting an implicit and highly relevant assumption, what I called the presumption of relevant membership. The question that comes up with regard to this component is, as suggested before, whether all three grounds for group classification are related to legitimate functions of governments. The second component is directed not to governmental justification as such, but to the criteria a group has to meet in order to be the proper object of classification. It is largely on this component that I have concentrated throughout the book by arguing that Hispanics do not meet one of the most salient criteria for purposes of inclusion in the federal standards. The criterion I am referring to of course is that of identity—and more specifically, the condition according to which membership in a group is central to someone's identity. I argued that given the conditions of membership and groups that tend to endow people with the kinds of memberships that are central to their identities, Hispanics fall short of satisfying these conditions. The end result is that Hispanic identity is not the sort of identity that can be said to play the conspicuous role that is assumed by the classificatory scheme. And thus the Hispanic group does not meet the identity criterion that could presumably give a good reason for its presence in the federal standards.

Moving away from the Hispanic group, and widening our scope the question for any group would be whether such group satisfies the relevant criteria for classification. I assume of course that a starting point for raising this question is that certain groups would be disqualified a priori because of overriding governmental interests. The best representation of nonqualifying groups makes us think immediately of religion. I also assume that a typological designation is not enough for classifying groups. So for instance, ethnoracial groups qua groups of a certain kind do not lead us to have enough motives for classification. The groups besides being designated as "ethnoracial"—which is certainly the case with German Americans, Arab Americans and Hispanics—would also have to meet the specified criteria. But given that we consider groups not according to their kind and designation but to the criteria they meet, maybe we need to consider whether groups that are not designated as ethnoracial, e.g., sexual orientation groups, may be qualifying candidates for official classification and recognition. If Hispanics do not qualify despite their designation, maybe other groups may qualify given their group and membership structure.[26]

Now consider, however, that maybe the grounds upon which group classification is justified may not be related in the right way to the proper function of governments, thus rendering the point of whether a group meets specific criteria or not largely irrelevant. Here we turn to the second normative question: To what ends should groups be classified?[27] I suspect that, at least apparently, the answer to this question would be more or less unanimous. The reason why governments classify certain population groups is in order to achieve integration, whether we construe integration economically, politically or in terms of justice.

But we must think of the fact that different philosophies of national integration will provide contrasting models. Compare, for example, France's civic-republican model with Britain's pragmatic conflict-resolution model and we will end up with two views of how classification contributes (or not) to integration. Under the French model, with its strong emphasis on citizenship, the general will and allegiance to the state, ethnoracial classifications only perpetuate group difference and thus hinder full integration. Not surprisingly some French demographers have been wary of asking the national origin question, a standard feature of other censuses, in their own census. Hervé Le Bras, for instance, claims that "the use of 'origin' in demographic classification is a source of racial discrimination."[28] So I think it is fair to say that under the French model, we must first ask about the terms of classification before we raise the question of purpose. If the terms are sound, then presumably the question of purpose follows. If the terms of classification are instead problematic, as is the case with ethnic and racial classifications, there is no point in asking what the purpose of classification is.

Under the British model, in contrast with the French model, classification, which is tightly bound with multicultural policies and the multiracial self-image of society, is part of a legislative and institutional framework that represents a "calculated, paternalistic attempt to engineer a kind of social harmony and multicultural equilibrium."[29] The aim of this equilibrium, which proceeds independently from public feelings about other racial groups, is to attain or preserve social order by avoiding intergroup conflict. The British model is in some respects similar to the American one, only that whereas the British model is motivated by concerns about social order the American model is primarily motivated by principles of justice. The important point for our current discussion is that given this model of integration, that accepts differences of a certain kind and aims to assess the performance of groups characterized by those differences, official classifications are not only natural but also necessary. To what ends do governments then classify their citizens? The answer to the question depends on the soundness of the classificatory scheme and the public philosophy that constitutes the starting point.

Assuming now that ethnic and racial classifications of some sort are legitimate for the purposes of integration, we then move on to the third question: How should governments make the determination of which groups to classify? Let us suppose that we do indeed need to single out, at an official level, particular groups whose integration needs to be monitored. We may in fact follow Kymlicka's multicultural argument here, or similar versions of the argument, and thus find it necessary to single out the groups and members that will be the object of privileges or measures for purposes of integration. The argument would go like this. Groups of a certain kind are accorded group-specific rights, or some type of special recognition even within the confines of individual rights,[30] by way of symbolic recognition, exemption, affirmative action or accommodation provisions because membership in the group has a certain status. In the specific case of the American context, we should add that members in the group have been historically and systematically discriminated against by virtue of class membership. The question now is, how do we determine which groups should be the recipients of these measures?

If we operate at the level in which we can clearly determine the kind of group and membership we are interested in, it follows that the group may indeed be the recipient of certain measures. But suppose now that we operate at a different level, one in which it is very hard to determine which groups, or a very particular group, should be the object of the integrative measures. Some cases will be more or less straightforward. African-Americans have clearly been discriminated against and, more controversially perhaps, seem to have a kind of membership that is central to their identities. And even if we undermine the claim that African-American membership has a special status, it is still true that they have experienced differential treatment for the most part of American history. As I suggested in chapter 10 and am suggesting now, African Americans are then an instance of group for whom the question of recognition or certain privileges may apply. If we do indeed follow the multicultural argument above and are able to determine the status of the group, we may yield a certain conclusion. Notice how in the case I have just described, two conditions are the case: the multicultural argument is sound and we operate at the level of determinacy. But now suppose that, as I said, we sometimes operate at the level of indeterminacy, without being able to determine whether a group should be the recipient of integrative measures. If this is the case, we may find ourselves in a situation in which we apply the multicultural argument to a group at the indeterminate level. Something very similar to this situation is what we see in the case of Hispanics: a classificatory scheme, that has a certain rationale, is applied to a group at the indeterminate level. As I have argued, the group does not possess, as a matter of fact, some of the traits attributed to it, once we place such group under a microscope and try to determine its status.[31] At the end, whatever one makes about the scope of government, and how much governmental functions should extend to identity matters, one point seems clear: The case for Hispanic classification and recognition, under the current federal standards, is weaker than it seems.

NOTES

1. Discrimination in this case does not simply refer to isolated incidents against a given individual. In *Hernandez v. Texas*, for instance, the case for showing discrimination against Mexican-Americans was made by establishing two conditions. First, it was necessary to prove that people of Mexican descent constitute a separate class. Second, the burden of proof lied on showing that the class, or members of the class, were discriminated against, an act that entails "systematic exclusion." 347 U.S. 475, 480 (1954).

2. See Barbara Schneider, Sylvia Martinez and Ann Owens, "Barriers to Educational Opportunities for Hispanics in the United States," in *Hispanics and the Future of America*, eds. Marta Tienda and Faith Mitchell (Washington D.C.: National Research Council, 2006), 180.

3. Schneider, Martinez and Owens, "Barriers to Educational Opportunities," 195.

4. As a consequence, groups and circumstances that were not intended to be protected under civil rights legislation end up reaping benefits. For example, the use of minority labels may make it possible for "employers to benefit from the 'brain drain' from the Third World . . ." "The hiring of foreign professionals and technical workers creates the statistical illusion of progress in minority recruitment and overall improvements in the life chances of U.S. ethnic minorities when in reality no significant positive changes can be documented." Martha E. Gimenez, "U.S. Ethnic Politics: Implications for Latin Americans," *Latin American Perspectives*, 19, 4 (1992): 9.

5. This claim assumes that civil rights considerations may be independent from identity considerations. Brian Barry makes the point that the "culturalization" of groups runs the risk of masking the sorts of traits that distinguish disadvantaged groups, which may not be cultural groups. Just as the cultural paradigm is not coextensive with a disadvantaged status, and perhaps the need for statutory protection, the identity of a group and its members is not coextensive with the kind of status that could give rise to civil rights considerations. See Brian Barry, *Culture and Equality: An Egalitarian Critique of Multiculturalism* (Cambridge, MA: Harvard University Press, 2002), 305–6.

6. "Recommendations from the Interagency Committee for the Review of the Racial and Ethnic Standards to the Office of Management and Budget Concerning Changes to the Standards for the Classification of Federal Data on Race and Ethnicity," in *Federal Register*, vol. 62, no. 131 (Thursday, Wednesday, July 9, 1997, Notices, 36883).

7. For succinct explanations of these terms and doctrines, see Richard H. Fallon, Jr., *The Dynamic Constitution: An Introduction to American Constitutional Law* (New York: Cambridge University Press, 2004), 106–29; and Charles Fried, *Saying What the Law Is: The Constitution in the Supreme Court* (Cambridge, MA: Harvard University Press, 2004), 207–17.

8. For a helpful review of how these elements and doctrines have developed through Supreme Court decisions, see *Adarand Constructors, Inc v. Pena*, 515 U.S. 200, 213–29 (1995).

9. See *Korematsu v. United States*, 323 U.S. 214, 216 (1944). See also *Regents of University of California v. Bakke*, 438 U.S. 265, 291 (1978).

10. The discussion of what represents benign versus malign forms of classification, and whether racial classification is permissible or not, is not a result of the civil rights era. There is a long historical strand that has set forth many of the arguments that did indeed prevail and became mainstream after the civil rights revolution. For a historical account on questions and arguments having to do with race as either a benign or malign form of classification, see Andrew Kull, *The Color-Blind Constitution* (Cambridge, MA: Harvard University Press, 1992).

11. In cases involving nonracial distinctions, the Court "has merely asked whether there is any rational foundation for the discriminations, and has deferred to the wisdom of state legislatures." In cases involving race, however, the statute has "the very heavy burden of justification which the Fourteenth Amendment has traditionally required of state statutes drawn according to race." *Loving v. Virginia* 388 U.S. 1, 9 (1967). On the kind of standard applied to classifications based on gender, see Fallon, *The Dynamic Constitution*, 129–33.

12. Or just generally, regardless of discriminatory effects as such, racial classifications might have negative effects due to a long history of racism. Some have even gone so far as to argue that the concept of "race" has pernicious effects and thus needs to be replaced with more precise terminology for purposes of statutory protection. The claim I am referring to is not that designations such as Jewish, Hispanic or African American are useless, since "these identities are central to many people's understanding of themselves in a way that is meaningful and empowering." The claim is rather that these designations should not be construed racially. Accordingly, the term race "should be replaced in future statutory texts and jurisprudence by other, more precise terminology." New terminology can include "color," "continent of origin," "national origin," and "descent from ancestors of a particular color." Claims of this sort, however, do not go to the heart of what I think matters most: how do we set the boundaries of groups that would seem to need statutory protection? See Sharona Hoffman, "Is There a Place for 'Race' as a Legal Concept?" *Arizona State Law Journal* 36 (2004): 1,100.

13. Racial classifications are inherently suspect as such, regardless of whether the classification imposes a burden or grants benefits to one of the groups involved. See *Adarand*, 224. See also *Bakke*, 289–90—a case which famously raised the question of whether an admissions program that classifies by race benefits a group, but imposes an undue burden on another group violates the Equal Protection Clause.

14. See *Bakke*, 291: "racial and ethnic distinctions of any sort are inherently suspect and thus call for the most exacting judicial examination."

15. The Supreme Court, in fact, has expressed opposition to racial classifications as such. In relation to racial gerrymandering, "racial classifications of any sort pose the risk of lasting harm to our society. They reinforce the belief, held by too many for too much of out history, that individuals should be judged by the color of their skin." *Shaw v. Reno*, 509 U.S. 630, 657 (1993).

16. *Adarand*, 239.

17. Racial classifications are sometimes necessary, but in such cases we have seen that racial classification needs to be subjected to strict scrutiny, the highest standard of judicial review. Under this standard, then the other criteria apply. In a case of racial gerrymandering, and the potential violation of the Equal Protection Clause, the decision puts it briefly: "to satisfy strict scrutiny, the State must demonstrate that its districting legislation is narrowly tailored to achieve a compelling interest." *Miller v. Johnson* 515 U.S 900, 920 (1995).

18. Racial "classifications are constitutional only if they are narrowly tailored measures further compelling governmental interests." *Adarand*, 227. Part of the reason why a program based on racial classifications needs to be narrowly tailored is because the Constitution protects individuals and not groups. See *Bakke*, 317–20.

19. Narrow tailoring is extremely important. Even two policies that may have the same compelling interest may be distinguished on the grounds of narrow tailoring. See *Gratz v. Bollinger* 539 U.S. 244 (2003), a case in which the Court examined University of Michigan's undergraduate admission's policies. The conclusion was this: "we conclude, therefore, that because the University's use of race in its current freshman admissions policy is not narrowly tailored to achieve respondent's asserted compelling interest [diversity], the admissions policy violates the Equal Protection Clause of the Fourteenth Amendment." *Gratz*, 275. Narrow tailoring was the criterion that separated the admissions policies discussed in *Gratz* and *Grutter v. Bollinger* 539 U.S. 306 (2003). Whereas one set of policies was narrowly tailored to serve the institution's interests, the other set of policies was not. See the concurring opinion of Justice Sandra Day O'Connor in *Gratz*, 276–80.

20. On the point of diversity as a compelling interest, see *Bakke*, 311–16. See also *Gratz*, 257; and *Grutter*, 327–33.

21. What constitutes a compelling interest? Interests of this sort need to be justified by moral and legal considerations and not simply judicial intuitions. Jeffrie G. Murphy makes the following remark: "What makes a state interest compelling or overriding? When one considers the interests that have actually been identified as compelling by the Supreme Court, one might wonder whether this is merely a laundry list or whether any coherent moral, political, and legal theory binds all these interests together in a systematic way." "Justifying Departures from Equal Treatment," *The Journal of Philosophy*, 81, 10 (1984): 592. He then goes on to identify sources for analyzing the concept, 592–93.

22. At the same time, a narrowly tailored program cannot be based simply on a set-aside or quota scheme; see *Bakke*, 315–19. The program must consider race among a set of other factors to insure that individuals receive individualized treatment; see the discussion of *Bakke* in *Gratz*, 271.

23. See Peter Skerry, *Counting on the Census? Race, Group Identity and the Evasion of Politics* (Washington, D.C.: Brookings Institution Press, 2000), 77–79.

24. The strong criterion I adduce rules out the possible grounds for affirmative action that Jorge J. E. Gracia proposes, i.e., identifiability and degree of participation. The question is not whether Hispanics are identifiable, but whether they are identifiable according to properties that would merit public recognition. See "Affirmative Action for Hispanics? Yes and No," in *Hispanics/Latinos in the United States: Ethnicity, Race, and Rights*, eds. Jorge J. E. Gracia and Pablo De Greiff (New York: Routledge, 2000), 211–14.

25. See Peter H. Schuck's discussion on themes related to this distinction. Peter H. Schuck, *Diversity in America: Keeping Government at a Safe Distance* (Cambridge, MA: Harvard University Press, 2003), particularly 320–31.

26. Or certain groups may simply be classified and recognized, for instance, on the grounds of what Owen M. Fiss has called "the group disadvantaging principle." See his article "Groups and the Equal Protection Clause," *Philosophy and Public Affairs*, 5, 2 (1976): 147–56.

27. Assume, for instance, that the proper function of governments entails fostering a robust public sphere and the kind of nation building that promote trust and solidarity such that it is easier to mobilize people in order to provide collective goods. If this is the case, then classification schemes that might potentially

compromise the kind of collective unity that facilitates other goods could become a matter of great concern. So the question of the ends toward which governments should classify citizens is one that needs a careful answer. For a defense of nationality and national identity as a means for fostering solidarity, within the confines of a political community, see David Miller, "In Defence of Nationality," in *Citizenship and National Identity* (Cambridge: Polity Press, 2000), particularly 31–33. For a full-scale development of his views, see, *On Nationality* (New York: Oxford University Press, 1999 [1975]).

28. See Riva Kastoryano, *Negotiating Identities: State and Immigrants in France and Germany* (Princeton: Princeton University Press, 2002), 24.

29. Adrian Favell, *Philosophies of Integration: Immigration and the Idea of Citizenship in France and Britain* (New York: Palgrave, 2001), 123.

30. This would be the case in the U.S., since the Constitution only officially contemplates individual rights. See, for instance, the characterization of rights in the case that established the "one man, one vote" principle in the electoral practice. *Reynolds v. Sims*, 377 U.S. 533, 561 (1964).

31. "Much of the difficulty in the creation of a consistent, rational classification system lies in the fluid nature of what race and ethnicity are. Race and ethnicity are inherently complex concepts, with multiple sources of definition. There is no scientific basis for the legitimacy of race or ethnicity as taxonomic categories. That is, although there clearly are many and varied racial and ethnic distinctions, their multiplicity of sources defies a single-variable classification scheme based on a single individual characteristic. The challenge of creating logically consistent standards is magnified even more by self-definitions of race and ethnicity, in which a devised set of categories may well not coincide with people's views of themselves." Barry Edmonston, Joshua Goldstein and Juanita Tamayo Lott, *Spotlight on Heterogeneity: The Federal Standards for Racial and Ethnic Classification* (Washington, D.C.: National Academy Press, 1996), 37.

Index

affirmative action, 24–25
African Americans: America and, 191–92, 194–200; basic membership and, 188–98; citizenship and, 195–96; civil rights and, 3, 40–41, 208; classification and, 40–41, 190, 220; community and, 191–92, 196–98; differential treatment and, 40–41; groups and, 188–98; Hispanics and, 193–200; history and, 191–92, 196–98; identification of, 188–92; identity and, 188–98; identity-making and, 188–92; immigration and, 195–96, 197; membership and, xiv, 188–98; nationality and, 190–98; presumption of relevant membership and, 40–41; race and, 188–92, 194, 198; recognition and, 40–41, 191–92, 198–200, 220; relevant identification and, 188–90; self-understanding and, 188–92; in Standards for the Classification of Federal Data on Race and Ethnicity, 202n23; terminology for, 46; traits and, 188–92. *See also* blacks
age, 7

agriculture, 65–66
Alcoff, Linda Martin, 144n24, 145n37
Amar, Akhil Reed, 183n22
America: African Americans and, 191–92, 194–200; assimilation and, 180–81; basic membership and, 129–30, 134, 135–36, 138, 148–49, 157–58, 194–200; citizenship and, 126–27, 129–30, 134, 135–36, 138, 190, 195–96; commonality and, 173–81, 180–81; community and, 173–81, 191–92, 196–98; conflict and, 127, 129–31; Constitution of, 174, 202n22, 210–15; cultural pluralism in, 187–88; culture and, 179–81; differentiation and, 157–58; diversity and, 175–76; empowerment and, 176–77; ethnicity and, 157–58; groups and, 148–49, 157–58, 175–79; heritage and, 175–79; Hispanics and, 126–27, 129–30, 134, 135–36, 138, 148–49, 157–58, 175–82, 195–200; history and, 157–58, 191–92, 196–98; identification and, 148–49, 157–58; identity and, 126–27, 129–30, 134, 135–36, 138, 157–58, 173–81, 191–92,

225

194–200; identity-making and, 173–81; immigration and, 179–81, 195–96, 197; Latin America and, 180–81; membership and, 129–30, 134, 135–36, 138, 148–49, 157–58, 180–81, 194–200; Mexico and, 143n13; multiculturalism in, 187–88; National Hispanic Heritage Month in, 157; nationality and, 126–27, 129–30, 134, 135–36, 138, 148–49, 173–81, 191–92, 194–200; partial basic membership and, 138; pervasive basic membership and, 138; politics in, 190; race in, 189–90; recognition and, 191–92; relevant identification and, 148–49; robust membership and, 180–81; self-understanding and, 138, 173–74; terminology for, xvi; traits and, 138
American Indians, 34–35, 44–45
Anderson, Benedict, 102, 143n18
Appiah, Kwame Anthony, 96n1, 166n23, 201n6
Arab Americans, 27, 39–40, 72–74. *See also* Muslims
Arel, Dominique, 13n21
Ascherson, Neal, 112
Asian Americans, 43–44
assimilation, 6–7, 11n2, 13n17, 54n18, 180–81. *See also* integration

Bali, 114
Bangladeshi, 54n31
Barone, Michael, xvi
Barry, Brian, 203n29, 221n5
basic membership: African Americans and, 188–98; America and, 129–30, 134, 135–36, 138, 148–49, 157–58, 194–200; birthplace and, 88–89, 132, 133, 148–49, 150–52, 157–58; citizenship and, 129–40, 195–96; civil rights and, 160–61; classification and, 148–49, 152, 157, 158, 209–10, 217–18; commonality and, 131–34, 153, 154–62; community and, 132–34, 191–92, 196–98; concept of, 84–93; conflict and, 127, 129–31, 132–34, 139–40; culture and, 94–96; differentiation and, 107–13, 131–34, 148–49, 150, 154–62, 167–68; discernibility and, 109–11, 154; empowerment and, 155–56, 158–60; as epiphenomenon, 150–53, 159–60, 162, 193; ethnicity and, 93, 155–62; groups and, 93, 94–96, 106–13, 114–15, 132–34, 137–40, 147–63, 188–200, 217–18; Hispanics and, 125–26, 129–41, 147–63, 167–68, 169, 193–200, 209–10, 217–18; history and, 155–60, 191–92, 196–98; identification and, 106–7, 114–15, 147–63, 188–92; identity and, 84–96, 106–7, 125–26, 129–40, 147–63, 167–68, 169, 188–200, 209–10; identity-making and, 167–68, 169, 188–92, 193–94, 199, 209–10; immigration and, 134, 136–37, 195–96, 197, 199; intrinsic identification and, 114–15, 167–68; justice and, 160–62; language and, 87–88, 89, 132, 150–52, 155–56; Latin America and, 129–40, 148–53, 156–60; nationality and, 86, 112–13, 125–26, 129–41, 148–53, 155–56, 157–58, 159–60, 162, 169, 190–200; origin and, 156–59; overview of, xiii–xiv; partial, 135–38; personhood and, 160–62; pervasive, 135–38; policymaking and, 217–18; politics and, 156–58; race and, 188–92, 198; recognition and, 148–49, 153, 191–92, 198–200, 209–10, 217–18; relevant identification and, 106–7, 147–53, 167–68; religion and, 86, 92; robust membership and, 149–53, 159–60, 169; self-understanding and, 84–93, 95, 106–7, 108–11, 131–32, 135, 136–38, 150–53, 154, 155–56, 158–60, 188–92, 193; social markers and, 148–49; sports and, 129–30; Standards for the Classification of Federal Data on Race and Ethnicity and, 209–10; traits and, 85–93,

Index

95–96, 108–12, 131–32, 135, 136–38, 147–53, 154, 155–62, 188–92, 193; value of, 94–96; well being and, 95–96
birthplace, 88–89, 132, 133, 148–49, 150–52, 157–58. *See also* heritage; origin
blacks, 46, 201n7. *See also* African Americans
Bolivar, Simón, 133
Britain, 54n31, 218–19
Brubaker, Rogers, 98n23
Bruelly, John, 143n17
Burundi, 165n10
Bush, George W., 157

censuses, 7–9, 26, 218–19. *See also* Standards for the Classification of Federal Data on Race and Ethnicity
Cervantes Saavedra, Miguel de, 177–78
chapter overview, xi–xv
Chavez, Hugo, 144n23
choice, 94–95, 138, 152–53. *See also* consensual; identification
citizenship: African Americans and, 195–96; America and, 126–27, 129–30, 134, 135–36, 138, 190, 195–96; basic membership and, 129–40, 195–96; birthplace and, 132, 133; commonality and, 131–34; community and, 132–34; conflict and, 127, 129–31, 132–34, 139–40; differentiation and, 131–34; groups and, 132–34, 137–40; Hispanics and, 126–40, 195–96; identity and, 126–40, 195–96; immigration and, 127–28, 134, 136–37; language and, 132; Latin America and, 126–27, 129–40; membership and, 129–40, 195–96; multiple, 128–29; nationality and, 126–40, 195–96; partial basic membership and, 135–38; pervasive basic membership and, 135–38; qualifications for, 163n2; race and, 190; robust membership and, 135–36, 138–40; self-understanding and, 131–32, 135, 136–38; sports and, 129–30; traits and, 131–32, 135, 136–38
civil rights: affirmative action in, 24–25; African Americans and, 3, 40–41, 208; American Indians and, 44–45; Arab Americans and, 39–40; Asian Americans and, 43–44; basic membership and, 160–61; classification and, xii, xv, 8–9, 23–25, 33, 37–47, 48–52, 206, 207–9, 210–14; commonality and, 160–61; Cuban Americans and, 42; differential treatment and, 38–45; differentiation and, 160–61; diversity and, 12n7, 24; employment and, 221n4; equality in, 6; ethnicity and, 39–40, 44–45, 160–61; exclusion, rectifying, 24, 191–92; groups and, 160–61; Hispanics and, xv, 41–43, 160–61, 206, 207–9, 210–14; identification and, 160–61; identity and, 160–61, 209, 210–14, 221n5; integration and, 6; membership and, 160–61; Mexican Americans and, 41–43; presumption of relevant membership and, 37–47, 48–52; race and, 40–41, 43–44; recognition and, 38–47, 206, 207–9, 210–14; religion and, 38–39; sexual orientation and, 39; Standards for the Classification of Federal Data on Race and Ethnicity and, xii, 23–25, 206, 207–9, 210–14; strict scrutiny and, 210–15. *See also* justice; rights
classification: African Americans and, 40–41, 190, 220; age and, 7; American Indians and, 44–45; Arab Americans and, 39–40; Asian Americans and, 43–44; basic membership and, 148–49, 152, 157, 158, 209–10, 217–18; in Britain, 218–19; censuses and, 7–9, 26; civil rights and, xii, xv, 8–9, 23–25, 33, 37–47, 48–52, 206, 207–9, 210–14;

criteria for, 15–16, 27–28, 36–37, 206–20; Cuban Americans and, 42; demography and, xi–xii, xv, 19–22, 25–29, 36–37, 206–7; differential treatment and, 38–45; differentiation and, 157, 158; diversity and, xi–xii, 19–22, 24, 25–28, 37–38, 45–46, 206–7, 210–11, 214–15; education and, 216; ethnicity and, 8–9, 15–19, 39–40, 44–45, 157, 158, 206–7; exclusionary, 8; in France, 218–19; groups and, 9–11, 20–22, 26–28, 148–49, 152, 157, 158, 216–20; Hispanics and, ix–x, xiv–xv, 27, 41–43, 148–49, 152, 157, 158, 168–69, 205–20; history and, 157, 158; identification and, xii, 17, 18–19, 45–47, 148–49, 152, 157, 158; identity and, xi, 14n25, 33, 38–39, 40, 45–47, 48–52, 157, 158, 206, 207, 209–10; identity-making and, 209–10, 215, 217; immigration and, 26–27, 216; inclusionary, 8–9; integration and, 7–9, 10–11, 218–20; membership and, xi, xii, 9–11, 33–37, 148–49, 152, 157, 158, 209–10, 217–18; Mexican Americans and, 41–43; multiculturalism and, 219–20; multiple, 17, 18–19, 46–47, 211–12, 214; origin and, 8; policymaking and, ix–x, 16–17, 19–29, 36–47, 48–52, 206, 216–20; politics and, 25–28, 156–58; presumption of relevant membership and, xi, xii, xv, 33–37, 48–52, 207, 209–10, 217–18; race and, 8–9, 15–19, 40–41, 43–44, 190, 206–7; recognition and, 9–11, 17, 38–47, 205–20; relevant identification and, 148–49, 152; religion and, 38–39; robust membership and, 152; sexual orientation and, 39; strict scrutiny and, 210–15. *See also* recognition; Standards for the Classification of Federal Data on Race and Ethnicity
cognitive capacity, 97n2

commonality, 131–34, 153, 154–62, 170–81. *See also* community
communism, 69–70
community, 132–34, 170–81, 191–92, 196–98. *See also* commonality
compelling interests, 211, 212–15
conflict, 127, 129–31, 132–34, 139–40
Connor, Walker, 121n26, 144n20
consensual, 91–93, 152–53, 174. *See also* choice; identification
Copp, David, 118n1, 119n10, 130
Corlett, Angelo, xiv, 154, 160–62
Coronado, Francisco Vázquez de, 177–78
Cuban Americans, 42
cultural pluralism, 187–88, 198–200. *See also* multiculturalism
culture: America and, 179–81; assimilation and, 180–81; of Bali, 114; basic membership and, 87–89, 94–96; birthplace and, 88–89; commonality and, 180–81; diversity and, 47–48, 74–75; education and, 47–48; ethnicity and, 60–76; freedom and, 63; groups and, 60–76, 94–96, 114–15, 118n6, 187–88, 221n5; Hispanics and, 169, 179–81; identification and, 114–15; identity and, 63, 73–74, 87–89, 94–96, 169, 179–81; identity-making and, 169, 179–81; immigration and, 61, 179–81; language and, 87–88, 89; Latin America and, 180–81; membership and, 59–76, 87–89, 94–96, 180–81, 187–88; nationality and, 60–76, 179–81; recognition and, 187–88; robust membership and, 180–81; self-understanding and, 87–89, 114–15; terminology for, 60–61; thick, 110–11; value of, 62–75, 187–88; well being and, 187–88. *See also* cultural pluralism; multiculturalism

demography, xi–xii, xv, 19–22, 25–29, 36–37, 206–7
destiny, 172

Index

differential treatment, 38–45, 206, 207–9, 210–16
differentiation: America and, 157–58; basic membership and, 107–13, 131–34, 148–49, 150, 154–62, 167–68; birthplace and, 157–58; citizenship and, 131–34; civil rights and, 160–61; classification and, 157, 158; commonality and, 154–62; discernibility and, 154; empowerment and, 155–56, 158–60; ethnicity and, 155–62; groups and, xiii, 107–13, 148–49, 150, 154–62; Hispanics and, 131–34, 148–49, 150, 154–62, 167–68; history and, 155–60; identification and, 148–49, 150, 154–62, 167–68; identity and, 131–34, 148–49, 150, 154–62, 167–68; identity-making and, 167–68; intrinsic identification and, 167–68; justice and, 160–62; language and, 155–56; Latin America and, 156–60; membership and, xiii, 107–13, 131–34, 148–49, 150, 154–62, 167–68; nationality and, 112–13, 131–34, 148–49, 150, 155–56, 157–58, 159–60, 162; origin and, 156–59; personhood and, 160–62; politics and, 156–58; recognition and, 148–49; relevant identification and, 148–49, 150; robust membership and, 150, 159–60; self-understanding and, 108–11, 154, 155–56, 158–60; social markers and, 148–49; traits and, 108–12, 148–49, 150, 154, 155–62. *See also* discernibility
direction, 62–75, 191–92. *See also* value
discernibility, 109–11, 154. *See also* differentiation
discrimination. *See* civil rights; differential treatment
diversity: America and, 175–76; civil rights and, 12n7, 24; classification and, xi–xii, 19–22, 24, 25–28, 37–38, 45–46, 206–7, 210–11, 214–15; commonality and, 175–76; community and, 175–76; culture and, 47–48, 74–75; education and, 47–48; ethnicity and, 74–75, 206–7; groups and, 20–22, 26–28, 74–75, 155; heritage and, 175–76; Hispanics and, 175–76, 206–7, 210–11, 214–15; identification and, 45–46; identity and, 175–76, 207, 210–11, 214–15; identity-making and, 175–76; integration and, 5–6; membership and, 22; multiculturalism and, 5–6; nationality and, 74–75, 175–76; politics and, 25–28; presumption of relevant membership and, 37–38, 45–46, 207; race and, 206–7; recognition and, 74–75, 206–7, 210–11, 214–15; Standards for the Classification of Federal Data on Race and Ethnicity and, xi–xii, 19–22, 24, 25–28, 45–46, 206–7, 210–11, 214–15; strict scrutiny and, 210–11, 214–15; value of, 74–75
Du Bois, W.E.B., 192

education, 42–43, 43–44, 47–48, 49–51, 216. *See also* school attendance
employment, 221n4
empowerment, 155–56, 158–60, 176–77
epiphenomena, 150–53, 159–60, 162, 193
equality, 6
ethnicity: America and, 157–58; basic membership and, 93, 155–62; birthplace and, 157–58; censuses and, 8–9; civil rights and, 39–40, 44–45, 160–61; classification and, 8–9, 15–19, 39–40, 44–45, 157, 158, 206–7; commonality and, 155–62; concept of, 29n8, 224n31; culture and, 60–76; demography and, 206–7; differential treatment and, 39–40, 44–45; differentiation and, 155–62; diversity and, 74–75, 206–7; education and, 47–48; empowerment and, 155–56, 158–60; groups and, 60–76, 121n26,

155–62; Hispanics and, 155–62, 206–7; history and, 155–60; identification and, 155–62; identity and, 34–35, 40, 73–74, 93, 155–62; integration and, 203n27; justice and, 160–62; language and, 155–56; Latin America and, 156–60; meaning and direction from, 62–75; membership and, 34–35, 35–36, 93, 155–62; minorities and, 61–62, 64, 78n40; nationality and, 155–56, 157–58, 159–60, 162; origin and, 156–59; personhood and, 160–62; politics and, 156–58; presumption of relevant membership and, 34–35, 35–36, 39–40, 44–45; race distinct from, 29n8; recognition and, 39–40, 44–45, 206–7; robust membership and, 159–60; self-understanding and, 93, 155–56, 158–60; Standards for the Classification of Federal Data on Race and Ethnicity and, 16–19, 206–7; traits and, 93, 155–62; of Yanomami, 68–69
ethno-racial classification. *See* classification
ethno-symbolism, 116
European Americans, 27, 159, 161. *See also* whites
experience, 35–36
extended membership, 102–4

family farms, 65–66
Fichte, Johann Gottlieb, 170, 171, 175
Fiss, Owen M., 223n26
Fletcher, George, 87–88
France, 171–73, 203n28, 218–19
freedom, 63

Garcia, Jorge L. A., 164n9
Geertz, Clifford, 114
Gellner, Ernest, xv, 183n10
gender, 14n24
generation gaps, 118n5, 142n12, 164n7
Germany, 170
Glazer, Nathan, 48, 192, 204n30

Gracia, Jorge, xiv, 121n26, 154–60, 223n24
Gratz v. Bollinger, 223n19
Grosby, Steven, 77n23
groupism, 98n23
groups: African Americans and, 188–98; agriculture and, 65–66; America and, 148–49, 157–58, 175–79; Arab Americans and, 72–74; basic membership and, 93, 94–96, 106–13, 114–15, 132–34, 137–40, 147–63, 188–200, 217–18; birthplace and, 148–49, 150–52, 157–58; citizenship and, 132–34, 137–40; civil rights and, 160–61; classification and, 9–11, 20–22, 26–28, 148–49, 152, 157, 158, 216–20; commonality and, 153, 154–62, 175–79; community and, 175–79, 191–92; conflict and, 139–40; culture and, 60–76, 94–96, 114–15, 118n6, 187–88, 221n5; differentiation and, xiii, 107–13, 148–49, 150, 154–62; discernibility and, 109–11, 154; diversity and, 20–22, 26–28, 74–75, 155; empowerment and, 155–56, 158–60; ethnicity and, 60–76, 121n26, 155–62; function of, 67–71; heritage and, 175–79; Hispanics and, xiv, 132–34, 137–40, 147–63, 175–79, 193–200, 216–20; history and, 155–60, 191–92; identification and, 45–47, 85, 101–18, 147–63, 188–92; identity and, 45–47, 66, 73–74, 82–87, 93, 94–96, 105–7, 132–34, 137–40, 147–63, 175–79, 188–200, 216–20; identity-making and, 175–79; immigration and, 61, 78n40; incorporation conditions and, 164n6; individuation of, 111–12; integration and, 4–5, 218–20; intrinsic identification and, xiii, 113–17; justice and, 160–62; language and, 150–52, 155–56; Latin America and, 137–40, 148–53, 156–60; membership and, xiii, 9–11, 22, 82–87, 93, 94–96, 102–4, 114–15,

Index

132–34, 137–40, 147–63, 187–200, 217–18; multiculturalism and, 219–20; Muslims and, 67, 72–74; nationality and, 60–76, 86, 112–13, 115–17, 132–34, 137–40, 148–53, 155–56, 157–58, 159–60, 162, 175–79, 190–200; neighborhoods and, 65–66; origin and, 156–59; partial basic membership and, 137–38; personhood and, 160–62; pervasive basic membership and, 137–38; policymaking and, 216–20; politics and, 26–28, 69–70, 156–58; presumption of relevant membership and, 67, 73–74, 217–18; primordialist view of, 86–87; race and, 188–92; recognition and, 9–11, 84, 103–4, 148–49, 153, 187–88, 191–92, 216–20; relevant identification and, xiii, 101–7, 147–53; religion and, 67–68, 72–74, 86; rights of, 61, 62–63, 64; robust membership and, 138–40, 149–53, 159–60; self-understanding and, 82–87, 93, 95, 105–7, 108–11, 114–15, 116–17, 137–38, 150–53, 154, 155–56, 158–60, 193; social markers and, 103–4, 110–11, 148–49; socialization and, 101–4; traits and, 85–87, 93, 95–96, 104–7, 108–12, 114–15, 137–38, 147–53, 154, 155–62, 188–92, 193; types of, 65–71, 81, 84–85, 109–13; unity and, 155; value of, 62–75, 187–88, 214–16; in Venezuela, 112–13; well being and, 95–96, 187–88. *See also* membership
Guevara, Ernesto "Che," 132–33

Haddad, Yvonne, 78n31
heritage, 148–49, 175–79. *See also* birthplace; history; origin
Hernandez v. Texas, 41, 220n1
Hijuelos, Oscar, 177–78
Hispanics: African Americans and, 193–200; America and, 126–27, 129–30, 134, 135–36, 138, 148–49, 157–58, 175–82, 195–200; assimilation and, 54n18, 180–81; basic membership and, 125–26, 129–41, 147–63, 167–68, 169, 193–200, 209–10, 217–18; birthplace and, 132, 133, 148–49, 150–52, 157–58; choice and, 138; citizenship and, 126–40, 195–96; civil rights and, xv, 41–43, 160–61, 206, 207–9, 210–14; classification and, ix–x, xiv–xv, 27, 41–43, 148–49, 152, 157, 158, 168–69, 205–20; commonality and, 131–34, 153, 154–62, 175–82; community and, 132–34, 175–82, 196–98; conflict and, 127, 129–31, 132–34, 139–40; culture and, 169, 179–81; demography and, xv, 206–7; differential treatment and, 41–43; differentiation and, 131–34, 148–49, 150, 154–62, 167–68; discernibility and, 154; diversity and, 175–76, 206–7, 210–11, 214–15; education and, 42–43, 49–51, 216; empowerment and, 155–56, 158–60, 176–77; epiphenomena and, 150–53, 159–60, 162, 193; ethnicity and, 155–62, 206–7; generation gaps and, 164n7; groups and, xiv, 132–34, 137–40, 147–63, 175–79, 193–200, 216–20; heritage and, 175–79; history and, 155–60, 196–98; identification and, 147–63, 167–69; identity and, xiv, 125–41, 147–63, 167–69, 175–82, 193–200, 206, 207, 209–10; identity-making and, 152, 167–69, 175–82, 193–94, 199, 209–10, 215, 217; immigration and, 127–28, 134, 136–37, 179–81, 195–96, 197, 199, 216; income and, 42; intrinsic identification and, 167–68; justice and, 160–62; language and, 42–43, 49–50, 54n18, 132, 150–52, 155–56, 169; Latin America and, 126–27, 129–40, 148–53, 156–60, 180–81; membership and, xiii–xiv, 125–26, 129–41, 147–63, 167–68, 169, 180–81, 193–200, 209–10, 217–18; nationality and, 125–41, 148–53, 155–56,

157–58, 159–60, 162, 168–69, 175–82, 193–200; origin and, 156–59; partial basic membership and, 135–38; as a people, 175–79; personhood and, 160–62; pervasive basic membership and, 135–38; policymaking and, 216–20; politics and, 156–58; population of, x; presumption of relevant membership and, 41–43, 207, 209–10, 217–18; race and, 194, 206–7; recognition and, 41–43, 148–49, 153, 198–200, 205–20; relevant identification and, 147–53, 167–68; robust membership and, 135–36, 138–40, 149–53, 159–60, 169, 180–81; self-understanding and, 131–32, 135, 136–38, 150–53, 154, 155–56, 158–60, 193; social markers and, 148–49; sports and, 129–30; in Standards for the Classification of Federal Data on Race and Ethnicity, 17, 125, 128, 157, 158, 168–69, 206–16, 220; strict scrutiny and, 210–15; terminology for, xv–xvi; traits and, 131–32, 135, 136–38, 147–53, 154, 155–62, 169, 193
history, 155–60, 171–73, 191–92, 196–98. *See also* heritage
Hobsbawm, Eric, 116
homeland. *See* birthplace
Horowitz, Donald, 93, 142n7
Huntington, Samuel, 179–81
Hutchinson, John, 121n24, 168

Ibañez, Jorge Larraín, 97n8
identification: of African Americans, 188–92; America and, 148–49, 157–58; basic membership and, 106–7, 114–15, 147–63, 188–92; birthplace and, 148–49, 150–52, 157–58; civil rights and, 160–61; classification and, xii, 17, 18–19, 45–47, 148–49, 152, 157, 158; commonality and, 153, 154–62; culture and, 114–15; differentiation and, 148–49, 150, 154–62, 167–68; discernibility and, 154; diversity and, 45–46; empowerment and, 155–56, 158–60; ethnicity and, 155–62; groups and, 45–47, 85, 101–18, 147–63, 188–92; Hispanics and, 147–63, 167–69; history and, 155–60; identity and, 105–7, 147–63; identity-making and, 167–68; intrinsic, xiii, 113–17, 167–68; justice and, 160–62; language and, 150–52, 155–56; Latin America and, 148–53, 156–60; membership and, 101–13, 114–15, 147–63, 188–92; multiple, 17, 18–19, 46–47, 211–12, 214; nationality and, 115–17, 148–53, 155–56, 157–58, 159–60, 162, 168–69; origin and, 156–59; personhood and, 160–62; politics and, 156–58; presumption of relevant membership and, 45–47; race and, 188–92; recognition and, 148–49, 153; robust membership and, 149–53, 159–60; self-understanding and, 105–7, 114–15, 116–17, 150–53, 154, 155–56, 158–60, 188–92; social markers and, 148–49; strong, 145n31; traits and, 104–7, 114–15, 147–53, 154, 155–62, 188–92; under Standards for the Classification of Federal Data on Race and Ethnicity, xii, 17, 18–19, 45–47, 168–69, 211–12, 214; *See also* choice; relevant identification
identity: African Americans and, 188–98; America and, 126–27, 129–30, 134, 135–36, 138, 157–58, 173–81, 191–92, 194–200; American Indians and, 34–35; Arab Americans and, 40, 73–74; assimilation and, 180–81; basic membership and, 84–96, 106–7, 125–26, 129–40, 147–63, 167–68, 169, 188–200, 209–10; birthplace and, 88–89, 132, 133, 157–58; blacks and, 201n7; choice and, 138; citizenship and, 126–40, 195–96; civil rights and, 160–61, 209, 210–14, 221n5;

classification and, xi, 14n25, 33, 38–39, 40, 45–47, 48–52, 157, 158, 206, 207, 209–10; commonality and, 131–34, 154–62, 170–79, 180–81; community and, 132–34, 170–79, 191–92, 196–98; concept of, 82–84; conflict and, 127, 129–31, 132–34, 139–40; culture and, 63, 73–74, 94–96, 169, 179–81; demography and, 207; destiny and, 172; differentiation and, 131–34, 148–49, 150, 154–62, 167–68; discernibility and, 154; diversity and, 175–76, 207, 210–11, 214–15; education and, 47–48; empowerment and, 155–56, 158–60, 176–77; ethnicity and, 34–35, 40, 73–74, 93, 155–62; groups and, 45–47, 66, 73–74, 82–87, 93, 94–96, 105–7, 132–34, 137–40, 147–63, 175–79, 188–200, 216–20; heritage and, 175–79; Hispanics and, xiv, 125–41, 147–63, 167–69, 175–82, 193–200, 206, 207, 209–10; history and, 155–60, 171–73, 191–92, 196–98; identification and, 105–7, 147–63; identity-making and, 209–10; immigration and, 127–28, 134, 136–37, 179–81, 195–96, 197; integration and, 198, 218–20; intrinsic identification and, 167–68; of Irish Americans, 93; of Jews, 110; justice and, 160–62; language and, 87–88, 89, 104–5, 132, 155–56, 169; Latin America and, 126–27, 129–40, 156–60, 180–81; Libertarian Party and, 34–35; membership and, xi, xii–xiii, 14n25, 34–35, 36–37, 63, 81–96, 105–7, 125–26, 129–40, 147–63, 167–68, 169, 180–81, 188–200, 209–10; multiculturalism and, 219–20; multiple, 128–29; Muslims and, 73–74; nationality and, 86, 99n31, 104–7, 115–17, 125–41, 148–53, 155–56, 157–58, 159–60, 162, 168–81, 190–200; origin and, 156–59; partial basic membership and, 135–38;

personhood and, 160–62; pervasive basic membership and, 135–38; phenomenon of, 83–84; policymaking and, 216–20; politics and, 34–35, 83, 156–58; presumption of relevant membership and, 34–35, 36–37, 38–39, 40, 45–47, 48–52, 203n26, 209–10; race and, 188–92, 194, 198, 201n7; recognition and, 14n25, 30n26, 40, 63, 66, 84, 191–92, 198–200, 203n26, 206, 207, 209–10; relevant identification and, 105–7, 147–53, 167–68; religion and, 73–74, 86, 92, 172–73; rights and, 166n25; robust membership and, 135–36, 138–40, 159–60, 169, 180–81; school attendance and, 104–7; self-understanding and, 82–93, 95, 105–7, 131–32, 135, 136–38, 150–53, 154, 155–56, 158–60, 173–74, 188–92; sports and, 129–30; Standards for the Classification of Federal Data on Race and Ethnicity and, 45–47, 48–52, 206, 207, 209–10; strict scrutiny and, 210–15; traits and, 85–93, 131–32, 135, 136–38, 147–53, 154, 155–62, 169, 188–92; value of, 66, 94–96, 216–17; vocabulary of, 83–84; well being and, 95–96, 170–71; of Yanomami, 83, 84. *See also* identity-making; personhood

identity-making: African Americans and, 188–92, 194; America and, 173–81; assimilation and, 180–81; basic membership and, 167–68, 169, 188–92, 193–94, 199, 209–10; classification and, 209–10, 215, 217; commonality and, 170–79, 180–81; community and, 170–79; culture and, 169, 179–81; destiny and, 172; differentiation and, 167–68; diversity and, 175–76; empowerment and, 176–77; groups and, 175–79; heritage and, 175–79; Hispanics and, 152, 167–69, 175–82, 193–94, 199, 209–10, 215, 217;

history and, 171–73; identification and, 167–68; identity and, 209–10; immigration and, 179–81; integration and, 181; language and, 169; Latin America and, 180–81; membership and, 167–68, 169, 180–81, 188–92, 193–94, 199, 209–10; nationality and, 152, 168–81, 199; policymaking and, 217; presumption of relevant membership and, 209–10; process of, 168–69; race and, 194; recognition and, 199, 209–10, 215, 217; relevant identification and, 167–68; religion and, 172–73; robust membership and, 169, 180–81; self-understanding and, 173–74; Standards for the Classification of Federal Data on Race and Ethnicity and, 209–10, 215; traits and, 169; well being and, 170–71

immediate membership, 102–4

immigration: African Americans and, 195–96, 197; America and, 179–81, 195–96, 197; basic membership and, 134, 136–37, 195–96, 197, 199; citizenship and, 127–28, 134, 136–37; classification and, 26–27, 216; commonality and, 180–81; community and, 197; culture and, 61, 179–81; generation gaps and, 142n12; groups and, 61, 78n40; Hispanics and, 127–28, 134, 136–37, 179–81, 195–96, 197, 199, 216; history and, 197; identity and, 127–28, 134, 136–37, 179–81, 195–96, 197; identity-making and, 179–81; integration and, 3–4, 181; Latin America and, x, 27, 180–81; membership and, 134, 136–37, 180–81, 195–96, 197, 199; nationality and, 127–28, 134, 136–37, 179–81, 195–96, 197, 199; partial basic membership and, 136–37; pervasive basic membership and, 136–37; recognition and, 199, 216; robust membership and, 180–81; self-understanding and, 136–37; Standards for the Classification of Federal Data on Race and Ethnicity and, 216; traits and, 136–37

income, 35, 36, 42, 44

individuation, 111–12, 144n28

integration, 3–11, 133, 181, 198, 203n27, 218–20. *See also* assimilation

interaction, 101–4

intrinsic identification, xiii, 113–17, 167–68

Irish Americans, 26–27, 93, 179

Isaacs, Harold, 109

Italy, 171–73

Jews, 110

Johnson, Lyndon, 175

justice, 160–62. *See also* civil rights

Kallen, Horace, 187

Kertzer, David I., 13n21

Kymlicka, Will: challenges to, 65, 71–75; on cultural groups, 60–63, 94–95, 118n6; on integration, 203n27; on multiculturalism, claims of, 63–65; overview of, xii–xiii, 5, 59–60

language: assimilation and, 54n18; basic membership and, 87–88, 89, 132, 150–52, 155–56; citizenship and, 132; culture and, 87–88, 89; differentiation and, 155–56; ethnicity and, 155–56; groups and, 150–52, 155–56; Hispanics and, 42–43, 49–50, 54n18, 132, 150–52, 155–56, 169; identification and, 150–52, 155–56; identity and, 87–88, 89, 104–5, 132, 155–56, 169; identity-making and, 169; membership and, 87–88, 89, 132, 150–52, 155–56; nationality and, 132, 150–52; relevant identification and, 150–52; robust membership and, 150–52; self-understanding and, 87–88, 89, 104–5

Latin America: America and, 180–81; basic membership and, 129–40, 148–53, 156–60; citizenship and, 126–27, 129–40; commonality and, 156–60, 180–81; conflict and, 127, 129–31, 132–34, 139–40; culture and, 180–81; differentiation and, 156–60; ethnicity and, 156–60; groups and, 137–40, 148–53, 156–60; Hispanics and, 126–27, 129–40, 148–53, 156–60, 180–81; history and, 156–60; identification and, 148–53, 156–60; identity and, 126–27, 129–40, 156–60, 180–81; identity-making and, 180–81; immigration and, x, 27, 180–81; membership and, 129–40, 148–53, 156–60, 180–81; nationality and, 126–27, 129–40, 148–53, 180–81; partial basic membership and, 135–38; pervasive basic membership and, 135–38; politics in, 69–70; relevant identification and, 148–53; robust membership and, 138–40, 180–81; terminology for, xvi

Latinos, xv–xvi. *See also* Hispanics

Le Bras, Hervé, 219

League of United Latin American Citizens, 199

liberal culturalism, 63, 74–75

Libertarian Party, 34–35

Lizot, Jacques, 68–69

Margalit, Avishai, 99n29, 118n1

marginalization, 4

Martí, José, 69–70

Mazzini, Giuseppe, 171–73, 175, 177

McKim, Robert, 145n31

Mead, G. H., xiii, 82

meaning and direction, 62–75, 191–92. *See also* value

membership: African Americans and, xiv, 188–98; America and, 129–30, 134, 135–36, 138, 148–49, 157–58, 180–81, 194–200; American Indians and, 34–35; assimilation and, 6–7; birthplace and, 88–89, 132, 133, 148–49, 150–52, 157–58; choice and, 94–95, 138, 152–53; citizenship and, 129–40, 195–96; civil rights and, 160–61; classification and, xi, xii, 9–11, 33–37, 148–49, 152, 157, 158, 209–10, 217–18; commonality and, 131–34, 153, 154–62; community and, 132–34, 191–92, 196–98; conflict and, 127, 129–31, 132–34, 139–40; culture and, 59–76, 94–96, 180–81, 187–88; differentiation and, xiii, 107–13, 131–34, 148–49, 150, 154–62, 167–68; discernibility and, 109–11, 154; diversity and, 22; education and, 47–48; empowerment and, 155–56, 158–60; ethnicity and, 34–35, 35–36, 93, 155–62; experience and, 35–36; extended, 102–4; freedom and, 63; gender and, 14n24; groups and, xiii, 9–11, 22, 82–87, 93, 94–96, 102–4, 114–15, 132–34, 137–40, 147–63, 187–200, 217–18; Hispanics and, xiii–xiv, 125–26, 129–41, 147–63, 167–68, 169, 180–81, 193–200, 209–10, 217–18; history and, 155–60, 191–92, 196–98; identification and, 101–13, 114–15, 147–63, 188–92; identity and, xi, xii–xiii, 14n25, 34–35, 36–37, 63, 81–96, 105–7, 125–26, 129–40, 147–63, 167–68, 169, 180–81, 188–200, 209–10; identity-making and, 167–68, 169, 180–81, 188–92, 193–94, 199, 209–10; immediate, 102–4; immigration and, 134, 136–37, 180–81, 195–96, 197, 199; income and, 35, 36; integration and, 6–7; intrinsic identification and, xiii, 114–15, 167–68; justice and, 160–62; language and, 87–88, 89, 132, 150–52, 155–56; Latin America and, 129–40, 148–53, 156–60, 180–81; levels of, 102–4; Libertarian Party and, 34–35; as limited, 102–4; nationality and, 86, 112–13, 125–26, 129–41, 148–53, 155–56, 157–58,

159–60, 162, 169, 180–81, 190–200; origin and, 156–59; personhood and, 160–62; policymaking and, 217–18; politics and, 34–35, 36, 156–58; race and, 188–92, 198; recognition and, 9–11, 59–60, 62–75, 103–4, 148–49, 153, 191–92, 198–200, 209–10, 217–18; relevant identification and, xiii, 101–7, 147–53, 167–68; religion and, 86, 92; rights and, 166n25; self-understanding and, 82–93, 95, 105–7, 108–11, 131–32, 135, 136–38, 150–53, 154, 155–56, 158–60, 188–92, 193; social markers and, 148–49; sports and, 129–30; Standards for the Classification of Federal Data on Race and Ethnicity and, 209–10; traits and, 85–93, 95–96, 108–12, 131–32, 135, 136–38, 147–53, 154, 155–62, 188–92, 193; value of, 59–60, 62–75, 81, 94–96, 150, 187–88, 214–16, 216–17; voluntary, 152–53; well being and, 95–96, 187–88. *See also* basic membership; groups; presumption of relevant membership; robust membership
Mexican Americans, 41–43
Mexico, 117, 143n13
Michelet, Jules, 171–73, 177
Mill, John Stuart, 174
Miller, David, 54n31, 200n4
Miller, Kerby, 179
minorities, 61–62, 64, 78n40, 187–88, 198–200
Miscevic, Nenad, 99n31
modernism, 115–16
Molina, Mario, 177–78
Morris, Christopher W., 202n24
multiculturalism: in America, 187–88; assimilation and, 11n2; challenges to, 65, 71–75; claims of, 63–65; classification and, 219–20; cultural pluralism and, 187–88; diversity and, 5–6; groups and, 65–71, 219–20; identity and, 219–20; integration and, 4–6; policymaking and, 219–20; recognition and, 219–20; terminology for, 11n1, 60
Murphy, Jeffrie G., 223n21
Muslims, 67, 72–74. *See also* Arab Americans

narrow tailoring, 211, 213–15
National Council of La Raza, 176–77, 199
National Hispanic Heritage Month, 157, 175–78
nationalist statements, 132–33, 157, 170–78
nationality: African Americans and, 190–98; America and, 126–27, 129–30, 134, 135–36, 138, 148–49, 173–81, 191–92, 194–200; assimilation and, 180–81; basic membership and, 86, 112–13, 125–26, 129–41, 148–53, 155–56, 157–58, 159–60, 162, 169, 190–200; birthplace and, 132, 133, 150–52; citizenship and, 126–40, 195–96; commonality and, 131–34, 159–60, 162, 170–79, 180–81; community and, 132–34, 170–79, 191–92, 196–98; conflict and, 127, 129–31, 132–34, 139–40; consensual v. non-consensual, 174; culture and, 60–76, 179–81; destiny and, 172; differentiation and, 112–13, 131–34, 148–49, 150, 155–56, 157–58, 159–60, 162; diversity and, 74–75, 175–76; education and, 47–48; empowerment and, 176–77; epiphenomena of, 150–53, 159–60, 162, 193; ethnicity and, 155–56, 157–58, 159–60, 162; ethno-symbolism on, 116; France and, 171–73; Germany and, 170; groups and, 60–76, 86, 112–13, 115–17, 132–34, 137–40, 148–53, 155–56, 157–58, 159–60, 162, 175–79, 190–200; heritage and, 175–79; Hispanics and, 125–41, 148–53, 155–56, 157–58, 159–60, 162, 168–69, 175–82, 193–200; history and, 157–58, 159–60, 171–73, 191–92, 196–98; identification and,

115–17, 148–53, 155–56, 157–58, 159–60, 162, 168–69; identity and, 86, 99n31, 104–7, 115–17, 125–41, 148–53, 155–56, 157–58, 159–60, 162, 168–81, 190–200; identity-making and, 152, 168–81, 199; immigration and, 127–28, 134, 136–37, 179–81, 195–96, 197, 199; individuation and, 144n28; integration and, 4, 133; intrinsic identification and, 115–17; Irish Americans and, 179; Italy and, 171–73; language and, 132, 150–52; Latin America and, 126–27, 129–40, 148–53, 180–81; meaning and direction from, 62–75, 191–92; membership and, 86, 112–13, 125–26, 129–41, 148–53, 155–56, 157–58, 159–60, 162, 169, 180–81, 190–200; Mexican, 117; minorities and, 61–62, 64, 78n40; modernism on, 115–16; multiple, 128–29; nationalist statements, 132–33, 157, 170–78; partial basic membership and, 135–38; pervasive basic membership and, 135–38; proto-nations compared, 116–17; in Quebec, 67; race and, 190–92, 198; recognition and, 191–92, 198–200; relevant identification and, 148–53; religion and, 67–68, 172–73; robust membership and, 135–36, 138–40, 149–53, 159–60, 169, 180–81; self-understanding and, 86, 104–7, 131–32, 135, 136–38, 150–53, 173–74, 190–92, 193; social markers and, 148–49; sports and, 129–30; symbolism and, 143n17; terminology for, 141n3; traits and, 131–32, 135, 136–38, 148–53, 190–92, 193; in Venezuela, 112–13; well being and, 170–71
neighborhoods, 65–66
Nobles, Melissa, 9, 25

Ochoa, Ellen, 177–78
Omi, Michael, 189–90, 194
One Nation, Many Peoples, 47–48

origin, 8, 156–59. *See also* birthplace; heritage

Parekh, Bhikhu, 5, 119n7, 120n19
partial basic membership, 135–38
people, 175–79
personhood, 160–62
pervasive basic membership, 135–38
Pogge, Thomas, 66
policymaking: basic membership and, 217–18; classification and, ix–x, 16–17, 19–29, 36–47, 48–52, 216–20; groups and, 216–20; Hispanics and, 216–20; identity and, 216–20; identity-making and, 217; integration and, 203n27, 218–20; justifications for, ix, 16–17, 19–29, 125, 160, 168–69, 206, 216–20; membership and, 217–18; multiculturalism and, 219–20; presumption of relevant membership and, 217–18; recognition and, 216–20; Standards for the Classification of Federal Data on Race and Ethnicity and, ix–x, 16–17, 19–29, 125, 160, 168–69, 206
politics: in America, 190; basic membership and, 156–58; classification and, 25–28, 156–58; in demography, 25–28; differentiation and, 156–58; diversity and, 25–28; ethnicity and, 156–58; groups and, 26–28, 69–70, 156–58; Hispanics and, 156–58; history and, 156–58; identification and, 156–58; identity and, 34–35, 83, 156–58; in Latin America, 69–70; membership and, 34–35, 36, 156–58; race and, 190; value of, 69–70
population, x. *See also* demography
Portes, Alejandro, 131, 134, 139
presumption of relevant membership: African Americans and, 40–41; American Indians and, 34–35, 44–45; Arab Americans and, 39–40; Asian Americans and, 43–44; civil

rights and, 37–46, 48–52; classification and, xi, xii, xv, 33–37, 48–52, 207, 209–10, 217–18; Cuban Americans and, 42; demography and, 36–37, 207; differential treatment and, 38–45; diversity and, 37–38, 45–46, 207; ethnicity and, 34–35, 35–36, 39–40, 44–45; experience and, 35–36; groups and, 67, 73–74, 217–18; Hispanics and, 41–43, 207, 209–10, 217–18; identification and, 45–47; identity and, 34–35, 36–37, 38–39, 40, 45–47, 48–52, 203n26, 209–10; identity-making and, 209–10; income and, 35, 36; Libertarian Party and, 34–35; Mexican Americans and, 41–43; overview of, 33–37; policymaking and, 217–18; politics and, 34–35, 36; race and, 40–41, 43–44; recognition and, 38–47, 207, 209–10, 217–18; religion and, 38–39; sexual orientation and, 39; Standards for the Classification of Federal Data on Race and Ethnicity and, 207, 209–10
primordialism, 86–87
principle of diversity. *See* diversity
properties. *See* traits
proto-nations, 116–17

Quebec, 67

race: African Americans and, 188–92, 194, 198; in America, 189–90; basic membership and, 188–92, 198; censuses and, 8–9; citizenship and, 190; civil rights and, 40–41, 43–44; classification and, 8–9, 15–19, 40–41, 43–44, 190, 206–7; community and, 191–92; concept of, 29n8, 224n31; demography and, 206–7; differential treatment and, 40–41, 43–44; diversity and, 206–7; education and, 47–48; ethnicity distinct from, 29n8; groups and, 188–92; Hispanics and, 194, 206–7; history and, 191–92; identification and, 188–92; identity and, 188–92, 194, 198, 201n7; identity-making and, 194; membership and, 188–92, 198; nationality and, 190–92, 198; politics and, 190; presumption of relevant membership and, 40–41, 43–44; recognition and, 40–41, 43–44, 191–92, 198, 206–7; relevant identification and, 188–90; Standards for the Classification of Federal Data on Race and Ethnicity and, 16–19, 206–7; strict scrutiny and, 210–15; traits and, 188–92
Rawls, John, 94
Raz, Joseph, 99n29, 118n1
recognition: African Americans and, 40–41, 191–92, 198–200, 220; America and, 191–92; American Indians and, 44–45; Arab Americans and, 39–40; Asian Americans and, 43–44; basic membership and, 148–49, 153, 191–92, 198–200, 209–10, 217–18; civil rights and, 38–47, 206, 207–9, 210–14; classification and, 9–11, 17, 38–47, 205–20; community and, 191–92; Cuban Americans and, 42; culture and, 187–88; demography and, 206–7; differential treatment and, 38–45; differentiation and, 148–49; diversity and, 74–75, 206–7, 210–11, 214–15; education and, 47–48, 216; ethnicity and, 39–40, 44–45, 206–7; freedom and, 63; groups and, 9–11, 84, 103–4, 148–49, 153, 187–88, 191–92, 216–20; Hispanics and, 41–43, 148–49, 153, 198–200, 205–20; history and, 191–92; identification and, 148–49, 153; identity and, 14n25, 30n26, 40, 63, 66, 84, 191–92, 198–200, 203n26, 206, 207, 209–10; identity-making and, 199, 209–10, 215, 217; immigration and, 199, 216; integration and, 10–11, 218–20; membership and, 9–11, 59–60,

62–75, 103–4, 148–49, 153, 191–92, 198–200, 209–10, 217–18; Mexican Americans and, 41–43; multiculturalism and, 219–20; nationality and, 191–92, 198–200; policymaking and, 216–20; presumption of relevant membership and, 38–47, 207, 209–10, 217–18; race and, 40–41, 43–44, 191–92, 198, 206–7; relevant identification and, 148–49, 153; religion and, 38–39; self-understanding and, 191–92; sexual orientation and, 39; social markers and, 103–4, 148–49; strict scrutiny and, 210–15; traits and, 191–92; value of, 62–75; well being and, 187–88. *See also* classification

relevant identification: African Americans and, 188–90; America and, 148–49; basic membership and, 106–7, 147–53, 167–68; birthplace and, 148–49, 150–52; classification and, 148–49, 152; commonality and, 153; differentiation and, 148–49, 150; groups and, xiii, 101–7, 147–53; Hispanics and, 147–53, 167–68; identity and, 105–7, 147–53, 167–68; identity-making and, 167–68; intrinsic identification and, 167–68; language and, 150–52; Latin America and, 148–53; membership and, xiii, 101–7, 147–53, 167–68; nationality and, 148–53; race and, 188–90; recognition and, 148–49, 153; robust membership and, 149–53; self-understanding and, 105–7, 150–53; social markers and, 148–49; traits and, 104–7, 147–53

religion: basic membership and, 86, 92; civil rights and, 38–39; classification and, 38–39; differential treatment and, 38–39; groups and, 67–68, 72–74, 86; identity and, 73–74, 86, 92, 172–73; identity-making and, 172–73; integration and, 4–5; membership and, 86, 92; nationality and, 67–68, 172–73; presumption of relevant membership and, 38–39; recognition and, 38–39; self-understanding and, 86, 92; value of, 67–68, 72–74

Renan, Ernest, 173, 177, 178–79, 183n15

rights, 61, 62–63, 64, 166n25. *See also* civil rights

robust membership, 135–36, 138–40, 149–53, 159–60, 169, 180–81

Rumbaut, Rubén, 131, 134, 139

Rwanda, 165n10

Sartre, Jean Paul, 110

Scalia, Antonin, 213

school attendance, 104–7. *See also* education

Schuck, Peter H., 12n7

self-government, 61

self-understanding: African Americans and, 188–92; America and, 138, 173–74; basic membership and, 84–93, 95, 106–7, 108–11, 131–32, 135, 136–38, 150–53, 154, 155–56, 158–60, 188–92, 193; birthplace and, 88–89; citizenship and, 131–32, 135, 136–38; cognitive capacity for, 97n2; commonality and, 158–60, 173–74; community and, 173–74, 191–92; culture and, 114–15; differentiation and, 108–11, 154, 155–56, 158–60; ethnicity and, 93, 155–56, 158–60; groups and, 82–87, 93, 95, 105–7, 108–11, 114–15, 116–17, 137–38, 150–53, 154, 155–56, 158–60, 193; Hispanics and, 131–32, 135, 136–38, 150–53, 154, 155–56, 158–60, 193; history and, 155–56, 158–60, 191–92; identification and, 105–7, 114–15, 116–17, 150–53, 154, 155–56, 158–60, 188–92; identity and, 82–93, 95, 105–7, 131–32, 135, 136–38, 150–53, 154, 155–56, 158–60, 173–74, 188–92; identity-making and, 173–74; immigration and, 136–37; intrinsic identification and, 114–15, 116–17;

language and, 87–88, 89, 104–5; membership and, 82–93, 95, 105–7, 108–11, 131–32, 135, 136–38, 150–53, 154, 155–56, 158–60, 188–92, 193; nationality and, 86, 104–7, 131–32, 135, 136–38, 150–53, 173–74, 190–92, 193; partial basic membership and, 136–38; pervasive basic membership and, 136–38; recognition and, 191–92; relevant identification and, 105–7, 150–53; religion and, 86, 92; robust membership and, 150–53; school attendance and, 104–7; self-understanding and, 193; traits and, 85–93, 108–11, 114–15, 131–32, 135, 136–38, 150–53, 188–92, 193; of Yanomami, 83, 84
sexual orientation, 39
Smith, Anthony, 88, 121n26, 172–73, 183n15
social class, 144n23
social markers, 103–4, 110–11, 148–49. *See also* traits
socialization, 101–4
Soto, Hernando de, 177–78
sports, 129–30
Standards for the Classification of Federal Data on Race and Ethnicity: adoption of, 16–17; African Americans in, 202n23; basic membership and, 209–10; civil rights and, xii, 23–25, 206, 207–9, 210–14; demography and, xi–xii, 19–22, 25–29, 206–7; diversity and, xi–xii, 19–22, 24, 25–28, 45–46, 206–7, 210–11, 214–15; education and, 216; ethnicity and, 16–19, 206–7; Hispanics in, 17, 125, 128, 157, 158, 168–69, 206–16, 220; identification under, xii, 17, 18–19, 45–47, 168–69, 211–12, 214; identity and, 45–47, 48–52, 206, 207, 209–10; identity-making and, 209–10, 215; immigration and, 216; membership and, 209–10; overview of, 16–19; policymaking and, ix–x, 16–17, 19–29, 125, 160, 168–69, 206; presumption of relevant membership and, 207, 209–10; race and, 16–19, 206–7; revision of, 17–19, 20, 46, 210–16; strict scrutiny and, 210–15. *See also* classification
strict scrutiny, 210–15
strong identification, 145n31
Suro, Roberto, 142n12
symbolism, 143n17

Taylor, Charles, 30n26, 97n10, 183n10, 187–88
terminology: for African Americans, 46; for culture, 60–61; for epiphenomena, 164n9; for multiculturalism, 11n1, 60; for nationality, 141n3; overview of, xv–xvi
territory. *See* birthplace
Thernstrom, Abigail, 30n29
thick cultures, 110–11
traits: accidental, 86, 89–90; African Americans and, 188–92; America and, 138; basic membership and, 85–93, 95–96, 108–12, 131–32, 135, 136–38, 147–53, 154, 155–62, 188–92, 193; choice and, 138; citizenship and, 131–32, 135, 136–38; commonality and, 154; community and, 191–92; consensual v. non-consensual, 91–93, 152–53; differentiation and, 108–12, 148–49, 150, 154, 155–62; essential, 85–93, 95–96, 105–7, 150–53, 188–92, 193; ethnicity and, 93, 155–62; groups and, 85–87, 93, 95–96, 104–7, 108–12, 114–15, 137–38, 147–53, 154, 155–62, 188–92, 193; Hispanics and, 131–32, 135, 136–38, 147–53, 154, 155–62, 169, 193; history and, 155–60, 191–92; identification and, 104–7, 114–15, 147–53, 154, 155–62, 188–92; identity and, 85–93, 131–32, 135, 136–38, 147–53, 154, 155–62, 169, 188–92; identity-making and, 169; immigration and, 136–37;

intrinsic identification and, 114–15; membership and, 85–93, 95–96, 108–12, 131–32, 135, 136–38, 147–53, 154, 155–62, 188–92, 193; nationality and, 131–32, 135, 136–38, 148–53, 190–92, 193; partial basic membership and, 136–38; pervasive basic membership and, 136–38; race and, 188–92; recognition and, 191–92; relevant identification and, 104–7, 147–53; self-understanding and, 85–93, 108–11, 114–15, 131–32, 135, 136–38, 150–53, 188–92, 193; well being and, 95–96. *See also* social markers

Truman report, 41–42

United States. *See* America
unity, 155. *See also* commonality
urban neighborhoods, 65–66
U.S. Constitution, 174, 202n22, 210–15

value: of basic membership, 94–96; of culture, 62–75, 187–88; of diversity, 74–75; of groups, 62–75, 187–88, 214–16; of identity, 66, 94–96, 216–17; meaning and direction, 62–75, 191–92; of membership, 59–60, 62–75, 81, 94–96, 150, 187–88, 214–16, 216–17; of nationality, 67–69; of politics, 69–70; of recognition, 62–75; of religion, 67–68, 72–74

Vasconcelos, José, 132
Venezuela, 112–13

Walker, Brian, 65
Walzer, Michael, 94, 110, 162
Waters, Mary, 93, 138
Weber, Eugene, 115, 164n8
well being, 95–96, 170–71, 187–88
whites, 27, 40. *See also* European Americans
Winant, Howard, 189–90, 194

Yanomami, 68–69, 83, 84
Young, Iris Marion, 5, 119n7, 119n8, 119n9, 120n17
Yzaguirre, Raul, 176, 179

About the Author

José Enrique Idler received his Ph.D. in philosophy at the University of Maryland, College Park. After a year as a post-doctoral fellow at the American Enterprise Institute for Public Policy Research in Washington D.C., he entered the private sector and now works as a government affairs consultant.